PIMLICO

542

THE FORTY-NINE STEPS

Roberto Calasso is the author of *The Marriage of Cadmus and Harmony*, *The Ruin of Kasch*, *Ka* and *Literature and the Gods*. He is the publisher of Adelphi Edizioni and lives in Milan.

John Shepley is a freelance writer and translator. His translation of Pier Paolo Pasolini's *Roman Nights and Other Stories* won the first Italo Calvino Translation Award in 1987.

THE FORTY-NINE STEPS

———

ROBERTO CALASSO

Translated by John Shepley

p262 Plato's quarrel with Homer in the Republic is metaphysical, not moral. He objects to the idea of the gods metamorphosing, as they do in myths, rather than being.

On Public Opinion is the subtlest essay and the most revealing of Calasso's central tenet of nihilism and his heroes: Nietzsche, Benjamin, Adorno and, above all, Kraus.

PIMLICO

Published by Pimlico 2002

2 4 6 8 10 9 7 5 3 1

Originally published as *I quarantanove gradini*, copyright 1991,
Adelphi Edizioni S.p.A., Milan, Italy
This translation first published in the United States of America
by the University of Minnesota Press 2001
First published in Great Britain by Pimlico 2002

Poetry by Bertolt Brecht is from 'Difficult Times', in *Bertolt Brecht: Poems, 1913-1956*,
edited by John Willett and Ralph Manheim (New York: Methuen, 1976),
p.449. Copyright 1976. Reproduced by permission of
Taylor & Francis, Inc./Routledge, Inc.

Pimlico
Random House, 20 Vauxhall Bridge Road,
London SW1V 2SA

Random House Australia (Pty) Limited
20 Alfred Street, Milsons Point, Sydney,
New South Wales 2061, Australia

Random House New Zealand Limited
18 Poland Road, Glenfield,
Auckland 10, New Zealand

Random House (Pty) Limited
Endulini, 5A Jubilee Road, Parktown 2193, South Africa

The Random House Group Limited Reg. No. 954009
www.randomhouse.co.uk

A CIP catalogue record for this book is available from the British Library

ISBN 0-7126-9740-3

Papers used by Random House UK Limited are natural,
recyclable products made from wood grown in sustainable forests;
the manufacturing processes conform to the environmental
regulations of the country of origin

Printed and bound in Great Britain
by Biddles Ltd., Guildford & Kings Lynn

To Francesco and Melisenda

Work method based on analogy?
(because that way one has
always to rethink . . .).

—*Simone Weil*

CONTENTS

Acknowledgments

I wish to thank Michela Acquati and Ena Marchi for their invaluable help in preparing this book.

R. C.

I Post-histories

I Fatal Monologue

As dream, as illusion, as a city of Gandharvas;
so are arising, abiding, and passing away
expressed.
—*Nāgārjuna,* Mādhyamikaśāstra, *VII, 34*

I

Ecce Homo opens with disconcerting words, compared to the beginning of *On the Genealogy of Morals,* a work that precedes it by only a year. "We are unknown to ourselves, we men of knowledge"—these are the first words of the *Genealogy,* and starting there, Nietzsche quickly arrives at the conclusion that in considering the whole of our lives and being, we "miscount"; not only are we "necessarily strangers to ourselves . . . we *have* to misunderstand ourselves." The argument then proceeds in the casual conversational tone Nietzsche assumed for the prefaces to his books, moves in other directions, and speaks of other things, never to return to those first remarks. Actually, these words do not sound odd to a reader of Nietzsche; rather, they seem like the momentary reemergence of a whole chain of thoughts already formulated in other writings, with restraint—as always in Nietzsche when he approaches the essential—and if anything, with a wish to conceal rather than to insist. It may also be because these thoughts were very close to confession, as shown by the use of "we": "I say 'we' to be polite," he would once have cautioned.

Now let us turn to the opening of *Ecce Homo.* Nietzsche starts by telling us that his writing will declare *what he is* and that this explanation

3

seems indispensable to him. In other words, he will provide an answer to that very question that the man of knowledge cannot put to himself without going wrong: "Who *are* we really?"[1] *This* is truly unheard-of, and we are all the more swayed by the italicized words with which the paragraph ends: *"Hear me! For I am such and such a person. Above all, do not mistake me for someone else."*[2] It is not the imperative tone that comes as a surprise but the claim to be able to present himself unequivocally, as well as the brusque manner, as though these words were uttered in the grip of necessity, with something immense looming and darkly suggesting "the most serious need" humanity has known. In this new act of presenting himself, one feels an approaching change, a change that turns above all against Nietzsche himself and threatens his most private self-image. He recognizes it at once: "a duty against which my habits, even more the pride of my instincts, revolt."[3]

So one wonders: What was it that in the space of little more than a year—the preface to *On the Genealogy of Morals* dates from July 1887, *Ecce Homo* from October 1888—drove Nietzsche to set himself a task that he considered doomed to failure and that wounded his instincts? Had not he himself shown how suspect and degenerative such a wound could be? Was the great tree of thought, which never knows what it will bring forth, perhaps preparing a monstrous fruit, a fruit representing in miniature the tree itself?[4] *Ecce Homo* has always aroused the most serious perplexities, though certainly not for these reasons. Since the book was published, people have never stopped wondering what to call it. A cosmic proclamation? A psycho-pathological document? A self-portrait? The loudest sort of anti-German invective? Or none of the above? But before asking these questions, which may all turn out to be beside the point, one ought to take a step back and pick up once more the ominous remains of the first questions Nietzsche himself asked when faced with any piece of writing: *Who* is speaking in these words? What necessity is speaking in these words?

Nietzsche's whole life has its unfathomable aspects, but this holds supremely true for the last year of his career as a writer. The constant fluctuation of force, the cyclical mockery and exaltation, recurrent and reverberating from things close at hand, so eloquently reinstated by Nietzsche himself, to those things that lie beyond any communicable life, the very element of his thought, his grand wager—to introduce thought into the actual flow of force, to remove its last restraints and defenses against the pressure of the world, which were characteristic of philosophy before being pounded by Zarathustra's hammer—seem to become more visible after a certain point. An irreversible transition is foreshadowed at every turn, as though everything Nietzsche had been so far was preparing to manifest itself in a new form. The first symptoms of this process can be seen in some letters written in December 1887. We see the same expression repeated to three different correspondents within the space of a week, thereby introducing the final phase: to close out his past by drawing a line under it.

> For I am, almost unwillingly but in obedience to an implacable need, in the process of settling my accounts as far as people and things are concerned and of putting my whole "till now" *ad acta*. Almost all I'm doing now is drawing a line underneath. The violence of inner fluctuations has been terrifying all these last years; from now on, since I must reach a new and higher form, I need in the first place a new separation, an even greater *depersonalization*.[5]

> What I've done in the last years has been to settle accounts, to sum up the past, and in the end I've freed myself from people and things and drawn a line under it all. *Who* and *what* I'll have left, now that I must pass on to the real main point of my existence (*I'm doomed* to pass on to it . . .), this is now an important question.[6]

> I feel like working but am in a melancholy mood and have by no means emerged from the violent shocks of these last years. Not yet "depersonalized" enough. Still, I know what is over and *done with*: I've drawn a *line* underneath my past existence.[7]

Nietzsche, having come to the end of his work and despite his "unconquerable mistrust of the *possibility* of self-knowledge"[8]—perhaps the sole critical point he shares with Goethe, the only other German he recognizes as his peer—then proceeds, by recognizing himself as object, to clash not only with his psychological acumen but with the harshest results of his thinking. Indeed, the condemnation of self-knowledge is only a corollary of the condemnation of any metaknowledge, which Nietzsche's criticism has by now established in a theorem that is likewise a death sentence: In the effort to know its own instruments, thought necessarily destroys itself, and in particular, Western thought, the only kind that has calmly ventured on this path. Turning then to personal experience, we see that whereas Goethe, at least in his maturity, had perhaps based his wisdom (the "perhaps" is essential) on the willed preservation of the ego in its most ordinary sense (a case of sublime hypocrisy) Nietzsche, in his most productive years, had instead pursued the active destruction of the subject, following the rule of a warrior monk by his systematic undermining of every reference point and by practicing the "magic of the extreme." So in considering this attempt at self-explanation, one would have more than ever to ask oneself, "Who says 'I' here?" And the answer, like the attempt itself, can only be paradoxical.

Throughout 1888, a year marked by harsh and hasty writings, the wish to establish an image of his own past will come increasingly to the fore, no longer in solitude in the darkness of the cave but now abruptly transported onto a stage as broad as the world, where Nietzsche himself will have the scandalous courage to display himself and say, *"Ecce homo."* During the winter in Nice, at a low point in the usual continual fluctuations in the state of Nietzsche's health, a secret transformation occurs, and like a negative film image what will be revealed a year later seems to become fixed in the silence. But for the moment Nietzsche is still in the cave, the site opposite to the stage. In the first months of 1888, he often, in speaking of himself, returns to the image of the *Höhle* (den, hollow, cave). This is for him a central and recurrent figure, and we will see it reappear amid the final signs of his life. "An animal, when it is sick, hides in its den; and so does the *bête philosophe* . . . inadvertently I have become a kind of cave— something hidden, which you would no longer be able to find, even if you went looking for it."[9] And earlier he had invited Georg Brandes to approach his "cave—i.e., philosophy."[10] From now on it is clear that in his underground work Nietzsche aims above all at *separating* himself from his past, certainly not at possessing it: "Basically everything in me now marks an epoch; everything mine till now crumbles away from me, and if I reckon what I have done in the past two years, it looks to me as though it has always been the same task: to isolate myself from my past and cut the umbilical cord that tied me to it."[11] This, from a letter to Paul Deussen, is Nietzsche's most explicit statement of his intentions; in the same letter the sound of the last phase could already be heard, a few words that might stand as an epigraph for the whole year 1888:

> Things do not prevail over the man who is able to put a will into them; even chance occasions end by arranging themselves in accordance with

our innermost needs. I am often surprised to see how little the extreme disfavor of destiny can do against our will. Or rather, I tell myself that the will must actually be destiny for always being right once more even against it, *hypèr móron*—.[12]

I I

If genius includes the capacity to take oneself literally, then Nietzsche, from the moment he settles in Turin (5 April), ingeniously applies the terms of his letter to Deussen about chance and destiny. If these phrases are accurate, then they *must* be fulfilled in every detail, first of all in the "closest things." From his first days in Turin we feel that Nietzsche is imprinting a positive sign, of ascendant life, on every aspect of the world surrounding him. "This is truly the city I need *now*!"[13]—so begins the transformation of Turin into the city of destiny. First to be transformed will be the city's general character and its aristocratic architecture; then all the circumstances of life, the prices, the food, the climate, the theater, manifest themselves as favorable signs. But by the last letters in autumn, in particular the last one to Jakob Burckhardt, everything is transfigured. By now the will has devoured the external world, devouring itself as well, and ecstatically watches the spectacle it has set in motion. During his first days in Turin, the "human cave" crosses an already prepared threshold, which his will, in the form of chance, now reveals to him. Early in April Nietzsche receives a letter from Brandes in which the Danish philosopher informs him that he will give a course at the University of Copenhagen "on the German philosopher Friedrich Nietzsche."

Today it is difficult to assess the enormous extent of Nietzsche's solitude at the time. Having become a shadow for most of his old friends, a difficult and invisible man, by now accustomed to publishing his books at his own expense, accustomed too to counting his loyal readers on his fingers and having to reduce their number as each new book comes out, Nietzsche seems to have circled as far from the world as possible, to a point of insurmountable alienation, which his old friend Erwin Rohde had felt at their last meeting, in the spring of 1886: "as though he came from a region inhabited by no one else." Brandes's letter arrives at this point as the first outside approval, produced by chance that has become destiny, the prelude to a stage, an action addressed to the world. Then, for the whole winter, rapid signs of an approaching upheaval kept flickering in Nietzsche, to erupt in the middle of his labors. August Strindberg's first letters in autumn represent a second threshold, where Nietzsche hears the "tone of universal history" resound and recognizes for the first time an interlocutor of his stature, and this at the beginning of his very last days in Turin, following the drafting of *Ecce Homo*. Between these two thresholds, spring and autumn, we have an entire cycle, a lightning advance on a single front, in *quickstep*, while his euphoria spirals upward. The first traces of this activity directed to the outside, the first steps of the *human cave* on the stage of the world, are already in Nietzsche's letter responding to Brandes's announcement. With this letter he enclosed a brief curriculum: three very simple pages seeking only to specify a few facts, but in them it is easy to recognize various observations that will reappear, sometimes almost word for word, in *Ecce Homo*, the writing of which had begun.

There is no reason to doubt Nietzsche's statement that *Ecce Homo* was written with the greatest speed and assurance between 15 October and 4 November 1888. This is not to deny the results of Mazzino Montinari's examination of the letters and manuscripts showing *Ecce Homo* to be a work in progress: Some fragments already appear off and on between April and October, and it is also obvious that after returning the proofs to his publisher, C. G. Naumann, on 6 December, Nietzsche went on correcting the text and writing variations on it during his very last days in Turin. So even if the outline of the work was established in a few days, one can say that many of its sentences and paragraphs had been on Nietzsche's mind for months, up to the moment of his breakdown. Besides, there is a close connection among all of Nietzsche's writings between April and October 1888. Each of these works is governed by the same gesture, the bursting forth of a wild theatricality, his self-presentation on the stage by concentrating his whole being in its most intense form. With *Ecce Homo* this impulse is fully displayed, but the style, tempo, and manner are similar in *The Case of Wagner, The Twilight of the Idols,* and *The Antichrist*—all of them composed between April and September 1888. First among them is *The Case of Wagner,* which Nietzsche already mentions incidentally to Peter Gast in April: "My fingers at the moment are busy with a little *pamphlet* on music."[14] By May the little book is finished, perhaps the most astonishing example in Nietzsche of the pure *art of gesture*. One might wonder why just now, ten years after his break with Richard Wagner and five years after the composer's death, Nietzsche should feel the need to write a savage attack on him. Here too the answer involves the whole process of Nietzsche's last phase. Indeed, as we will see, only the preexisting, albeit unformulated, thought of *Ecce Homo* can account for his need to write *The Case of Wagner.*

The first big problem that looms for Nietzsche at the beginning of his Turin spring is the acceptance of the theater, of the stage. Having thought all his life *about* the theater, he now finds himself faced with the imperative to *practice* it. And for Nietzsche, theater has always been synonymous with Wagner. The stage *is* Wagner, and to mount the stage himself Nietzsche must rid it of Wagner, must set down and etch the differences like scars. The tenor of the text is derisive; the action has an unseemly mobility; here for the first time Nietzsche tries out the *Prado style,*[15] the mask of the "decent criminal."[16] The Nietzsche who is quick to assume the role of *histrio* [actor] raises the *histrio* Wagner to the sinister archetype of the simulator, that deadly category that had been on his mind ever since *The Birth of Tragedy.* Here, for the last time, Nietzsche stares at the features of the being who is his exact opposite, before meeting him on the same stage, his own features set firmly for the last time *in a role,* in the last pages of *Ecce Homo.* This dual movement already recalls the gesture of the tragic hero who wills "the utter collapse into his opposite";[17] otherwise, why should Nietzsche choose to present himself with the greatest theatricality, the very weapon of his antipode? Attacking, in the name of music, the perversion of the actor who *makes use* of music, and thereby breaking the supreme spell of decadence—this is *The Case of Wagner.* Using the weapons, gestures, masks, and indiscretion of the actor to make music of oneself, a monologue that forgets *itself* and is "the music of forgetting"[18]—this will be *Ecce Homo.*

The real response to *The Case of Wagner* was to come more than seventy years later. Just as Nietzsche recognized in Wagner his only existing antagonist, thereby rendering him the highest tribute, so it was to Nietzsche that Martin Heidegger devoted his most articulate piece of writing on the subject of a modern, though still untimely, thinker, paying him the supreme compliment of calling him "the last Western metaphysician."[19] And just as Nietzsche distanced himself in everything from Wagner's opponents, so Heidegger had little to do with all the generations of critics and impugners of Nietzsche; much more important, he was the only one to *respond* to Nietzsche. To be sure, the style and tone are different, not to say opposed. Where Nietzsche indulged in sarcastic clowning and violent confrontation, the exacerbation of thoughts expressed quite otherwise in his private letters, Heidegger instead chose Wagnerian envelopment, the capacity to absorb any outside argument into his own idiom; for the thrust of the fencer, he substituted the undulation of the octopus. Heidegger's praise is as lethal to Nietzsche as Nietzsche's scorn is to Wagner. To be the last metaphysical thinker, the last *tableau vivant* of the West before its destiny flows into the glades of Being, revealing in the darkness what the West has never had the good fortune to see, while a Swabian shepherd leads us to the sound of spellbinding music (which, by the way, reminds us of something: perhaps the English horn of the watchful shepherd, he too the guardian of being, who forever enthralls us at the opening of the third act of *Tristan*?) is the most ironic nemesis that could befall Nietzsche. For Nietzsche's intention—and he was sure he had succeeded—was to break out of the enchanted castle of metaphysics. He himself had already defined that castle, in Heidegger's sense, one would say today, as a site of marvelous spells where the inhabitants are unaware of living under a spell. Of course, having emerged from this place, he claimed to have found not silent country paths but a desert that extends endlessly and easily swallows one up, where there is no marked goal. Heidegger has splendidly demonstrated how Nietzsche can be absorbed into Heidegger's thought: In a grandiose historical perspective ranging from the pre-Socratics to today, Nietzsche comes to represent the last period that has a name.[20] The great thinkers parade in succession across the stage of the West, each quietly uttering his formula, *his* thought, that unique thought that belongs only to great thinkers; others have so many thoughts. On this stage Nietzsche says, "Will to Power." His words are a seal, whereupon the curtain comes down on metaphysics; it will no longer have anything to say but will continue to act in the *Gestell,* Heidegger's word for our world as the fulfillment of metaphysics.

Let us look for a moment at this huge spectacle before questioning its legitimacy, an old metaphysical vice. Who could have invented it but a man of the theater, a prodigious director, who knows how to manipulate the strings of thought with the automatic perfection of the great puppet masters? And yet we know that the virtues fostered by Heidegger are sobriety, steady and solitary reflection, and silence. How can this be? Let us turn now to Heidegger's language: From *Sein und Zeit* through his last writings, throughout multiple variations, we are always faced with an omnivorous organism that reduces everything to a substance homogeneous with itself. At first the movement is slow, sometimes inadvertent, punctuated with tautologies; but these tautologies, Heidegger warns us, are always *something else*—and so they are. They may be hypnotic devices, for in a few pages we find ourselves ensnared, sweetly drawn to precise, unforeseen conclusions of great importance, and yet not one of them has convinced us; we have not seen any gesture of persuasion. Perhaps it is the uninterrupted murmur of being that has dragged us along with its ultimate power. Heidegger's lexicon changed several times over the course of forty years, yet the process of his writings remained the same while the spell he cast grew even greater. One would say, in short, that Heidegger's thought, in order to act, needed all his machinery. The word is deliberate. Is it not from their equipment, the very principle of modernity, that these texts derive their strength?

Let us now look more closely at how Heidegger's machinery works, which is above all by *etymological chains.* He begins by reflecting on a word. We choose the first word: "thought." In the space of a few pages, a chain is forged on the thread of etymology, no matter whether certain or dubious: *Gedanke—Gedanc—Dank—Andenken.*[21] Briefly, before our very eyes, a transformation has taken place: The indeterminate "thought" has become "grateful memory." Take another fundamental word: "representation." Here the chain is formed from *Vorstellung,* through the many compounds of the verb *stellen,* up to the obscure final term *Gestell;* the whole history of metaphysics is prefigured in this single transition. Or from *Grund* in the sense of "reason" and *Grund* in the old sense of "soil," one jumps, through *Satz* in the sense of "principle" and *Satz* in the sense of "leap," into the *Grundlosigkeit,* "the lack of foundation" of the *Abgrund,* "abyss."[22] It will be said that this implicit phonetic cabala has a long tradition in Germany, that Jakob Böhme and other seventeenth-century theosophists were no less daring. But there it was precisely a question of theosophy, knowledge of God—and the word "God" does not often turn up in Heidegger, though at times the adjectival form "the divine" is allowed. But that, as we know, is something quite different. And what can a phonetic cabala be without God, without a God who divinely establishes language, *phýsei* and not *thései,* against the prime axiom of Western metaphysics? It will no longer be a *sophía,* but it will certainly still be thought, even very complex thought, in which, however, it will not be only the traditional figure of the philosopher who acts but also the likewise mysterious

one of the funambulist. By now we are no longer in the promised land beyond metaphysics but in a more familiar sphere, the one Nietzsche called
the sphere of the *Artistik,* an indispensable word, closer indeed to the life
of the acrobat than to that of the philosophy professor. It is the farthest
area of decadence, the seductive spot where all the treasures of the modern lie hidden, including the intoxication of nihilism. We are even very
close to Nietzsche, since this is just what Nietzsche wanted to leave behind him after living to the point of exhaustion. Is not Zarathustra's first
stand-in a tightrope walker? Is it not Zarathustra himself who buries him,
with immense respect, as the victim of his mortal risk? We are back to
Wagner, hero of the *Artistik,* who wanted to be a hero of something quite
different, as did Heidegger. Now perhaps we can better explain the bewitching quality of Heidegger's *etymological chains:* Are they not somehow equivalent to Wagner's compositional procedure? And was not Wagner perhaps, like Heidegger, an advocate of the *authentic*? Heidegger
responded to Nietzsche's stated injustice toward Wagner with a more devious injustice, by denying Nietzsche the first privilege he had claimed for
himself, that of not being, by Western standards, a philosopher at all, but
a nomad who plunders the crumbling temples of philosophy and then returns to *his* desert. The will to power is not Nietzsche's answer to the
question of Being *[Sein],* reduced to a question of being *[Seiende],* but the
obscure criterion for understanding any possible answer to the question
of knowledge, as a symptom of the rise or collapse of force, of the various
degrees of affirmation or denial of the world. Whatever the will to power
may be, it is even more obscure than the obscurity recognized by Heidegger.
Nietzsche himself, by likening it to a "chimera," warned against the dazzle
of clarity. The irreducibility of this formula—and of the eternal return,
which is the formula's other version—to the basic coinages of Western
thought, systematically set forth by Heidegger in the second volume of
his *Nietzsche,* is virulently expressed in all of Nietzsche's last writings, in
the whole phase that culminates in *Ecce Homo* and the letters from Turin,
before being lost in silence. And it is precisely this final chapter that shat-
ters the framework suggested by Heidegger. Moreover, Heidegger was
quite sparing in his references to the ultimate Nietzsche and rightly saw
the question as an open one. But all of Nietzsche is an open question, and
not all of his horizon coincides with that of the metaphysical theater set
up by Heidegger. But one can still say that in the end Heidegger has never
been more faithful to himself than in his book on Nietzsche, for there he

has shown thought in progress as *Andenken,* "grateful memory," bestowing on Nietzsche that singular *gratitude* that years before had inspired *The Case of Wagner.*[23] The tempo of astral friendship differs from earthly rhythms, responses roam through names, years, and things, and yet a certain order is observed in these movements. Would it not be time now to expect a *Case of Heidegger*?

III

If the phase that begins with the draft of *Ecce Homo* and ends with madness tends to elude even the most subtle speculative analysis, such as Heidegger's, it is because Nietzsche has tried something that already lies outside the sphere of representative thought. What he seems to have wanted to demonstrate visibly is the passage, already implicit in his previous thinking, from a theory that is radical but still respectful of formal conventions to a *practice* of an unprecedented nature, which remains forever his most mysterious point.

The trail of the theatrical manifestation of this *practice* leads through everything that Nietzsche wrote between October 1888 and the very first days of January 1889: *Ecce Homo* is the only work completed in this period, and in a certain way it is the prelude to this practice. Faced with these last writings, which ought to be taken as a whole—*Ecce Homo,* last notes, last letters—one has only a single choice: Either to consider them as clinical material, documents of the outbreak of insanity, or to read them in terms of their own necessity, linking them on the one side to all of Nietzsche's previous work and on the other to the silence that follows them. Here we will ignore the first possibility, not because it is devoid of interest in itself but because of its necessarily heavy-handed approach to the material it is called upon to treat. To choose the other path, however, does not mean to shun the final outcome of madness, with the excuse that one should concentrate on Nietzsche's texts. On the contrary, it presupposes—and we will see in the end in what sense it can be demonstrated—that madness was implicit in all the activity of Nietzsche's last years, which can even be seen as the systematic *construction of madness.* At this point, one might wonder *what sort* of madness we are dealing with, with the understanding that the word is used here as a term of convenience, taken up and left in its natural imprecision.

How does it happen that Nietzsche feels the need to write *Ecce Homo*?

Did he not see from the beginning that the very plan of this work runs counter to his secret sense of etiquette? It is one thing to settle accounts with his past by silent study in the cave, quite another to settle them by the most exaggerated self-dramatization on the stage. This prospect opens wide for Nietzsche during his first stay in Turin. *The Case of Wagner* represents the removal of the first obstacle: the tracking down of theatrical falsity where it pretends not to exist and claims to present an authentic essence. Then finally the stage has been cleared: Nietzsche can appear on it to assert the need for the *false theatrical,* deliberately willed. But this *false theatrical* has to be Nietzsche himself, the real Nietzsche: *"Above all, do not mistake me for someone else."*[24] Here a knot appears, at first sight inextricable, a new form of vicious circle. And it is precisely this knot that was succinctly put forward by Nietzsche as one of his four great "questions of conscience" in *Twilight of the Idols,* that is, just before *Ecce Homo*: "Are you genuine? Or merely an actor? A representative? Or that which is represented? In the end, perhaps you are merely a copy of an actor. *Second* question of conscience."[25] A few lines later, having exhausted the list of "questions of conscience," Nietzsche wrote: "Those were steps for me, and I have climbed up over them: to that end I had to pass over them."[26] But Nietzsche does not tell us *how* he responded to his "question of conscience," he only says he overcame it. And the answer will come in *Ecce Homo,* which is the theatrical event par excellence in Nietzsche's life.

The question of the theater in Nietzsche is quite other than one of aesthetics. If anything, it is the very question of knowledge that opens out in it. Ever since his notes from the period of *The Birth of Tragedy* (1869–71), Nietzsche had acknowledged the antithesis that was to torture him to the end: the one between the Dionysian man and the actor. It is the Dionysian man who generates the tragedy, the man who is able to experience it in its endless metamorphosis. But alongside this ecstatic being looms a shadow, which will always accompany him: the actor. In him, "this world midway between beauty and truth manifests itself as a game with rapture, no longer being totally swallowed up by it. In the actor we find the Dionysian man, the poet, singer, and instinctive dancer, but as an *imitation of the Dionysian man.*"[27] "We no longer believe in this language, we no longer believe in these men, and what otherwise moved us as the most profound revelation of the world, now strikes us as a repulsive masquerade. . . . We feel something similar to a desecration."[28] The actor appears here as a parasite drawing substance from the sacred power of the transformation. He is the very doubt that undermines the tragic affirmation, the constant possibility of emptying it, and he empties as well any human action through simulation. From the time of these early observations until 1888, Nietzsche will never stop thinking about the actor. And for him, Wagner will be the most potent catalyst, the one who will truly show him the extent of the terrible trap concealed in the question.

Moving ahead by eighteen years to consider the situation of Nietzsche's thought on the eve of *Ecce Homo*, we see that in the course of many transformations the initial terms have been in a sense reversed. The critical point in this evolution was the moment when the problem of the actor came in contact with Nietzsche's radical gnosiological criticism, already set forth in *Human, All Too Human* and carried relentlessly forward to the end. The first thesis Nietzsche wanted to refute was the fundamental one of all Western thought, affirming truth as *adaequatio rei et intellectus*. Nietzsche's dogged inquiry tolerates no doubts on this point: Every form of representation is a *necessary* falsification, which immensely reduces reality but presents itself to us *as if* it comprised the whole of reality. This intrinsic falsity of representation is, moreover, our greatest organic defense, for without it we would only be the chaotic movement of the will for truth, which is basically suicidal will. The dilemma of knowledge is posed in these terms: Either thought wants everything (and then it kills the subject that thinks it), or thought renounces everything (and then it kills life). For Nietzsche, this would hold true for all Western philosophy beginning with Socrates.

Representation is thus a *feigned* relation with reality: This is the only basis of our knowledge, and it is arbitrary besides. If the unconscious simulation manifested in cognitive activity is defined by its character of necessary *incompleteness* in reproducing what it simulates and at the same time by its claim to be at all moments the whole of what it simulates, then the man of representations is first of all the actor—a passive actor who does not know and must not know he is such. This, of course, applies not only to his relation with the world but, primarily, to the subject's relation with himself; or rather, here simulation appears in its pure state, since it lacks any possibility of verification. The subject himself, in fact, is the first simulation, the one that makes all the others possible, a simulation characterized by maximum persistence. At this point, it is already clear that the more Nietzsche pushes on with his criticism of the actor, the more he is obliged to grant him importance and the closer he brings him to the center of the very nature of man. Eventually the terms have switched positions: No longer is it the actor who grows like a parasite on the trunk of the Dionysian man; on the contrary, it is the Dionysian man who can reveal himself only on condition that he don the garb of the actor, in a certain way grow over him. As Nietzsche proceeds with his devastating inquiry into the gnosiological question, he shows with increasing clarity that knowledge is primarily a *comedy of knowledge,* an ineradicable theatricality that operates within the individual, constantly reproduces itself in solitude, and *must* reproduce itself for the economy of life to be maintained. Here it is not even a question of tracing "what really happens." About the "inner process," about the ground—if there ever is a ground— what little Nietzsche had to say is obscure. But the upheaval produced by his thought lies in his having considered thought itself as exteriority, pure symptomatology, a series of gestures, like nature itself. Here is the question that Nietzsche raises: "To what extent can thought, judgment, all of logic be considered as the outer aspect, or symptom, of a much more inner and fundamental occurrence?"[29] The answer is: completely. "The world of thought only a second degree of the phenomenal world."[30] This is the final limit of Nietzsche's gnosiological criticism: to turn all knowledge and thought *inside out,* presenting it as a continual surface across which the fabric of nature extends, something that serves for *manifesting* a process but never for making a judgment back from the process to its beginning; thought belongs to the *circle of signs.* One does not, therefore, in the face of knowledge, now raise the question of truth: Is it correct or incorrect? Knowledge cannot even insist on the standard of correctness. The question is instead the very question of the theater: What and how much reality is knowledge capable of asserting and supporting? How much reality does it exclude?

The actor thus continues to reappear at the center. We met him at the beginning as the protagonist of decadence, that is, as a historical figure, but by now it would seem that his presence cannot be eliminated, since decadence itself has turned out to be something more than a historical process that can be engulfed by time. Decadence is produced by the action of our consciousness and is the direct operation of thought. The Dionysian man, the man defined by his capacity to emerge from himself through metamorphosis, now becomes a special example of life, a happy exception. And to what will the Dionysian man return when he is once more within himself? Haven't we seen that the subject himself is a simulation?

The theatrical nature of Western thought, the continuous identity of its scenario, its look of a game in which the pawns always move on the same chessboard—these result from the implicit acceptance of a rule: that the *primum* is always in the midst of the numbers, that the origin lies along the way and asserts itself all the same as origin, while the origin can only lie outside the chessboard, the chessboard being already the dispersion. But the other, complementary rule of the scenario is that the dispersion never be stated as such, that it always be reabsorbed into something, that the game not be uninterrupted, as called for by its nature, that it always stop at some opportune point in the game itself. If philosophy is thought that starts from zero, thought without foundation, then Western philosophy is thought that starts from zero and always manages to establish a *primum.* But there is no path between zero and one. Nietzsche has given away the rules of this game and is therefore the great *traitor* of Western thought.

 When Descartes, with his genius for the falsely self-evident, stated in his *Regulae ad directionem ingenii* that the operation of knowledge should be preceded by the enumeration of the facts pertinent to the problem,[31] the model latent in all Western thought came to light for the first time in the crudity of a practical suggestion. The device of enumeration is certainly not a calm measure of the intellect; it has immense power, a power that still suffuses scientific thinking. To require that the facts be enumerated is the first step leading to the much more rigorous requirement of a formal system. But with this step, exclusion is already admitted; the renunciation of the whole and the practice of simulation is explicitly introduced: Given an enumerable set of facts, simulation is the process that allows one to consider that set equivalent to the whole of the problem raised. Descartes is said to have merely revealed a model already latent in the dominant line of Western thought, its appearance being only a transition in the progressive manifestation of a single potential: formalization. Nietzsche, in the course of his criticism of knowledge, his inquiries into the "secret history of philosophers," sniffed out this *identity of place* in Western thought, this constant complicity of the most diverse speculations, and he gave it a name, implicating all of it in a single vicissitude: the history of nihilism. And formalization is only another name for nihilism.

If the common feature of metaphysics, the index fossil of the West, is precisely the tacit claim that thinking about the world can and should present itself as a formal system, and if, for this very reason, even thinking about God, which would seem to be exempt from this compulsion, has been increasingly transformed in our history from theosophy, as exegesis of a given and unattainable word, into theology, the rudiment of a deductive argument and chain of proofs, then it is no wonder that philosophy professors are scandalized over the numerous contradictions found in Nietzsche's writings. In fact, the sense of contradiction in Nietzsche is quite new; he is speaking by now from somewhere else. His argument may be incongruous, but it can no longer be refuted *because* it is incongruous: Here it is not a question of incorporating the contradiction into a lax and disguised formal system, as it is in the grandiose attempt of German idealism and especially of Hegel. Here the contradiction is stated as an independent and unrelated power, which does not expect to be justified; it is the very game of thinking that wants it and continues to insist on it. Nietzsche represents the advent of thought that has no wish to expend itself in the construction of formal systems, conscious or unconscious. Such thought cannot, nor does it want to, provide proofs; rather, it offers itself as pure imperative, a succession of forms, basically unaware at every step of what has gone before and what follows. What can such thought do with its contradictions? Maybe it forgets them.

If thoughts are gestures, like the forms of nature—"We must consider our thoughts as *gestures*"[32]—then one of the more suitable criteria for considering them will actually be style, which is the "art of the gesture," as Nietzsche repeats for the last time in *Ecce Homo*. The style of decadence is Wagner's, but it is also Socrates', and *almost* all our history is included between these two extremes. But by what signs does one recognize the style of decadence? First of all, decadence always appears as a representative system, since it needs to exclude from itself a part of the world that it is not ready to support and lacks the strength to sustain the pain and death implicit in all perception. This is the withering diagnosis that Nietzsche, man of decadence, let fall on himself and on our history.

"Since each thing is so connected with everything, to try to exclude any one thing means to exclude everything."[33] In this sentence Nietzsche presented his fulcrum, *his* gesture that compels him to seek beyond the man of decadence. The direction of this search, however, reveals at once that it is a matter not of replacing one image of man by another but of denying man himself. Indeed, exclusion is not a temporary or secondary characteristic of knowledge but what defines it. We cannot help excluding, even if we consider knowledge a fiction, because our bodies cannot do otherwise. Hence the despair of nihilism: One recognizes the illusory nature of knowledge but cannot give up knowing; one lives in a *compulsion to know,* and such knowing is groundless. At this point it would no longer be possible for Nietzsche simply to counter, as he did in the period of *The Birth of Tragedy,* with the antithetical image of the Dionysian man. The analysis has already been pushed too far along the suicidal path where one has to verify knowledge, and there are no more exits. To abandon the man of decadence means by now to abandon man. It is now that the eternal return appears in a flash. And it will be the basis for the enigmatic image of the superman, the metamorphosis of the Dionysian man: the being who proclaims the eternal return and lives it.

Above the rubble of knowledge and the fragmentation of chance, the sun reaches the "moment of the briefest shadow," the Panic clarity of noon; as the true world *and* the apparent one are engulfed, the fable goes on telling stories about its fate: The "escutcheon of necessity" appears from the sky, and the world asks to be expressed in another language.[34] First in the guise of his double Zarathustra, then, with *Ecce Homo,* presenting *himself* as the double, Nietzsche abandoned the path of philosophy with an abrupt gesture, the ongoing result of his vision of the eternal return. The fact that Nietzsche himself did not write much about the eternal return, despite the supreme importance that that doctrine assumed in his thought; moreover, the fact that what he did have to say in no way justifies making any unequivocal statement on the idea of the eternal return, since it combines other, often incompatible elements, whereby the argument would appear at times as a chain of proofs based on scientific fact, at others as instant certainty—all this would suggest that we are in the presence of something that can be approached only on its own terms. Actually, the eternal return is not a thought that can be added to another thought but a *practice* that overturns the very state of thinking about the world as the sole imperative making it possible to endure the whole of existence. Nietzsche's attack on representative thought was now concluded: By its very nature, any representative thought is forced to exclude some parts of the world; it is obliged to build a lazaretto where that part of existence not admissible in good society must live. This is above all pain, constantly opposed by thought in an effort at anesthetization (and this effort is almost the definition of the modern), and time, which thought keeps separating from itself, thus laying the foundations for revenge. Anesthetization of pain and evocation of revenge: this is the final residue left by thought after Nietzsche's disrespectful inquiry. These two features already comprise all of metaphysics; the attack on Christianity and morality will be only a derivation from them.

Now Nietzsche's aim is to abolish the permanent structure of Western thought: the clash between ego and world. Nietzsche wants to emerge from representation, but by rejecting the Vedantic path of identification, he maintains all the terms of the confrontation and illuminates and preserves the biological need for representations, while transporting them into another space, which is no longer that of knowledge or of any kind of objectivity. Now it is the sea of force, where each epistemological gesture, the feat of a fictitious subject, becomes a savage wave amid the immensity of others. We are made not for knowing but for acting as if we know—this "as if" is the necessary guarantee of thought, but it is a guarantee that has always had to remain unconscious because to acknowledge it is unbearable. For the *bête philosophe* it means paralysis and derision. Nietzsche chooses to put this "as if" at the center of the action and *insists* that the action be exalted by it, because only now does it lose all reference and appear in its pure form as an aggregate of signs that do not, cannot, and do not even *want* to know their origins. With this last transition to the wholly groundless will, the world is once more an enigma, an enigma composed also of its various solutions.

But how do we emerge from the circle of exclusion? Let us go back to where we started: "Since each thing is so connected with everything, to try to exclude any one thing means to exclude everything." Given this necessary connection of everything, each instant will therefore include within itself, in extremely abbreviated form, all preceding ones. And yet we live it as a separate entity, bowing in this to the constraints of representation. To bow instead to the necessity of the whole, we should, in opposition to our immediate impulse, discover a *practice* that allows us to live the abbreviated whole in the instant. And this practice is only one: to live the instant *as if it were to be endlessly repeated,* that is, recovering in the necessity of an unlimited future, in which the same is repeated, the unlimited past of the necessity that has constructed the present instant. This practice *is* the eternal return. Thought has shed its skin. It is no longer a subject representing the world, but it is *as organ of the world* that it asserts itself, and therefore the world in its entirety. But this transition has occurred by making use of the specific means of representative thought. In order to approach necessity, thought has need of simulation—is this not the practice of the eternal return?—just as it had needed it to defend itself from necessity itself. The world is two-faced at every point: Its elements remain constant, their use is forever twofold. Perhaps never before has this suspicion come to light as it does in Nietzsche, and not by chance in theatrical form. The attack on representative knowledge, accused of being unable to recognize necessity, does not lead to not knowing or to the construction of *another* kind of knowledge; rather, the very elements of representation and its process—simulation—are now turned toward necessity and converge on the closest approach to the affirmation of necessity: the eternal return. "*To stamp* on becoming the nature of being."[35]

We have so far been following a single track in the boundless Nietzschean labyrinth, the track that might ultimately lead to answering the question "What necessity gave rise to *Ecce Homo*?" We have seen how the pair of *theatrical twins,* the man of decadence and the Dionysian man, appear in Nietzsche from the start and accompany him ever after, through multiple nuances, transitions, and disguises, yet representing themselves each time as inseparable companions, mutually hostile but accustomed to the same instruments, the same weapons. After the lightning flash of the eternal return, the seal of the final phase, a word that had always pertained to Nietzsche finds itself being glorified and once again placed violently at the center. It is the word "destiny." In *Ecce Homo* Nietzsche faces his destiny, in his dual aspect as man of decadence and Dionysian man, in his single aspect as harbinger of the eternal return.

IV

Ecce Homo is the work that Nietzsche devoted to destiny. The subtitle— *How One Becomes What One Is*—already offers the book as an education in destiny. This important notion, continually impoverished by the West throughout its history and finally relinquished to the exclusive use of palm readers and sentimentalists, resurfaces in Nietzsche with both its archaic and its newest features, since now the context in which the notion thrived has disappeared; to conceive destiny amid chaos is a task that thought sets itself for the first time with Nietzsche. *Fate and History* and *Free Will and Fate*—these are the titles of two school themes by the eighteen-year-old Nietzsche. We find in them a transparent prefiguration of the final Nietzsche, as though with a steady but unwitting hand he was already outlining his thought as destiny. Even at that time, Nietzsche, in his invincible determination, could not conceive the will except as "fatal will," or rather, as the "supreme power of fate."

And the will sought in *Ecce Homo* is no different, except that now, having completed the circuit, Nietzsche wants to bring his thought closer to a *practice,* insisting that his own destiny be visibly configured in his writing and recognized as such by the world. In this intention, Nietzsche dealt with the penultimate consequence of his thought, obeying his impulse with the "ancient sovereignty of mind."[36] Now that thought has abandoned the claims of representation and has itself become a fragment of the world, the task can now be only to discover its own necessity. But if this task presents itself as the story of one's life, it obliges one to describe and *enumerate* oneself. The word defining the thought that Nietzsche wanted to avoid here reappears. But this time enumeration is not reduced to a *mere* practical measure. Here, on the contrary, it becomes an insolent challenge: to express one's destiny by gathering what one has casually squandered in life under the sign of necessity. The threat that we feel hanging over this enterprise is analogous to the ancient tradition about the baleful nature of the census. Nietzsche simultaneously approaches the utmost consistency and the utmost contradiction—a word that here does not designate a logical objection but *nefas* [the impious] itself.

Ecce Homo is constructed as a set of superimposed impossibilities: to don the garb of the actor (that is, of the person with no destiny) to tread a huge stage and present the figures of one's own destiny; to point to Dionysus with the same words, *ecce homo,* used for Christ *dressed up* as king ("And the soldiers platted a crown of thorns, and put it on his head, and they put on him a purple robe");[37] to say simultaneously "I am dynamite," and "I am a nuance";[38] to pass through one's destiny as a familiar place and even open the doors casually on one's future; to prepare humanity for "the most difficult demand ever made of it"[39] with a short book of indiscreet autobiography, thus indulging in one of the most obvious vices of decadence—all these discordant and misleading characteristics, by their very excess, end by convincing us that *Ecce Homo* is exactly what it promises to be, a sort of prodigious compendium of a polymorphous being who offers us a complete explanation and enumerates not only all the passages but all the gestures of his destiny. The mosaic of quotations from previous works inserted into *Ecce Homo* thus reveals in hindsight its formal justification, instinctively chosen by a great "fanatic for expression": to enclose in a single frame the entire repertory of tones and nuances, to compel oneself for the first time to make a frontal presentation. In *Ecce Homo* "I'll be seen completely all at once,"[40] and this because, as Nietzsche was to write a month later, "now I no longer write a line in which I don't appear *completely* on the stage."[41] In this sense *Ecce Homo* is one of the outstanding successes in Nietzsche's work. Its lightness and flexibility of language, its capacity to move simultaneously and continuously on many levels, its combination of opposing rhythms—the aristocratic *lento* of certain abrupt openings, the nervous *prestissimo,* the judgment expressed in a staccato drumbeat—are the signs of maturity, of the grand style that embraces and holds in its grasp the discordant forms of a man who, like few others, was able to pass through the whole circle of appearance. A perfect work—but what occurs in *Ecce Homo* is also something quite different. The great changes of madness unfold in the hidden chamber of this work, something mysterious haunts these pages, and the mystery is destined to remain such. This will come as no surprise to a reader of Nietzsche: That his book of maximum exposure should also be one more cave, perhaps more inaccessible than the others, is part of Nietzsche's game.[42] And *Ecce Homo* may even be a sign of modesty, the distraction of a masquerade to cover a discreet event that requires obscurity and silence: Nietzsche taking leave of himself.

Before recapitulating history and all that said "I"—the last days in Turin—Nietzsche recapitulated his own history, reviewing his whole past, as the saying goes, in the hour of his death. There is no intention in all this, only a temporary submergence, the biological foreshadowing of great transformations, like dreaming of the dead: "*Indication of violent changes.*—If we dream of people we have long since forgotten or who have for long been dead, it is a sign that we have gone through a violent change within ourself and that the ground upon which we live has been completely turned over: so that the dead rise up and our antiquity becomes our modernity."[43] In *Ecce Homo* Nietzsche dreams of himself as dead and looks at himself, the posthumous man, with a posthumous gaze before his flight into all that is other has begun. To evoke the whole image of one's own destiny means to evoke one's own death. This anticipation of destiny is the transgression that transforms *fas* into *nefas,* what is lawful into what is unlawful. At the end of his journey, in *Ecce Homo,* the very book devoted to destiny, the will to destiny is transformed in Nietzsche into the will to *nefas,* and even Nietzsche, who had been able to dissolve the superstition of facts in the theory of knowledge, falls under the spell of *destiny as fact.* In *Ecce Homo* he dares to set down the facts of his life as destiny, before preparing, in his last days in Turin, to make his actions coincide directly with destiny itself. This movement violates the law implicit in the notion of destiny—namely, that the time required to anticipate oneself is, at the most, equal to the time needed for the anticipated event to take place. Only Friedrich Hölderlin found a word for this impulse to violate fate *for the love of* fate. Nietzsche did not name it because he was to die of it.

The sin of Oedipus, according to Hölderlin,[44] is neither the murder of his father nor incest. It is in questioning Tiresias that Oedipus evokes the real *nefas* in his life. Oedipus sins because "he interprets too infinitely," as if it was he who first experienced the exaltation Nietzsche felt when a world subject to infinite interpretations was thrown open by his own provocation.[45] For this reason as well, Oedipus has become one of the primordial emblems of the West. Infinite interpretation is the savage, brutal power that bursts secretly into history with the classical age in Greece. Oedipus, from the start, is unable to discriminate in the presence of the oracle: He thus finds the twofold solution that once and for all indicates our ultimate ambivalence. First, the solution that allows him to escape death at the hands of the Sphinx; then, the solution, torn from the soothsayer, that will sentence him to death. Only Oedipus succeeds in avoiding death from the oracle, and only Oedipus finds himself subject to a death sentence by the oracle. The indissoluble link between the two solutions governs the whole space of thought as solution, within which we still find ourselves. Hölderlin writes that Oedipus ought to have interpreted the oracle in this way: "Establish, in general, a pure and rigorous judgment, maintain good civil order." Oedipus rejects generality; he wants the particular, the person. But what is the real difference between the two interpretations? That the first relinquishes a private solution and settles for the first derivation from the oracle, while the second gives itself over to an indefinite process, which will stop only when the particular is irreparably unveiled? To be sure—but there is also another, less obvious difference. The interpretation offered by Hölderlin is a response obedient to tradition, to an exegetic orthodoxy, whereby any interpretation is the reading of a sign that represents the state of the world, a process involving always and solely images of the whole. Oedipus's interpretation, on the other hand, looks for a chain of fragments. Even an exegetic orthodoxy can allow an indefinite series of superimposed levels of interpretation. But between them there must always be a homology, without gaps. Oedipus pursues a series of fragments that have only a single tie, the most particular and thoughtless: Each one points endlessly to the next. And this is the crux: Oedipus chooses the path, blasphemous and at the same time priestly ("But Oedipus in response at once, as priest"), of infinite interpretation, but he rejects its inner law: the endless, boundless, unstoppable multiplication of signs, now no longer subject to a judgment, orthodoxy, that could halt their proliferation. Thus for Oedipus it is not his interpreting but his sin that becomes truly infinite. Oedipus chooses the path of no appeal because there is no judgment, but nevertheless he still violently craves judgment; thus there is no way to appeal his sentence, and he is condemned to execute it himself on his own body. With Oedipus's judgment on himself, a new image of ruin is born, to be reproduced through metamorphosis right down to ourselves, down to the most awkward, most vacuous "coming to awareness"—a final, modest echo of that original "almost shameless effort to take hold of oneself, the mad wild pursuit of a conscience."

"Empedocles, long disposed by his feelings and his philosophy to hatred for culture and to contempt for every well-determined occupation, every interest directed at different objects, the mortal enemy of every one-sided existence," seems to us a man who suffers because "as soon as his heart and mind grasp what exists, they become bound to the laws of sequence."[46] The opposite extremes of nature and art—or, in Hölderlin's terms, of the organic and the aorgic—live in this man in their most exacerbated form. He is, as Nietzsche writes of himself, under cover of the language of the feuilleton, "at the same time a *decadent* and a *beginning*."[47] Empedocles is by nature a poet, but he is not destined for poetry. "The destiny of his time, the violent extremes in which he had grown up, did not require song. . . . the destiny of his time did not even require true action, which has an immediate effect and is a help. . . . it required a *victim,* in which the whole man became actually and visibly the one in which the destiny of his time seems to dissolve, in which the extremes of his time seem truly and visibly to be reunited in one."[48] But let there be no misunderstanding: The victim must not simply suffer the penalty, otherwise we are back in the Christian circuit of revenge. The victim *must* be guilty, he must be the one who collapses in his own guilt. And precisely this was Nietzsche's great obsession, expressed for the last time in *Ecce Homo*: "not to take the punishment upon oneself but the *guilt,* only this would be truly divine."[49] The mysterious sin of Empedocles is that he makes destiny *too visible,* dissolving it prematurely in the too intimate reunion of extremes:

> [Because of this action] the individual collapses and must collapse, since the tangible reunion, prematurely produced by crisis and dissension, has been shown in him, the reunion that dissolved the problem of destiny, but which can never be resolved individually and visibly, for otherwise the universal would be lost in the individual, and (what is still worse than all great movements of destiny and is the only impossible thing) the life of a world would be extinguished in a single entity.[50]

Instead, it is precisely this single entity that must be dissolved as a "premature result of destiny," because it was "too intimate and real and visible." And finally: *"Thus Empedocles had to become a victim of his time. The problems of destiny, in which he was born, had only apparently to be resolved in him, and this solution had to reveal itself as only temporary, as it does more or less in all tragic individuals."*[51] The affront to destiny, as the will to *nefas,* corrodes the defense of being in its creatures and thus necessarily drives them to ruin. But then this is not a punishment corresponding to a sin, *since that sin is itself a way of dying.*

Shortly before writing *Ecce Homo,* in a passage in *Twilight of the Idols* where a fragment of *Human, All Too Human*[52] clearly reappears in different words, Nietzsche described in *his* terms this way of dying, but he kept completely silent about the tragic mechanism that would prepare it for him. His words are a defense of the *construction of death:* "then a real farewell is still possible, *as the one who is taking leave is still there;* also a real estimate of what one has achieved and what one has wished, drawing the *sum* of one's life. . . . One never perishes through anyone but oneself. . . . From love of *life,* one should desire a different death: free, conscious, without accident, without ambush."[53] To have so altered the terms of an indiscreet Rousseauian autobiography, the height of decadence, into one of the unknown "hundred tragedies of knowledge" is the wonder of *Ecce Homo.* In this transformation no term is lost. From start to finish, the text thrives on the bitterest contradiction; the two theatrical twins, the actor and the Dionysian man, divide the last scene between them. The contradiction appears above all in the alternation of two opposite gestures that run through the whole text, leaving doubts as to which of the two, if either, will prevail in the end. We recognize in them the transposition of a similar dual movement in *Zarathustra,* the movement that at the same time made that work "a book for everyone and for no one." The first gesture appears immediately in the opening appeal of the work: *"Hear me! For I am such and such a person. Above all, do not mistake me for someone else."* Nietzsche does not customarily ask to be heard, and this is doubtless something, as he says, his pride instinctively rebels against. But the course of his movement now requires such a gesture: Once he has decided, in the will to *nefas,* to take literally his transformation of representative thought into a *practice* (and his practice is the presage of the eternal return), once he has recognized the absolute theatricality of thought, the stage of the world opens for Nietzsche, and then we also witness—with surprise, given Nietzsche's distaste for any kind of propaganda in itself—the determined effort to prepare the public for *Ecce Homo.* We see the birth of the idea of having the book appear simultaneously in four languages, the choice and sovereign courting of translators, the announcement of the book itself as a decisive *fact* of history. In this view, *Ecce Homo* becomes an event of "great politics," an initial skirmish in the "war of spirits."[54] This also accounts for the stupendous anti-German fury condensed in this book, more than in any other of Nietzsche's works. There is little to add, after a hundred years, to the clairvoyant precision with which Nietzsche treated the German spirit. As in the case of Wagner, here too he was able to choose something that *deserved* his fury: Germany as the ultimate bearer of the great thought of the West and *therefore* the origin of its corruption and a dismal end—the only possible interlocutor and antagonist for his words, as time has shown all the more clearly.

The second gesture, on the other hand, never manifests itself in explicit statements, but it is constantly asserted in the form. Only with the final dithyramb does it flare up in its violence. But there was already a trace in a few words at the beginning ("and so I tell my life to myself"), where the public has now vanished and the telling of *Ecce Homo* means talking to himself in the solitude of the monologue. And a monologue is exactly what the whole form of *Ecce Homo* will turn out to be. Nietzsche, to be sure, will don an actor's costume in these pages, since it is *also* his own, but unlike his antipode Wagner, he will not thereby try to become an expert operator on the sensory apparatus. That is not what interests Nietzsche. His art is something else, discreetly, almost fleetingly, hinted at in a few writings from the last years; indeed, he called it "monological art," the art of one who speaks with the void in front of him, the art of one who has created the void in front of him: "I do not know of any more profound difference in the whole orientation of an artist than this, whether he looks at his work in progress (at 'himself') from the point of view of the witness, or whether he 'has forgotten the world,' which is the essential feature of all monological art; it is based *on forgetting,* it is the music of forgetting."[55]

Monological art is first of all art without witnesses, but in it the other two obligatory terms in the analysis of art—the work and the artist—likewise disappear, since monological art is the art of forgetting and of forgetting oneself. There is only one other activity that is pursued in solitude, in the necessary elimination of the subject and indifference to the outcome—namely, solitary play, a monological and cosmological practice par excellence, where everything arranges itself according to necessity in a spectacle without spectators. The cosmic player "has forgotten the world," just as the solitary player forgets himself in playing and forgets the world because this time the player is the world itself.

Such a conception hurdles the usual boundaries of art in one leap; nor does it try to establish others. Nothing would be so deadening as to treat it in terms of aesthetics. Of course, if ever a writer's oeuvre could be considered, in its entirety, as an example of monological art, it would be that of the man who stated the formula, the work of Nietzsche himself. Whichever way we move in it, backward, forward, sideways, we hear a sound that may also be private, the echo of a vast monologue, a counterpoint of musical phantasms that pass across years and contradictions. Destiny does not ask of us consistency; it imposes its own, while thoughts and wishes serve it as pretexts. In the face of the overwhelming degradation of thought reduced to prosthesis, almost all the organs in direct contact with the world having been amputated (all that remains, upright on the head, is the defective antenna of thought about thought, *metathought,* while immediate thinking has atrophied), Nietzsche appears as a tree that grows "not in one direction but equally upward and outward and inward and downward,"[56] able to forget the trunk in every branch and each branch in the trunk, a power of expansion, the power of great form, governing what is written, experienced, dreamed. As the last example, not by chance a literal monologue, we discover the tumultuous loquacity of *Ecce Homo,* which overcomes all obstacles and concentrates too many things in every nuance, in a steady erotic connection with language, only possible by starting from perfect solitude. There, every visible interlocutor disappears, and nothing remains but the labyrinth of the monologue, the sound of inner voices in endless pursuit of each other: Zarathustra, the Cynic, Ariadne, Wagner. This premise alone can allow Nietzsche such felicity in the indiscreet task of judging himself.

V

In the realm of facts, *Ecce Homo* emerges as the last part of *Twilight of the Idols,* a quick self-portrait, which then becomes autonomous and takes shape as a work in its own right. In the realm of destiny, *Ecce Homo* is the book that represents the tragic breakdown of Nietzsche's life, death as his conscious farewell to himself, the ultimate discursive result of his previous thinking, offering again in theatrical form all its fundamental features at their most intense, even their most incompatible.

Many signs show that Nietzsche clearly felt the fatal significance of *Ecce Homo.* In two letters to Gast in November, five days apart, he already, unexpectedly, ends by asking his friend to give his words a "tragic meaning."[57] And yet so far nothing seems to threaten him; Nietzsche is in a period of unprecedented creative fervor: "I go on and on, ever more, in a *tempo fortissimo* of work."[58] At the beginning of December, Strindberg's letter discloses the first interlocutor; now that Nietzsche has begun to turn so violently outward, he proclaims himself and wants to proclaim himself to the world. In these same days, Nietzsche once more revises the manuscript of *Ecce Homo,* weighing it "on a golden scale." After sending it back to Naumann, he writes to Gast, "This work literally breaks the history of humanity in two!"[59] Before entering the series of enigmas of his last days in Turin, Nietzsche again twice mentions with obvious clairvoyance, what he has accomplished with *Ecce Homo* and what remains to be fulfilled.

"Meanwhile I don't see why I should hasten the course of the *tragic* catastrophe of my life, which begins with *Ecce Homo,*" he writes abruptly in a letter to Gast otherwise devoted to the subject of operettas, and this theme, too, as we will see, is coded.[60] Finally, on 27 December, he writes to Carl Fuchs, "All things considered, dear friend, from now on there's no point speaking and writing *about* me; with *Ecce Homo* I have put *ad acta* the problem of *who I am.* So there will no longer be any need to worry about me, only about the things for which I'm here."[61]

The first active signs of delirium, which would last until Franz Overbeck's arrival in Turin on 8 January 1889, now began to manifest themselves in Nietzsche. A number of letters from these days, sent to friends and political leaders, are variously signed "Dionysus" or "The Crucified" or "Dionysus the Crucified." Only the letter to Burckhardt, the longest, is signed "Nietzsche." In order to fathom the meaning of these "notes of madness," one must grasp what has happened with *Ecce Homo:* Nietzsche, ever the posthumous man, has now *become* posthumous, has buried himself ("This fall . . . I twice witnessed my funeral"),[62] and he now reveals the *comic* finale of the tragedy. But what in ancient Greece had been the satyr play now reappears, in the Europe of *Le Figaro* ("Of course, I maintain close relations with *Figaro*"),[63] in the guise of perfect frivolity. "That the most profound spirit should also be the most frivolous, this is almost the formula of my philosophy."[64] In his new mask as "jester of the new eternities," Nietzsche comes forth with a series of dreadful witticisms, culminating in the sublime sarcasm of the second letter to Burckhardt, which ends as follows: "You may make any use of this letter which will not degrade me in the eyes of the citizens of Basel."[65] As the final consequence of his practice, Nietzsche loses his mind and his name; he strips himself of a mode of expression that coincided with his person.

"Don't read books!"[66] is one of the last entries in Nietzsche's notebooks. Every line of the so-called notes of madness sets up vibrations with the rest of his work. Each sentence seems to be uttered under the seal of his previous thought, but the form of that thought is no longer apparent; its structure has been submerged. In the second and lengthier letter to Burckhardt, Nietzsche's language seems to consist wholly of what before had lived in its interstices: the burst of irony, the riddle, the sudden disguise. The fabric of his thinking is no longer visible. What has happened? Meanwhile, one can see that Nietzsche's perfect duality is maintained to the end: The Dionysian man is now Dionysus himself; the actor has become the feigned madman. Every symptom can still have a double interpretation, and every interpretation now lacks any foundation. If, then, one would like a true picture of what happens in Turin, seen from the standpoint of the actor, there is no point leafing through the various pathological explanations that have been proposed. Nietzsche himself comes to our aid, in a passage about the modern artist written precisely in 1888:

> The absurd excitability of his system, which makes him create crises out of every experience and puts a dramatic element into the smallest incidents of life, makes it impossible to count on him in any way; he is no longer a person, at most a rendezvous of persons, among whom now this one, now that one, appear with shameless assurance. For this very reason, he is a great actor: All these poor creatures, lacking in will, whom doctors study closely, are astonishing for the virtuosity of their mimicry, their capacity to transform themselves and take on almost *any character they desire.*[67]

Thus, once again, the usual scene is rewritten: It is the last appearance of the Dionysian man and the actor, but this time a split and a final interfusion take place, with no return. One of the two characters is fated to disappear into the secret; the other, to survive for a few more years as a clinical case. Before our eyes, for the last time, the Dionysian man is transfigured into the god who, together with Ariadne, governs "the golden equilibrium of all things,"[68] and alongside him, the actor is transformed into the madman who astonishes the psychiatrist by his acting talents.

The actor is a coward not because he takes leave of himself but because he *returns* to himself (in self-defense he has persuaded himself that he has an identity), because he makes a distinction between the stage and offstage, and because he comes to a halt—like the process of knowledge, by its nature *regressus in infinitum,* which instead always stops at some point: "What stops movement (to a presumed first cause, something unconditional, etc.) is *laziness,* weariness."[69] In obeying the suicidal will to truth that he had recognized as a will hostile to life, as the destruction of life itself, Nietzsche in his last year was increasingly forced to realize the *letter* of his thinking, which is moreover the most radical cancellation of the letter and thus also of the being who thought it. This affirmation of the letter accordingly requires that the declarative form of thought disappear. Thus, the notes of his madness can be considered as the last experiment in a way of thinking that in them denies its own form. This experiment puts life at stake: "To make an experiment of one's very life—this alone is *freedom* of the spirit, this then became for me philosophy."[70] In this final practice, all of thought becomes silent monologue, interrupted at intervals by forceful epigrams, just as the self-generation of the world is a soliloquizing and inaccessible activity, which proclaims itself only at intervals in fragments of forms. Any other disappears. Thus each of the letters seems to imply a thought, as though the addressee knew it already. It is impossible to bring them together in a consistent argument, these scattered tesserae of a vast mosaic, which has never been shown because it *could not* be and did not *want* to be shown.

More than thirty years after stating that the chief task of Nietzsche's thought is the abolition of identity, "disindividuation,"[71] Pierre Klossowski finally worked out a complete, convoluted, and masterful development of his theses on Nietzsche, creating a design with the "Turinese euphoria" as its center—corresponding to the hypothesis of departure, according to which Nietzsche's thought "rotates around delirium as around its axis"— and with the vicious circle precisely as its circumference. The first commentator on the theology of the *circulus vitiosus deus,*[72] Klossowski is also the first to tackle the last letters from Turin as a form of thought and to try to reconstruct, at least in part, their inner connections and progression. Previous attempts are valid at most as conscientious documentary evidence. Klossowski's intention, in a way the opposite of Heidegger's, is to remove Nietzsche from any context and to try, instead, to reconstruct his thought as the *unique sign* of something distinctive and incommunicable. In pursuit of this goal, Klossowski has made a number of memorable discoveries, but in the final analysis it appears that Nietzsche, that most elusive of human beings, has once again refused to be pinned down. Swayed by the impetus of his commentary, Klossowski also attempts a *reading* of the Turin messages. But what particularly distinguishes these messages is that, in their extreme transparency, they refuse to be read: Illusory statements, random outbursts—in them the discriminating play of truth and simulation comes to nothing. At this point, any reconstruction of their inner movement, as though one were dealing with some other text by Nietzsche, seems doomed from the start. And we see this confirmed when Klossowski subtly tries, for example, to explain the allusion to magic in the second letter to Burckhardt ("from time to time there is magic")[73] by tracing it back to what is also the biographical labyrinth of Ariadne–Cosima Wagner and Dionysus-Nietzsche.[74] For the first time, we feel that there is an unbridgeable gap between this short text and not only this explanation but any other as well. No commentator will ever emerge from that labyrinth. Madness may simulate, even with virtuosity, the language of reason ("We artists are incorrigible"),[75] but where the play of truth and simulation has been forever suspended, there is no way for reasonable language to exercise its interpretation in accordance with the discipline of philology. "O Ariadne, you yourself are the labyrinth: it is no longer possible to get out of it."[76]

Necessity and chance are each the mask of the other. The total acceptance of this double mask means coinciding with the world's movement and at the same time abdicating the fictitious necessity for an identity of one's own. Therefore, there is no "endpoint where necessity and the fortuitous meet;"[77] rather, chance and necessity always correspond, even though the conditions of existence require the two realms to be rigidly separated so that life can go on. Once this defense of life against itself is shattered, a third realm is opened, in which the discriminating play between truth and simulation is no longer possible, and this realm is madness.

With *Ecce Homo,* Nietzsche had been prematurely separated from his own identity, which, according to the doctrine of the eternal return, is nothing but a *cyclical syndrome.* In Nietzsche's previous thinking, the will to everything, the condemnation of exclusion, required each state to affirm in itself the succession of all other states and thus deny any claim to *exclusivity.* Nietzsche is now governed by a literal application of this doctrine, having been compelled to establish the image of his destiny in *Ecce Homo,* and it drives him to wander in a vast series of states, the *plural destiny* that follows the collapse of his own individual destiny. "We should not desire *a single* state, but we should *want to become periodic* beings: become, that is, equal to existence."[78] In this fragment, Nietzsche provided perhaps the most concise formulation, without naming it, of the eternal return. To abandon the *state* of one's identity is a particular instance of the process described: It means to put oneself into the cycle of the whole, which must come back to that identity, but only after completing its *period,* that is, passing through the chain of all other states. The sequence that now opens out is that of all simulations ("What is disagreeable and offends my modesty is that at bottom I am every name in history"):[79] Man, who is nature but who by nature denies being so, must simulate nature in order to rediscover that he himself is nature. The being who has become equal to existence generates the world from himself: The signs of this process are distributed throughout the last letters from Turin. "Siamo contenti? son dio, ho fatto questa caricatura" [Are we content? I am the god who has made this caricature].[80]

In August 1889, on one of her visits to the clinic in Jena, Nietzsche's mother realized that her son had secretly taken a pencil and some paper from her: "When I said to him jokingly, 'My old Fritz, you're a little thief,' he whispered in my ear, with a look of satisfaction, as we said good-bye, 'Now I have something to do when I hide in my den' *(Nun habe ich dich etwas zu tun, wenn ich in meine Höhle krieche)*."[81] *Höhle,* as we have already seen, is a key word for Nietzsche. Zarathustra's cave, philosophy as a cave, the den where the wounded beast hides, as does the *bête philosophe*—Nietzsche's remark to his mother evokes a chain of thoughts and in the end recalls the lone man who in Nice silently separated himself from his past. After a year on a huge stage, he went back into hiding. The "shining constellation" had passed forever: "a premonition that the end is near, like the prudence animals have before they die: they go off by themselves, become still, choose solitude, hide in caves *[verkriechen sich in Höhlen],* and become *wise.* . . . What? Wisdom as a screen behind which the philosopher hides from—spirit?"[82]

Once again, if *Ecce Homo* is a work intended to show "how one becomes what one is," if the madness in Turin is primarily the manifestation of a *practice* constructed by all of Nietzsche's previous thought, it will come as no surprise to find a text from the beginning of this journey that already seems to delineate all its phases in happy ignorance. I refer to the 1873 dissertation *On Truth and Lying in the Extramoral Sense,* where in a few brilliant pages, which remain among Nietzsche's finest, the arduous process that we have been following seems to take shape before our eyes. There, simulation, as a dominant force of the intellect, is already affirmed from the start: "The intellect as a means for the preservation of the individual reveals its principal forces in simulation." Mask, stage, and performance are recognized at once as constituent elements of knowledge; the truth itself as "a mobile army of metaphors"; veracity is defined as the obligation to "lie in accordance with a fixed convention."[83] Man appears as a *meta-*

phorizing being: "that instinct for constructing metaphors, that basic instinct of man, which we cannot leave out of account at any moment since
we would thereby leave man himself out of account."[84] There it is stated
that the simulative laws of knowledge are already given in the construction of language, where all the categories—subject, predicate, cause, and
so on—are prepared, categories that knowledge would claim to establish
by means of language. Knowledge is a *templum,* a columbarium, a sepul-
cher. Knowledge makes it possible to avoid pain.[85] Dumbfounded, we peruse these pages, recognizing in the swift progress of the argument the
endless underground passages that Nietzsche would spend fifteen years
digging after drafting this text. It all proceeds with fatal assurance. So
might we not find foreshadowed there not only the intermediate writings
but the dissolution of Nietzsche's thought as well? We do indeed: After
describing the history of knowledge as the history of concealed simulation, Nietzsche offers us another possibility, a perpetual alternative to
knowledge as a defense against the world and the threat of being crushed
by it. It is the path of active, self-aware, playful simulation, the one he
himself would later follow. And here we find perhaps the only adequate
description that could apply to Nietzsche's final state, as it appears in the
notes of his madness:

> That huge scaffolding and structure of concepts to which the man who
> must clings in order to save himself in the course of life, for the liberated
> intellect is merely a support and a toy for his daring devices. And should
> he break it, he shuffles it around and ironically reassembles it once more,
> connecting what is least related and separating what is closest. By doing so
> he shows that those needful ploys are of no use to him and that he is no
> longer guided by concepts but by intuitions. There is no regular path lead-
> ing from these intuitions into the land of spectral patterns and abstrac-
> tions: There are no words for them; man falls silent when he sees them, or
> otherwise speaks solely through forbidden metaphors and unprecedented
> conceptual structures, in order to respond at least in a creative way, by de-
> molishing and deriding the old barriers of the concept, to the feeling of
> powerful intuition that dwells within him.[86]

Nietzsche has been such a *forbidden metaphor* from his day to ours.

2 The Sleep of the Calligrapher

In this sense writing is a deeper sleep, or rather, death, and since you neither can nor would pull a dead man out of his grave, so you cannot get me away from my desk at night.
—*Franz Kafka,* Letters to Felice

From the moment Jakob von Gunten starts describing the Benjamenta Institute until the last lines in Robert Walser's eponymous novel, where we see the young hero preparing to leave for the desert, we get no sense of time. It may all be happening in days, months, or years; there is no way of knowing; duration is unspecified. A different measure of time is the real fence that separates the Institute from the rest of the world. Nor is there any indication of the seasons. Only once does Jakob observe that it is snowing, and he is quickly reminded of another snow, the vision of snow that he experienced on his visit to the "inner chambers" of the Institute, and we have no idea on what ground this snow fell. And yet the subtitle reads: *A Diary.* We are faced with a design and a rhythm, but they do not match what is going on. "One thing is true: Here nature is lacking." This is how the Benjamenta Institute is presented: as life delivered from cycles, as a sky beyond the most distant revolution of the stars, and at the same time, as the waters of the abyss. Walser, who considered discrimination in general to be an extravagance, was certainly not one to make a sharp distinction between mirrors.

The Institute proposes to teach its pupils how to serve. The teachers "are asleep, or else they're dead, or only apparently dead, or maybe they're fossils." The pupils have little to do. They memorize the precepts that govern the place. Or they peruse the book *What Is the Goal of the Benjamenta Boys' School?* They learn how to behave, devoting themselves to hours of imitative repetition of "everything that can happen in life." Specific knowledge is not imparted. At first young Jakob thinks of the place as a scam. But he will immediately change, forever. His loyalty to the Institute and his distance from every other form of life will keep growing. "What had then seemed to me ridiculous and idiotic looks fine and decent to me today." At the end, with the Institute in ruins, the faithful Jakob will be the last to leave. A transformation has taken place, and it has been brought about by instruction. "There, at the gymnasium, there were a lot of notions, here there's something quite different. We pupils are taught something quite different here." And what is this "quite different" something that Jakob finds at the Institute? Later we will discover cryptic traces, boundless echoes, eddies of prehistory, but in speaking of Walser one must first of all take note of his style, which goes forever off the track, shies hastily away from any hidden or obvious meaning, and calms down only as it approaches the lull of the insignificant. Writing is born from scribbling and must return to it. With Walser, we keep chasing around this circle.

Like Jakob von Gunten, Walser could only breathe "in the lower regions"; he looks primarily at minuscule events, scattered bits of life, whatever is negligible; his tone may be light or childish or rambling, the tone of words that go by and cancel each other out. At symbols Walser can only smile. Above all, he would find it a dreadful task to connect one meaning with another—and tactless pedantry to consider such a connection permanent. The titles of some of his prose pieces, however, seem to suggest weighty issues: "Something about Jesus," "Caesar," "Essay on Bismarck," "The Red Thread" (of history). But here the letdown is even greater. After a few opening words that appear to foreshadow serious, panoramic observations on the world, there is a sudden wavering, a change of direction that becomes ever more abrupt over the years, sometimes revealing a little of its darker meaning, and then Walser falls back on the first small, or at any rate extraneous, things that lie within range of association and from there begins to digress until he reaches an arbitrary stopping place, with nothing more to remind us of whatever major thoroughfare we had first set out on.

Last heir of the great romantics, Walser has a steady irony that presupposes the certainty that words are superfluous. Hence the prevalence of chitchat. "Here We Chatter" is the title of one of his short prose pieces and could also be the motto for all his works. The labyrinthine chatter in which Walser writes is a sign, a bulwark of murmurs and doodles against the threat of the Minotaur, a spell cast on the reader that allows the author to disappear. Whoever fails to recognize that each of Walser's words implies a previous catastrophe is likely to get him all wrong. Something has cut the moorings, and the hallucinatory vessel of Walser's prose sets sail without a crew, obeying impulses from wherever they may come. This wandering course certainly does not suggest free association; rather, it suggests the shifting receptiveness of matter.

> THE ROMANTIC WOMAN: I used to be more
> disheveled and spontaneous. For the sake of
> order I lost a sound. A largeness, a freedom, an
> ease, which was already sufficiently restrained,
> forsook me. In purifying myself, I repressed
> something essential, but with what's left of
> my ego I still get up to all sorts of mischief.
> —*Robert Walser,* Kleines Theater des Lebens

Impatient with any sort of meaning and indulgent toward all styles, Walser would read trashy novels in order to have the pleasure of recycling their plots, with the addition of a few particulars, and he was satisfied by his invention.[1] In his thousands of pages of short "prose pieces," he spoke of everything while judging nothing—or rather, letting it always be understood that judgment was to be considered suspended each time at the moment of improvisation. Tact, which he pushed to an extreme, kept him from assuming solid convictions. Over the impassive surface of this void, Walser furtively unleashed language, his only confidant, with a lack of scruples seldom equaled by his more eager and aggressive contemporaries. "When I really let myself go in writing, it may have looked a bit comical to serious people; and yet I was experimenting in the field of language in the hope it might conceal some unknown brightness that it would be a joy to reawaken."[2]

Walter Benjamin spoke of the "inhuman, imperturbable superficiality" of Walser's characters,[3] who are so imperturbable that Walser is always discouraging anyone who might go looking for secrets in his writings, and in particular for the secrets of his secret novel. At a distance of some years, he recalled *Jakob von Gunten* as the book closest to his heart but also as perhaps "a bit rash,"[4] probably for fear of having, despite it all, revealed too much in his tale. Discovering Walser is a little like Jakob von Gunten discovering the Benjamenta Institute: You go from suspecting a hoax, to being sure of a mystery, and finally to discovering that the heart of this mystery is its near identity with a hoax. Jakob discovers that there is really no thought behind the facade of the Institute ("Is there perhaps some general plan here, a thought? No, nothing"), but the true secret of the Benjamenta brother-and-sister pair, and Walser's as well, is the *flight from thought.*

Time is suspended in the Institute but not suppressed. No one in that dull enclosure, a disguised Eden, is able to reckon time; all are engulfed in a common unconscious state, an abnormal kind of sleep, that absence that Jakob notes in his teachers and in Benjamenta himself. And Benjamenta tells him, "Jakob, you're a little surprised, aren't you, at the lazy way we spend our lives here at the Institute, almost as though we were absent in spirit?" In the face of such scandalous behavior, Jakob thinks briefly of rebelling; but nothing comes of it, and later he will understand that this kind of sleep is the supreme result of the curriculum. "Today, you see, religion is no longer worth anything," he will observe. "Sleep is more religious than all your religion. Maybe when one sleeps one is closer to God."

The Benjamenta Institute is the diametric opposite of Goethe's "pedagogic province." Moreover, we know that Walser had studied Goethe's *Wilhelm Meisters Wanderjahre* and was very fond of it.[5] Instead of forming a personality, as they say in pedagogic jargon, the Institute breaks it down and dissociates it. Here the obstacle the pupils must overcome is consciousness itself. They therefore train themselves in empty repetition and mimetic obedience: They follow any external order to rid themselves of the compulsion to think. They tend to reduce themselves to zero—in the end Jakob will be able to say, "And if I go to rack and ruin, what will get broken, what will be lost? A zero"—and these zero subjects know they have nothing of their own and are thus perfect servants; above all they know that their own thoughts do not belong to them. The first, and least important, reasons that convince young Jakob von Gunten of the deep meaning of the teachings imparted by the Institute relate to society. The last descendant of a decayed aristocratic family, Jakob already has an inkling that in a world where everyone claims to be free and everyone is a slave (are not even those who seem to be most free actually "slaves, governed by a maddening, gross, scourging idea of the world?"), uniform obedience restores that ultimate asymmetry that is the indispensable sign of sovereignty. Reversing Hegel's thesis, in the realm of slavery the sovereign can only try *not* to be recognized, to approach the nonexistent and invisible, in accordance with the example that Jakob sees in his perfect companion Kraus: "Kraus is a genuine divine work, a nothing, a servant."

But this is only a preliminary lesson in the Institute's curriculum: The pupils are preparing themselves not to enter the world but to leave it, unseen. The world consists of time and wakefulness; the idea is to suspend them. The first weapon for bringing about this silent, stealthy upheaval is uninterrupted repetition, the category of the perpetual, a hybrid transition from the measuring of time to an indivisible continuum. Every gesture is deprived of its function, everything becomes exercise, meaning is eroded, automatism is regained, and the symbolic function is sabotaged: "The eyes act as a go-between for thoughts, and that's why I close them every so often, so as not to be forced to think." Finally, a declaration of principle: "If only they knew how many things they spoil, the thinkers. Someone who applies himself to not thinking is doing something; well, that's just what's needed most."

> Und gesellt sich zum Verborgnen,
> Zu den Lieblingen des Schlafes.
>
> [And is joined with the hidden,
> With the favorites of sleep.]
> —*Goethe*, Siebenschläfer

There is an old legend of Christian origin—one that for centuries lent itself to Islamic speculation, having been recorded in the enigmatic *Sura of the Cave* (Sura 18) in the Qur'an—wherein we find the same sleep that is re-evoked, ambiguous, and counterfeit but secretly faithful in Walser's novel. It is the story of the Seven Sleepers. An underground passage impossible to find runs from the cave at Ephesus to the "inner chambers" of the Benjamenta Institute. In the chain of witnesses constituting the history of the myth, this last and most recent one is so subdued as to be unrecognizable, as though the genealogy of the gods were compressed into a nursery rhyme. The connection between sleep and the suspension of time can now be seen in perspective, no longer in the life of a boarding school but in the story of the cosmos. Fleeing persecution by the idol-worshipping emperor Decius, the seven Ephesian youths who take refuge in the cave sleep without physical decay for 309 years. Their reawakening prefigures eschatological time in the most violent way that the order of the world can offer: After one of them goes forth among men "in search of whoever has the purest food" (18:19) and to testify involuntarily to the miracle, which guarantees the resurrection of the body, the Seven will finally die.

"Time can only be reckoned by means of movement; when no movement is perceived, no time is perceived, as in the story of the Seven Sleepers," wrote Avicenna (*Najāt*, 189). But this story was itself a variation, and in following its wanderings we fall into prehistory. There is a passage in Aristotle that matches Avicenna's words: "Thus there is no [time] without change; indeed, when our mind does not undergo changes, or does not notice them, it does not seem to us that time has passed, just as it did not seem when they reawakened to those who, according to the myth, lay beside the heroes in Sardinia: They connect the prior moment with the moment after, combining them in one and abolishing the interval they have not perceived" (*Physics,* 218 b 21). According to Simplicius, Aristotle is here referring to another variant of the myth of *uncorrupted sleepers*: the story of the nine sons of Herakles and the daughters of Thespios, who died in Sardinia and whose bodies remained intact, looking like men who had fallen asleep. The passage presumably alludes to a practice of *incubatio,* of lying next to these bodies in order to commune with them in dreams.[6] But this is only one of the many ramifications of the theme to be found, both before and after. Most important, there is a rich variety of sources to show the connection between the Seven Sleepers and Canopus, the star close to the celestial South Pole and belonging to the constellation of Argo Navis, the ship on which, according to Islamic tradition, the Seven Sleepers were to embark.[7] Certain words in the Qur'an supposedly refer to the roll of the waves in the celestial abyss, a movement outside of movement: "You would have thought they were awake and instead they slept, and we turned them to right and to left" (18:18). It is in the same region of the sky,[8] and not on some Ogygia that cannot be located on terrestrial maps, that Kronos, the now deposed god of the Golden Age, is said to reside: "For Kronos himself sleeps imprisoned in a deep rock cavern that shines like gold; he sleeps the sleep ordained by Zeus to hold him fast, and the birds that fly over the rock bring him ambrosia and the whole island is drenched by the fragrance that descends from the rock as from a fountain" (Plutarch, *De facie in orbe lunae,* 941 F). And yet his sleep governs the world; immersed in slumber, he still "oversees all creation" (*Orphicorum Fragmenta,* ed. O. Kern, n. 155).

By making one's way through the labyrinths of the symbolic, one would reach in the end the opposition of the two celestial poles, where the north stands for perfect wakefulness and the south for the divine sleep that sustains the world. Both are connected with Saturn, who holds the umbilical cord entwining heaven and earth,[9] but in accordance with cosmic inversion they have opposite meanings, like the two corresponding halves of an hourglass-shaped drum.[10] The seven stars of the Bear, points of light from outside the cosmos, are associated with the seven Abdâl, "mysterious characters who follow and replace one another from one cycle to the next. . . . they themselves [are] the eyes through which the Beyond looks at the world":[11] The Seven Sleepers are received aboard the ship *Argo.* They are apotropaic guardians, some of the initiatory vigil, the others of seafarers *walled-up alive* in the storm.[12]

Walser, with no conceivable conscious reference on his part, was impelled by what Aby Warburg called the "mnemic wave" to develop a new variation on the theme of the *uncorrupted sleepers,* once again exposing the essential feature of that myth, the *suspension of time,* but leaving the whole grandiose cosmological structure that supports it submerged. It could hardly be otherwise, not only for the obvious reason that Walser was unaware of what he was doing, but precisely because of the supplementary meaning that the myth takes on in his hands. "Here nature is lacking," says Jakob in the Institute. Reference to any order whatsoever is ruled out; the rapture of nihilism presupposes indeterminancy of meaning and is gratified by it. But by canceling meaning and abolishing a time frame for all that happens, this rapture leads back to the very category that finds its supreme demonstration in the story of the Seven Sleepers: pure abandonment; abandonment wherein Islam identifies its own essence; abandonment that in the Christian tradition is held to be somewhat suspect, the quietist heresy having been evoked to exorcise it, and that accordingly appears in heterodox forms, as in Molinos or Jean-Pierre de Caussade. This also explains why there has been so little speculation about the Seven Sleepers in the West, where the legend has been transmitted mostly in naive poetic versions, some of them full of charm, like Charbry's little Anglo-Norman poem.[13]

As Louis Massignon's illuminating analyses[14] have shown, the slumber of the Seven Sleepers is an image of eschatological expectation beyond verbal expression. Thus the pupils at the Institute, in this most recent version of the image—childish, minuscule, but perfectly corresponding—know "only one definite thing: We are waiting! That's all we're good for." It is only by shunning all discourse that experience, enclosed in a lethargic and stubborn silence, is transformed into a symptom of the *Hour,* the one "perfect, self-sufficient moment," while any other moment of common consciousness can only be split off, its fulfillment postponed to the future:[15] "Thus we made all sign of them disappear so that people would know that the promise of God is true and that the Hour is sure to come" (Qur'an, Sura 18:21). Consciousness is doubled by losing itself *in a certain way* ("a certain kind of sleep is useful, if only for the fact that it leads a specific life of its own"),[16] just as the inability to do something, for the pupils of the Benjamenta Institute, "is like pretending to do it in some other way."

One of the many meanings of the story of the Seven Sleepers is thus the retaliation of wakefulness against itself. If the common human condition is a fictitious wakefulness that signifies sleep, the slumber of the Seven Sleepers is a wakefulness beyond wakefulness, where a possibility precluded by the constitution of the living is realized mythically: the blur between wakefulness and the flux of what is happening, which consciousness is *forced* to watch. The Seven Sleepers do not have the measure of time because they live in a flow that itself counts time and is counted by it.

"I am a dethroned king," the surly Benjamenta tells Jakob on one occasion. This ambiguous giant, the absent man who grumbles as he reads the newspaper, has "nothing beautiful, nothing magnificent" about him but allows "lengthy vicissitudes, serious strokes of fate" to be glimpsed within him, so that for Jakob it is "this human element, this almost divine element that makes him beautiful."

Benjamenta is Kronos, earliest model of the dethroned king, god of the Golden Age, whom the later gods relegated, in the seeming inconsistency of great myths, both to the horrid cave of Tartarus and to the cave dripping with ambrosia on the fortunate isle of Ogygia. In either case, he is *buried,* as Benjamenta says of himself: "I've actually . . . buried myself here." And Ogygia is at the same time a fortunate isle and the Isle of the Dead.[17] The face of Kronos that we first see in Benjamenta is the one so often reproduced by more recent tradition: sinister melancholy; the old man who contains in himself the knowledge of *numerus, mensura, pondus* [number, measure, weight] and the power of destruction; the *praefectus carceris,* lord of destitution. But the Benjamenta Institute is also the happy Ogygia, where Kronos awaits in sleep the ultimate revolution of the stars that will reestablish his order, the resplendent earth of the Golden Age. Behind the dismal stairways and corridors of the Institute, "an old abandoned garden" can be seen, which the pupils are not allowed to enter, even though they know about it: "In our Benjamenta Institute there are plenty of other gardens. We are forbidden to enter the real garden." One day, "if one of us were, or rather had been, a hero who had performed some courageous exploit and put his life at risk, he would be permitted (thus it is written in our book) to enter the marble portico adorned with frescoes that lies hidden amid the greenery of our garden; and there a mouth would kiss him." To the sudden strains of *The Magic Flute,* Saturn's paradise opens and snaps shut.

> Est ignota procul nostraeque impervia menti,
> vix adeunda deis, annorum squalida mater,
> immensi spelunca aevi, quae tempora vasto
> suppeditat revocatque sinu. Complectitur
> antrum, omnia qui placido consumit numine,
> serpens perpetuumque viret squamis caudamque
> reductam ore vorat tacito relegens exordia lapsu.
> —*Claudian,* De Consulatu Stilichonis, *424–30*

The one truly visionary scene in *Jakob von Gunten* is when Jakob visits the "inner chambers" of the Institute, following the wand of Lisa, Benjamenta's sister and magical go-between. As always in Walser, the oddness of the event is diminished and trivialized by the tone of the narrative, as though someone were relating a true fact while warning at every moment that he is probably lying. But this in no way detracts from the scene's specificity: This time it is the darkness of the cosmic cave that is thrown open. "I had the feeling of being at the center of the earth": dampness, cold, darkness.

The divine consort of Benjamenta-Kronos, Lisa here assumes the role of Adrastea, born "of foresight and inevitability" (*Orphicorum Fragmenta,* no. 105), who joins the old god in governing the world.[18] During the regular initiatory journey to which Lisa subjects Jakob—immersing him in the "pyre of light" and in "crypts and ambulatories," finally guiding him onto the "skating rink of ice or glass"—one of her remarks sums up the lesson: "One must learn to love necessity, to care for it." The reader, by now accustomed to the *transcendental buffoonery* of the various gnomic expressions encountered at every step in the Institute ("Little, but in depth," "Hands are the five-finger proof of vanity and human concupiscence," and so on) may be disconcerted to realize that a similar thought about necessity was uttered by Zarathustra a few years earlier. But the sorceress Lisa is a necessity about to be undermined and got rid of: The cosmos designed by her lord and brother in the Institute is a fragile image, a temporary and at the same time rigid calculation. Once again the dethroned king will have to move on.

All these comparisons may seem irreverent—and with good reason. Probably no one would be more surprised than Walser to see gods and celestial bodies circulating in *Jakob von Gunten*: He used a great many words, but it would be hard to find "mythology" among them. And so? Writing has a life of its own unknown to its author; this, at least, was something about which Walser was never in any doubt. Few authors have succeeded in effacing themselves to such perfection, becoming cocooned in their own words, happy in their invisibility; few authors have been so secure in the self-sufficiency of their writing, and today, many others are ready to take it on faith, as a new dispensation. Yet this is not enough; there must be a double leap: It is a question not simply of writing but of the independent life of images. Treacherously, "like thieves in the night," images burst in. One does not "do" mythology by filling pages with the names of gods—an illusion that goes back to Carl Spitteler and Theodor Däubler—but neither can one be sure of avoiding mythology by imbuing one's prose with disruptive charm, in radical indifference to meaning and with the extinction of will. On the contrary, it may be that it is just such a practice that summons the images back. But it would be too disheartening to find a rule in this, for the involuntary would then turn out to be merely a subterfuge of the will. Walser instead shows us that, if anything, the reverse is true.

Lisa mysteriously wastes away and dies, and with her the Institute is likewise consumed, unstable experiment in emerging from the *aion*. Now there is no protective space. Lisa's death follows an offense committed by her brother. It is up to Jakob to redeem the offense. With these two movements, the Institute dissolves and the way to the desert opens for the old man and the boy. In a final Saturnine shock, Benjamenta first tries to strangle Jakob and then to kiss him. Saturn, *Mercurius senex,* as the alchemists called him, would like to restore his whole vast and ageless image, his "crooked thought," and loosen up his old man's useless rigidity: *"Saturnus cum sit senex, posse fieri puer fingitur"* (*Mythographi Vaticani,* 3,8). *Senex* [old man] and *puer* [boy] are transformed, each becoming the other's guide. Jakob seems to possess by nature the virtues fostered by the Institute and thus has no need to will them. Benjamenta, on the other hand, collapses before the contradiction of having *willed* to bury himself in non-will. Neither fences outside the world nor those hidden in the world are allowed. But in the end, everything dissolves, once again in sleep. A new earth appears to Jakob in the night, Walser's real earth: "It was nature and yet it wasn't, image and body at the same time." And hidden in Jakob's exquisite, ridiculous Middle Eastern fantasy appears the final motto, which absorbs and sets its seal on the previous ones: "Stop explaining." The pataphysical pair Benjamenta-Saturn and Jakob-Mercury now set out on the road; they will never come back to tell us about their final getaway: "It was as though we had escaped forever, or at least for a very long time, from what it is customary to call European civilization." What is certain, however, is that they will not be going to Samoa, where Walther Rathenau, in an operetta-like gesture reminiscent of Robert Musil's Arnheim, offered to find Walser a job so that he could live as a free artist. Walser's reply to such invitations sums up perfectly his conception of his role: "I thank you, but I consider it unnecessary that you take me by the arm. The world is thousands of years old and full of unhoped-for prospects."[19] Walser's journeys were always motionless. As he had already said in his first novel, *Geschwister Tanner:* "Does nature go abroad?"

The Benjamenta Institute is a temporary regression of utopia to its cosmological origins, which annihilate the very concept of it. Nature-culture, that pairing of opposites and our impertinent identity card, is eliminated by exhaustion in an intermediate world of pure fluid, a new *natura nymphydidica,* where the signs that identify the individual or group, but especially the species, are drained away in a sleep that is a biological commonplace, where consciousness is reabsorbed into what nourishes it. But for this very reason, it is not surprising that many have seen in the Benjamenta Institute an image of oppression, one among many representations of a wicked society. The mistake is understandable: Society these days sins *through excess of spirit* and dispels the letter, in an infernal similarity to the practices of the Institute. Society has become a single esoteric body, but with nothing to cover it, wherein all that is most awful and secret passes for everyday banality. No one who stands in its light can see: So rigorously closed as to be equally hidden from its leaders and its followers, it puts rulers and ruled up against the same wall, and neither are aware that they cannot know what they are being forced to do. The great criticism of culture, the line that runs from Friedrich Nietzsche to Theodor Adorno and survives today mostly in spurious variations, established an exact portrait of the *new man:* mediocre above all, good, malleable material for society's experiments. But only in rare glimpses did it foresee the dazzling parody into which the whole structure would be transformed: cities hard as diamonds, tautology riddled by a multiplicity of opinions, and those opinions weighed by an invisible jeweler, in order that the sum of all disorders might be the best equilibrium—"gnats of subjectivity," wrote Hegel, destined to be burned in the great central fire of repetition. At the end of a long battle with nature, almost unprecedented in the roster of societies for the crudeness of its established methods, the new nameless society— "industry," its only name so far, is laughably inadequate—tends to replace nature: By now self-sufficient, it assimilates itself to the one accessible image of self-sufficiency. Nature itself has become a particular instance of this huge operation, which does not require a purpose but a litany, a mystical machine that can do without any of its parts and disown its operators, the ultimate stylization of power, ready for diffusion and contagion, as in the beginning. Names are only its precarious supports, straw dogs.

Max Brod tells how Kafka suddenly came to see him one day to express his enthusiasm for *Jakob von Gunten.* He also says that Kafka enjoyed reading Walser's prose aloud and couldn't stop laughing[20]—laughter that recalls that of Kafka and his friends when he read them *The Trial.* Finally, Kafka had an office supervisor named Eisner who noted a certain resemblance between Kafka and Simon Tanner, the hero of Walser's first novel.[21] This detail already seems to belong to a remote civilization. The affinity between Kafka and Walser was noted by Musil in a 1914 review, where Kafka is even described, unjustly, as a "special example of the Walser type."[22] Of course, it is not unusual to find passages in Kafka and Walser that seem to reflect one another naturally. When we read in *Jakob von Gunten* that "in a very simple, and in a certain way stupid, exercise, there are greater benefits and truer notions than in learning a lot of concepts and meanings," we can immediately find in Kafka an illustration of what Walser meant: "to nail a plank with patient, careful skill and at the same time not do anything, and without anyone being able to say, 'For him nailing is nothing,' but 'For him nailing is really nailing and at the same time nothing,' whereby the nailing would indeed become more reckless, more decisive, more real, and, if you like, more foolish." In Walser, as in Kafka, prehistoric winds blow from the Ice Mountains. But whereas Kafka firmly and increasingly transformed writing into a steady confrontation with power ("Of all writers, Kafka is the greatest expert on power"),[23] Walser, incurably damaged before taking the first step, was too weak and unsubstantial for such a challenge. He must always have known it, since only once in his life as a writer—with *Jakob von Gunten*—did he face up to what later would slowly destroy him. The short prose pieces of his last years are quick, often splendid, attempts at escape by dissociation. While Kafka left a number of testimonies, both magnificent and embarrassing, of his chronic clash with what he still called "life," Walser always pretended to be talking about himself without really confessing a single word. "No one is entitled to behave toward me as though he knew me"[24]—these words are tacitly posted at the beginning of everything Walser wrote. In his boundless helplessness, Walser never lacked the strength to keep silent. His loyal friend Carl Seelig, who continued to visit Walser in the various psychiatric clinics where the writer spent the last twenty-eight years of his life, recounts an episode in which we see the shadow of the Benjamenta Institute reemerge for a moment: "I will never forget that autumn morning when we were walking from Teufen to Speichen, through a fog as thick as cotton wool. I told him that day that his work might last as long as Gottfried Keller's. He stopped as though rooted to the spot, gave me a most serious look, and said that if I valued his friendship I should never again pay him such compliments. He, Robert Walser, was a zero and wanted to be forgotten."[25]

The Castle and *Jakob von Gunten* have obvious similarities. Both revolve around a *site of power;* both arouse a craving for symbolic interpretation and disappoint it in the end. Walter Benjamin, the most enlightened reader of both Walser and Kafka, avoided the temptation to identify them too closely by relating Kafka's work to prehistory and Walser's to fable— regions where that later invention, symbolism superimposed on litera- ture, does not exist. The Castle and the Benjamenta Institute are concrete expressions of power and as such contain the germs of every image, but in a dubious and still undifferentiated state that precedes the subdivision into ambivalences that constitutes the symbol. We will never be able to decide whether the Castle is a place of grace or hell or whether the Ben- jamenta Institute is an image of oppression or the liberated life. The im- ages lie hidden and entangled at the bottom of the well. What makes the difference is not so much their positive or negative meaning as the two re- verse axes on which they rest: for *The Castle* the axis of wakefulness, for *Jakob von Gunten* the axis of sleep. K. constantly struggles, without success, to stay awake, in order to match the Castle's relentless wakefulness. He *tries* to discover its secret and falls asleep just when the secretary Bürgel, a marginal figure and chance emissary, calmly reveals to him some of the Castle's—crucial?—rules. And K. immediately wonders "why he couldn't put up with a few bad nights and one sleepless night, why it was here that he had been overtaken by such irresistible fatigue, here where no one got tired, or rather where everyone was continually tired without it affecting their work, indeed their fatigue seemed to encourage it." Conversely, Benjamenta fails for having *tried* to establish the walled chamber of sleep within the big city. He will have to go far away. Both K. and Jakob are caught up in a journey where neither ever gets anywhere.

Moral issues aside, abjection is the disturbing pleasure of linking up with what is given, whatever it may be; abjection always leaves meaning out of consideration and bows only to presence, in order to guarantee the separa- tion of the absent; the sum of possible actions is embraced once and for all, and henceforth the process begins of debasing anything that might recall an ego's choice. Such a vice does not have many devotees, but Walser is one of them. This is the fundamental origin of the great obsession that runs throughout his life and work: to serve. The mask of the servant as life's supreme possibility appears in all of Walser's novels, from *Geschwister Tanner* to *Gehülfe* to *Jakob von Gunten* and the lost novel *Theodor,* of which only one hilarious chapter survives.[26] And we know that in his various jobs, Walser always sought subordinate roles, that of domestic servant being his highest aspiration.

Enoch/Elias, according to Ibn ʿArabī, becomes completely animal, and thereby loses speech as well, thus undergoing a mute unveiling forbidden to the human being;[27] Hugo von Hofmannsthal's Lord Chandos, himself struck dumb, is gripped by a dizzying paralysis: "Even my own heaviness, the general torpor of my brain, seems to acquire a meaning; I experience in and around me a blissful, never-ending interplay, and among the objects playing against one another there is not one into which I cannot flow. To me, then, it is as though my body consists of nought but ciphers which give me the key to everything."[28] Likewise Walser, by the pure force of dissociation, and certainly without laying claim to any sort of revelation, patiently slackened all the threads that might have given dignity or consistency to his ego. He likens himself to zero, which can be added to any element without changing it, other than imparting to it a touch of nullity. And if abjection has a sign, it is most certainly zero. Jakob, Walser's agile double, says, "Nothing gives me greater pleasure than to give a false image of myself to those I have locked in my heart. . . . For example, I imagine it would be indescribably beautiful to die in the terrible knowledge of having offended and inspired the worst opinions about myself in those I hold dearest in the world." And finally, he alludes in passing to the pleasure aroused by such a reckless way of life: "What a strange perversion, to rejoice secretly at seeing that you're being robbed a little." For Walser the literary form of the abject is the gloss; it too "represents a perversion," certainly reprehensible in terms of "literary morality." The gloss attracts Walser because it "operates in all directions,"[29] is determined by indifference in the presence of impulses, thwarts all contours, continually duplicates itself, and is multiple and erratic.

Between his many jobs as an underling—among others, bookstore clerk, law clerk, employee in two banks and a sewing-machine factory, and finally butler in a castle in Silesia, and only readers of *Jakob von Gunten* will be able to understand his delight—Walser from time to time withdrew to the "Writing Room for the Unemployed" (the name is Walserian but true) in Zurich, and there, "seated on an old stool in the evening, by the weak light of an oil lamp, he made use of his graceful handwriting to copy addresses and do other such jobs assigned him by stores, firms, and individuals."[30] It is not only these periods but Walser's whole existence that take us back to Herman Melville's Bartleby, the impeccable scrivener who revealed nothing and accepted nothing except ginger cakes. In these vegetal creatures, disguised in the clothes of the common man ("I am not particular," Bartleby liked to repeat) negation thrives. All the more radical in going unnoticed, their destructive breath is often not registered by any instrument: For many, Walser remains a cozy figure. His nihilism has even been described as "delicate and domestic, good-natured as a Swiss bourgeois."[31] On the contrary, he is a remote man, a path parallel to nature, an almost indiscernible thread. Walser's obedience, like Bartleby's disobedience, presupposes a total removal. An original failing bars them from the body of communicants, and this failing constitutes their riches. As sovereigns, they make no effort to find a remedy for their condition or even to comment on it. They copy. They transcribe letters, which pass through them as through a transparent plate. They express nothing of their own. There is nothing they would alter. "I do not develop," says Jakob in the Institute; "I would prefer not to make any change," says Bartleby. In their affinity, we see the equivalence between silence and a certain ornamental use of words. In the thousands of pages written by Walser—an oeuvre indefinitely extendable, elastic, devoid of bone structure; endless chatter to conceal the lack of any forward movement in its discourse—Bartleby's words, though never uttered, are a constant refrain: "I would prefer not to."

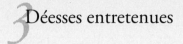

3 Déesses entretenues

> Avis aux non-communistes: Tout est commun,
> même Dieu. [Warning to noncommunists:
> Everything is common, even God.]
>   —*Baudelaire*

(After long and roundabout wandering, I found myself back in Sonnenstein park, under a green tent of leaves that became ever more transparent. A serrated crack opened in them and there, a little farther ahead, I
saw the Königstein fortress: If the Stone of the Sun is also—and who can
doubt it?—the Stone of the King, then the judge had discreetly yielded
his place, for the time being, to Frank Wedekind. The latter, jailed in the
fortress for committing the crime of lèse-majesté in cabaret songs, was in
the first months of the year 1900 working on the second and final draft of
Mine-Haha. The vegetation before me kept thinning out, and I came
upon, as in a sudden drawing room, a small table and a chair, both of
stone. An envelope stamped with red sealing wax stood propped on the
table, and I recognized the judge's alchemical eagle. It was one of his letters of instruction:

"Dear friend,

"I thought it well to absent myself for a short time from the park and
leave it at your disposal for a glotto-theological appendix on the real social
situation of my girls, the bird-maidens, something very close to my heart.
Frank Wedekind, land agent for my house and ringmaster of my circus,
keeps watch from the height of the fortress on everything that goes on in

the park, and at times he also trains his long-range binoculars on the sky, which is crawling with worms. He has already taken note of many things. He is trustworthy. I advise you to take a good look at his impeccable account ledgers. The economic connections, in this regard, need to achieve their proper luminescent obscurity, which only a rigorous paralogical analysis can release from those regions of nature and the spirit that are themselves muddled and arbitrary.

"Your insistence on maintaining relations with me beyond the prudent measure of two books will probably do you no good from the scientific standpoint, but I make bold to whisper in your ear that so far there has not been much hope for you.

Yours,
D. P. Schreber")

Life in the Königstein fortress had turned out to be agreeably eccentric. The prisoners were treated like officers in a frontier garrison, with cigars and liquor and readings while the wind whistled around the walls, doors banged, and windows creaked. There was a suggestion of paradise in the air, of the memory of Lenzburg Castle, almost hidden by the dense trees. There, in territory open for the impudence and dangerous games of childhood, Wedekind had already absorbed many of the phantasms in his work, later to be developed in advertisements for Maggi bouillon cubes until the clumsy mythological dramas of his last years. From one extreme to the other, he had touched on almost all the delicate topics of the time and had traced their nervous intertwinings at length. His words flowed doggedly between sex and money, the press and the circus, intrigue and the body, while always keeping an eye out for the police.

A first draft of *Mine-Haha,* now lost, dates from July–October 1895. The second and final one was written in the Königstein fortress, between September 1899 and March 1900. In those same months, Wedekind also reworked the manuscript of *The Marquis von Keith:* "The fact is, my eyes now turn only to that region where the cross between philosopher and horse thief is appreciated for its true worth"; "People never know whether they should look out for me or if it's my duty instead to look out for them"; "There's nothing I can do about my insatiability," says the marquis, the only possible consort for Lulu. *Mine-Haha* was published in *Die Insel* (vol. 2, no. 3) in 1901. In 1903 it appeared in the Little Library series

published by Langen, who was responsible for many of Wedekind's legal
and financial difficulties, with the addition of the prologue, fourth chapter, commentary, and the specification "From the letters of Helene Engel,
edited by Frank Wedekind."

The Marquis von Keith had the "coarse red hands of a clown," and so
Wedekind hid his own in cool gloves. When Wedekind appeared on the
scene, his figure immediately created confusion and nervousness, and so
in his mature years his demeanor was distant and formal. Bertolt Brecht
looked on him with admiration: "There he stood, ugly, brutal, dangerous,
with his short red hair, his hands in his trouser pockets, and you felt that
not even the devil could carry him off."[1]

In the beginning there were visits by seagulls to Lenzburg Castle, the
Senatus poeticus of the grammar school pupils, an epidemic of suicides.
Benjamin Franklin Wedekind, named after that mean and thrifty hero
of liberty, reads Heinrich Heine's poems to his companions, and the female images that vampirize the medulla are immolated in the attic: Palma
il Vecchio's *Venus,* but also Hans Makart's *Leda,* Lossow's *Galatea,* and
J. van Beers's *Ada,* this last swiped from a secret drawer of his father's; in
the background are the protective shadows of a "philosophical aunt" and
an "erotic aunt." Having fled the paternal roof, he finds in Zurich two
things that will never desert him: words written for money, "philanthrop-
ic buttresses for earning cash" at the firm of Julius Maggi; and the Herzog
Circus: "Every time I set foot under that tall tent, airy and light, I feel a
truly voluptuous shiver run through me. Here I am enveloped by an air of
celebration, something sumptuous and grand, and yet in its way so un-
speakably childish." (We are in Zurich in 1888; still in the future lies that
evening of 7 February 1920 in Paris, when a delightful bunch of party-
goers broke up at the door of the Fratellini brothers—"On se rendait dans
leur loge comme dans celle d'une danseuse" [One went to their dressing
room as to that of a dancer]—while the Comte Anne d'Orgel cordially
greeted young François de Séryeuse, thus throwing the latter's friend Paul
Robin, impenitent *cachottier,* into despair: "Il y avait là des épaves gran-
dioses, des objets dépouillés de leur signification première, et qui, chez ces
clowns, en prenaient une bien plus haute" [There was grandiose wreckage, objects stripped of their prime significance, and which, among these
clowns, took on a much higher one]. The entire heroic period of modernism was gently snuffed out at that moment). In Munich, the manda-

tory bohemia of those years, the general imperative was *sich ausleben,* to live to the full, to drain the cup to the dregs (which very much worried his landlady), and it was mostly proclaimed by lifeless and talentless poets. But Wedekind was driven by a particular preference for the lower depths and was already perfecting his rare ability to descend lucidly into the sewers. He was especially interested in these categories of men: the speculator, the plagiarist, the acrobat, the gambler, the pimp, the swindler, the journalist, the fire eater, the runaway schoolboy. And of women: the whore, the grisette, the hetaera—three categories among which he then tried desperately to draw sharp distinctions. In Paris, between 1891 and 1895, he attends the Cirque d'Hiver, the Cirque d'Été, the Nouveau Cirque, the Jardin de Paris, the Casino de Paris, the Hippodrome, the Eldorado, and the Élysée Montmartre. He is accompanied by Rachel; the *artiste lyrique* Léontine; Kadudja from Alexandria; Henriette, *mourant sans regrets à l'âge de 26 ans et n'ayant jamais vécu* [dying at the age of twenty-six without regret and having never lived]; the morphine addict Marie Louise; Alice; Madame Fernande; Germaine; Madeleine; Raymonde; and Lucie. He again runs into the legendary Rudinoff, a wanderer and jack-of-all-trades, albeit temporary and disreputable ones, known in all the circuses and cabarets of the time. He acts as secretary to Willi Grétor, inspired adventurer, forger, and cultural agent for money and the pleasure of creating messy situations. Among these characters, exotic plants at her court, resound the first strains of Lulu's delinquent saxophone.

Paradox of *Mine-Haha*: It is Wedekind's single perfect text but lacks his peculiar virtues—the jarring notes, the knowing degradation, the frantic puppetry, the grotesque natural background. And yet all these qualities lie at the bottom of the pond in the park, as gigantic carcasses, underwater plants feeding the waters with their juices. On the surface: little ripples of transparent, elusive laughter.

The paradox of *Mine-Haha* leads to an equivocal and secretly fertile rapport between Wedekind and his text. The girls' park appears for the first time in *Der Sonnenspektrum,* an "idyll" in the form of a play, on which Wedekind worked until the summer of 1894 but never completed. The park is here the yard of a bordello. The inmates are named Melitta, Kadudja, Elise, and Franziska—finally Minehaha—and they clearly foreshadow, though in another sphere of style and meaning, the girls being trained in the park in *Mine-Haha.* They are watched over by a sharp-eyed madam, who bursts into colorful soliloquies over what goes on in her house ("With my guests I assume the responsibility of acting in such a way that they leave restored in body and soul, and come back soon and as often as possible") and who has nothing in common with the mystery-cult discretion of the instructresses of Hidalla and her companions. The upbringing of young girls had, in any case, been on Wedekind's mind for many years: For more than twenty years, we can reconstruct the signs of a grandiose project, wavering between novel and utopian drama, of which *Mine-Haha* would presumably have been a fragment. As a novel it was to have the title *Hidalla, oder Das Leben einer Schneiderin* (Hidalla, or The Life of a Seamstress); as a utopian drama, *Die grosse Liebe* (The Great Love).

There is no way to make a detailed analysis of the notes for *Die grosse Liebe,* contained in notebooks 38–42 in the Wedekind Archive, since they have yet to be published. Their overall content, however, is clear: Wedekind was developing a "utopia of life in the park," in which *Mine-Haha* would have represented the phase of the girls' education from birth to puberty. There is an echo of such a utopia in the secret treatise by the "giant dwarf" Karl Hetmann, protagonist of *Hidalla,* which is entitled "Hidalla, or The Moral of Beauty." This was to be followed by the parts devoted to the erotic and sacrificial rites of spring and autumn and to the education of boys. A vaguely ridiculous sacral aura, reminiscent of the myths revived in those years on the ceilings of opera houses, hovers over the project. Now there is talk of "divine lads" and "divine maidens," and the park has expanded to become the site of a theocracy based on "voluptuous death," the immolation of boys and girls as the highest point of the erotic journey. The boys, in truth, do not seem all that happy: The handsomest ones are made available as sacred prostitutes to aristocratic ladies of any age who desire them. After some years, exhausted by their work, "they feel attracted only by things of the spirit"—proof of the failure of utopia and a sign of Wedekind's ambivalence toward this Spartan-Babylonian dream. Indeed, one might almost say that Wedekind would rather try all the wrong paths than recognize that he has already laid out the only right one, in *Mine-Haha*. The fragments of *Die grosse Liebe* are all inexorably linked to the period and its anxieties: The form is awkward, and in the background one notes an intense need to make use of the African folklore collected by Leo Frobenius and the description of Aztec rites compiled by Bernardino de Sahagún. The idea of sacrifice would accordingly be freed from the inevitable décor of Arnold Böcklin and Makart, and Isadora

Duncan's prefigurative tunics, which covered the flaming heart of the matter, would fall after a few final flutters: "Exactness, reality, is the sacrifice" (*Maitrā yanī-Samhitā*, 1, 10, 11).

Wedekind's uncertainty before the mirror of *Mine-Haha* is matched by the consistent banality of the few critics who have paid it any attention. So far the greatest homage to this text has been the shadow of restless nostalgia that passed across Theodor Adorno's face when he mentioned it, perhaps the same shadow that dwells in his words about the sleeping Albertine. But not even he published anything about *Mine-Haha,* though he must often have dreamed of a paradise of little girls. However, Arthur Kutscher, author of the imposing official monograph on Wedekind, three volumes still indispensable for many details, devoted a page to *Mine-Haha* that is most useful for plumbing the pataphysical abysses into which the treacherous light of literature can cast upright scholars: "The work *Mine-Haha,* as we know it, strikes us as extremely bizarre or remarkably vacuous. The formal artistic element is insignificant, unless one cares to give a certain weight to language as such. No longer, as in *Der Sonnenspektrum,* are we faced with an ideal image of the joy of the senses, drawing its sparkling colors from nostalgia and unreality. Here the element of content prevails, offering us the closed formulation of a system, an educational method that totally excludes the spirit and puts the accent solely on the body. Of course, as an image of a dream of desire, unmindful of the problem of its realization, this text presents, in a poetic exaggeration, some notable elements from the hygienic, moral, and aesthetic standpoints. Jaques-Dalcroze was inspired by it when he founded his school of eurythmics in Hellerau. Wedekind himself practiced nudism and gymnastics. To the last, he kept in his studio a wooden sphere half a meter in diameter and a large drum, which he, along with his wife and daughters, used for exercises in balance and running. But all this is not enough to make his interest in this work comprehensible or to resolve its many enigmas."[2]

Appropriate commentaries on *Mine-Haha* speak neither of rhythmic gymnastics nor of hygiene. I posted a provisional list of these writings at the tall iron gateway, topped by gilded grillwork, that led into the park. Here it is:

Marx, *Capital*
Marx, *Grundrisse*

Marx, *A Contribution to the Critique of Political Economy*
Klossowski, *La monnaie vivante*
Mauss, *Essai sur le don*
Elwin, *The Muria and Their Ghotul*
Baudelaire, *Fusées*
Baudelaire, *Mon coeur mis à nu*
Benjamin, *Zentralpark*

PARK

"Knowledge consists in setting up collections of evocative oddities. The king's garden or his hunting park should contain all the animal and vegetable curiosities in the world. Those that no explorer has been able to find are nevertheless actually represented there: sculptured or drawn. The collections aim to be complete, especially with monstrosities, since the purpose of collecting is not so much knowledge as power, and the most effective collections consist not of realities but of emblems."[3]

"Then the emperor built the palace of *Kien-chang;* it was so large that it had a thousand outer gates and ten thousand small inner ones; the first hall exceeded in height the one in the palace of *Wei-yang.* To the east was the Phoenix Gate, more than two hundred feet high. To the west, in the middle of the avenue, lay the Tiger Park, which extended for several dozen *li.* To the north, [the emperor] had a large pond dug, in the middle of which rose the Terrace Bathed with Water, more than two hundred feet high; he called it [the pond] *T'ai-ye.* In the pond were the islands of *P'ong-lai, Fang-chang, Yng-cheou,* and *Hou-leang,* imitations of what is in the sea, holy mountains, turtles, fish, and so on. To the south was the Hall of Jade, the Gate in the Shape of a Jade Ring, the Great Bird, and so on. Later [the emperor] had the Terrace of the Gods built, and the Tower of the Well Barrier, which measured five feet; a road, wide enough for the emperor's chariot, connected these buildings."[4]

". . . unde multis accessionibus tale Theatrum auguri possit, et tota rerum universitas in unam domum compacta spectatoribus exhiberi."[5]

Ever since the time when the park was Paradise, the fluid and fleeting powers of nature have been concentrated there in simulacra: names, until the *lingua adamica* became muddled; stone statues for the Son of Heaven;

a turquoise tree similar to a palm tree in Rûzbehân's dazed eyes; stuffed crocodiles hanging from the ceiling; severed heads; hedgehogs and ant-eaters—in the still air of the *musaeum clausum,* when the funeral pomp of the seventeenth century required that nature withdraw into the *biblio-theca abscondita.* While *nihil* kept gnawing at the images until they wasted away to parchment masks, to be adapted to circumstances in accordance with the brutal dictates of Cardinal Mazarin, the gardens filled up with artificial ruins; Moorish, Chinese, and Gothic pavilions stood face-to-face amid the overgrown grass, signifying history's impending resolution in rubble and toys. And finally, good citizens wanted to have nature as a guest in their city; they installed benches, fountains, and paths; then they found it useful to bring in animal specimens in special boxes. Whereas parks had once reproduced nature on a reduced scale, now all of nature is already a park in itself, encircled by society on every side. Visible history thus arrives at the picnic and festive desolation, but the invisible history of the park is celebrated within the walls of *Mine-Haha,* where the shreds of past and present forms are caught in a single spiderweb: Eden, zoo, boarding school, bordello, garden-of-the-flowering-bulbs of Indra, enclosure for hierodules, riding stable, path of initiation, warehouse of commodities.

Where are we? In a place that rules out all contact with the surrounding world; the walls are insurmountable; outside does not exist. Those who live in the park can have no notion of any other life; those outside the park can only gaze at it in ignorance, as at a sealed heart. And yet there are two points at which this excluded place opens now and then to circula-tion with society: by welcoming female infants in swaddling clothes, who later, of course, have no recollection of how they were taken into the park; and by restoring them to the outside, through show business and finally emergence from the dead-end structure of the theater into the external world. And from that world, through the box offices of theaters, flows the money to maintain the life spread out over the vine-covered cottages in the park. Within that enclosure, as in a large alchemical retort, a transfor-mation takes place: The raw material of little girls is transformed by their upbringing into a different material. Into what? For what purpose?

The classic fiction of political economy is the Robinsonade. Problems are thought up to be put to Robinson Crusoe, *Homo oeconomicus:* choices of production, division of labor, use of the technics offered to him on the island. All around lies the big sea, fluid society that watches while he operates in solitude. At most, he will be approached by his savage shadow. But paradoxically, the primitive image of economic activity presents it as solitary action. Here I propose a new fiction, taken no longer from the transparency of the beginning but from the frivolous fires at the end: This time we might call it the fiction of the park in *Mine-Haha.* Given a sealed enclosure inhabited by female children and young girls committed to a subtle upbringing, whose cost is paid by the society outside the enclosure, of which we know nothing, it will be a matter of reconstructing how and on what terms the unknown society around the island of the park permits it to exist, just as the reconstruction of Crusoe's activity was to make it possible to project an operative model on the sea of society around him.

At the very beginning of the *Grundrisse,* Marx lashes out at Robinsonades, "conceits devoid of imagination," which serve to let the end product of a historical evolution pass for natural fact: in this case, the individual as isolated entity. His theological hatred for the *primum* forced him to condemn it, but by adding the observation that such "nonsense, which had sense and reason for men of the eighteenth century," had been reintroduced "right into the middle of the most modern economics"—and he cites Claude-Frédéric Bastiat, Henry Charles Carey, and Pierre-Joseph Proudhon—Marx implied a recognition of the power of images lying in ambush behind the rude prose of economists. Indeed, he himself would be the most prodigious creator of phantasms within economic discourse, so it comes as no surprise that later, in *Capital,* he decided, albeit ironically, to discuss the Crusoe hypothesis. And the ticklish place where he chose to do so is revealing: at the end of the first chapter of the first book, as an introduction to a series of Robinsonades. The others are devoted to "the darkness of medieval Europe" and then, after mentioning the *"naturwüchsig"* (natural and spontaneous) primitive community (an ever recurring *fictio* in *Capital* and certainly no less extravagant and improbable than Crusoe's island), to the "patriarchal peasant family" and an "association of free men." All these hypotheses are examined against the world of the production of commodities, for in them (though to varying degrees and even for opposite reasons) "the social relations of men with their labors and with the products of their labor" tend to remain "simple and transparent."[6]

The *demonstrandum* had been presented by Marx at the beginning of the passage: "The whole mysticism of the world of commodities, all the magic and phantasms that enshroud the products of labor with fog and result from the production of commodities, is immediately dispelled as soon as we take refuge in other modes of production."[7] There thus exists a specific perversion in the world of commodities, which distinguishes it from every other social form: a mystical perversion, as if phantasms, having been cleared from the sky, had all insinuated themselves intact into the seams of economic circulation. No sooner does Marx evoke the phantasmagoria of commodities than he abandons himself to a proliferation of images, and yet he does not offer a crypto-mythological structure adequate to represent the totality of that world, unless it would be the whole vast, overflowing, and unfinished edifice of *Capital*. Years later, however, a tiny, highly precise emblem of that world was to appear, a miniature bathed in that opalescent light that libertines say is actually a distinctive product of the "mysticism of the world of commodities": the park of *Mine-Haha*.

The girls in the park do not belong even to a family, much less to themselves. Like the exposed children of mythology, they are pledged to a mission—not, however, the heroic kind reserved for unique beings. On the contrary, their training will streamline them to endless permutation, to interchangeability, that is, to *equivalence*—to the great Western practice of substitution, separation, and arbitrariness. They will become algebraic and erotic beings. The girls in the park are a *social property*, which society sacrifices to itself. Behind the Isis-like veil of the walls, the phantasms of the exchange process become bodies, and in particular freshly minted female bodies, by that inversion mechanism that Marx encountered at every step as the *countersign* of capitalism and that he called the "personification of things and reification of the relations of production." The girls' bodies will, in their turn, again become phantasms, by being sold on the stage of the theater. The initiatory aura comes as no surprise; these are clearly the secret ceremonies of the most bigoted and devious of religions: the "religion of everyday life."[8]

HIDALLA: We are live coin, he told us, remember?—that hospitable Huguenot-Slav teacher of ours—and we squealed with laughter at those words uttered with such liturgical gravity. But when I too found myself with a riding crop in my hand, and was introducing on the stage the younger companions they'd entrusted to me, when I had got used to gazing into the hazy darkness of the audience and hearing its awful breathing, which sucked us in every time and spat us out again, us nimble *épaves* [waifs], ready to repeat our pantomime every evening with increasing fluidity—I felt with a pang the certainty that it was precisely ourselves who were that element into which everything was converted, that which arrived on the stage from the darkness *extra muros* and returned to it shining in drops of mercury, or others say in gold coins.

An elusive happiness dwells in the park. A spell emanates from the little yellow boots and white stockings, the tightly laced shoes, the pale green garters, the broad-brimmed straw hats, the red bricks covered by Virginia creeper, the darting tongue of the salamander Simba, Gertrud's slender rod, the windows illuminated at night, where one glimpses the little girls' white dresses—a spell that still haunts the memory of the female narrator and seduces the reader into regions that *Mädchen in Uniform* and *Olivia* suggest but do not attain. "We were happy, all of us, but that was all." An apparently innocuous sentence, which conceals the secrets of the park. Might this suspended and unreasonable happiness perhaps be coerced, imposed by machinations that chemically separate it from everything? It is certainly based on ignorance: of the world, which is never seen, of feeling, of function, of society—all obscure unknowns. The little girls, absorbed in the exercise of their own bodies, can know nothing of all that. "To do things without knowing what they are": This is how Adorno at Darmstadt described "the form of every artistic utopia today": translating in his pathos Samuel Beckett's dry *"dire cela, sans savoir quoi,"* which he used as an epigraph for his lecture "Vers une musique informelle."

The girls in the park behave precisely in accordance with this incongruous rule, indispensable as it is for whoever has encountered it. By exercising themselves, they tattoo the physiology of their bodies and transpose it into phantasm. "The flesh has its own spirit": This was almost Wedekind's motto, and the same goes for the forms of things unknown, those raw yet prodigiously animated materials that Charles Baudelaire found at the bottom of the *gouffre* [abyss] and christened *le Nouveau*. Scouring the city streets around the park, Walter Benjamin discovered that *le Nouveau* had another name as well: commodities. The unblemished happiness of reclusion, which allows one to experience forms as pure exercise, is made possible precisely by the functions of a world that does not have symbols and therefore wants the park to produce phantasms and sell them.

So we find ourselves faced with a variation of *le bonheur dans l'esclavage* [happiness in slavery]. As coin and phantasm, the girls in the park get ready to circulate. They process themselves, and in this they discover a happiness the outside world cannot know. As persons, they are slaves: locked in imponderable rapture for as long as they are such, in the park; destined for mockery, brutality, and torture once they become free in the outside world. They must, in any case, be killed. Either slowly, in the park, if they break its rules and want not to be mere phantasms but *to touch life,* whether by trying to escape from the park or by seeking erotic pleasure *as persons.* This is what had happened to the two horrible, ominous old women who wait on table for the girls in the park and who remind us of the slaves supposed by Hugo von Hofmannsthal to be moaning faintly in Goethe's cellars. Or else they can look forward to a symbolic immolation in the outside world as soon as they leave the park, as happens to the female narrator. It is only a question of time. These menacing truths dawn slowly on Hidalla; the omens gradually pile up as the end of her training nears. The transition to the theater then intensifies the whole process. The phantasms offered to the spectators by the girls are their bodies, which have no way of knowing what a body, upon which the whole discipline of the park is inscribed in minute arabesques, must represent for the howling public in the dark. But the pantomime these bodies enact is a ceaseless repetition of the rape committed by the Prince of Mosquitoes, who with equanimity sticks princesses, magicians' daughters, court ladies, and peasant girls in a barely disguised prefiguration of the second and final rape that will take place in the basin of the Campidoglio, thus now in the outside world, the final stage of the initiation: the sacred nuptials.

Indeed, the world does not care to give up its traditions, and in its ceremonies it has certainly not stopped following the august pattern of all theaters. The girls in the park will unwittingly go through it all again. Born from the water that eliminates all traces of prelife, naked at the beginning of the journey as they will be naked at the end of it on the stage, confined in baskets to enter from darkness into the new phase, then locked up to undergo the various trials imposed by their training, later selected as worthy initiates after a careful zootechnical examination conducted by ladies in long white silk gowns, and finally, led through hellish underground passages to the blinding light of reflectors illuminating the sacred marriage with the prince before a multitude of avidly staring eyes, though not so many as the countless ones that will exult around the basin of the Campidoglio, the site of the final immolation, which is called an encounter with life and marks its end.

Whereas a careful reading of the economic structure of *Mine-Haha* shows that the girls in the park are commodities, and in particular "excluded commodities," the "universal equivalent," *Geldkristall* (money crystal), a careful reading of the psychical structure of *Capital* shows that the prime commodity is woman. The first chapter of the first section of *Capital,* the only great demonology text produced by the bourgeois age, is already shaken by convulsions: Marx, like a rude exorcist, clutches at skirts, jackets, and pieces of cloth in mad pursuit of the metamorphoses of commodities, that "social hieroglyphic" with its restless mobility, which still seems "at first sight like something obvious and banal." Instead, it will turn out to be "something very twisted, full of metaphysical cunning and theological whims," something "sensitive and supersensitive."[9]

These commodities, which "come into the world in the form of use-values or of bodies of commodities," are quick to betray their "natural domestic form"[10] to devote themselves to the perversion of the "value-form," the "money-form" that by its spectral uniformity contrasts brutally with the "multicolored bodies" of commodities in their "natural forms." At the beginning of the second chapter, which takes up the "process of exchange," men also appear explicitly as *maquereaux* [pimps]: "Commodities cannot go to market by themselves and be exchanged. We must therefore seek out their guardians, the possessors of commodities. Commodities are things and therefore unable to resist man. And if they do not consent, he can use force; in other words, he can take them over." One of the few irrefutable practical rules of psychoanalysis is to look for symptoms more in the notes than in the text. At the end of the quoted sentence, Marx adds a footnote: "In the twelfth century, so celebrated for its piety, very delicate things often happen among these commodities. Thus a French poet of the period lists among the commodities to be found in the Landit marketplace, along with clothes, shoes, leather, farm tools, skins, etc., also *'femmes folles de leur corps'* " [wanton women].[11]

The training of the bodies of the young girls in the park represents, as it progresses, the triumph of *l'art pour l'art,* that first and still rather crude formula of great modern formalism: a pure exercise in the sealed chamber of nothingness, unmindful of any function, which no longer even knows what a function might be. Just as the "body of commodities" is transformed and perverted by succumbing to the pervasive breath of the "value-form" that translates it into money and transforms the object into a fetish, so the training of the girls in the park instills the erotic phantasm in the natural existence of the body. Thus a *communicatio idiomatum* is created among bodies, which no longer relate to an ego but all stand for the repetition of the "fetish character."

As phantasms, the girls in the park deftly replace each other. They are equivalence itself and communicate in the coin of pleasure that they represent but that they must not explicitly know: "Due to the total ignorance in which we lived, our relations were limited to the simplest elements. So I don't even remember that any of those girls in the park ever seemed to me spiritually different from another one. Each thought and felt like the next one, and if one of them opened her mouth all the others always knew beforehand what she was going to say. And so we spoke very little. Often at meals no one said a word. They all ate sunk in silence. It was only by their physical differences that you could tell them apart. When one said "I," she meant her whole self, from her head to the tips of her toes. We almost felt our I in our legs and feet more than in our eyes and fingers. I have no recollection of how any of the girls spoke. I still know the way each one walked." Edenic perfection, dreamt by Rousseau and the romantics as a triumph over the unhealthy split, by Marx as reappropriation—that is, a return, once the forces of production had achieved their most complex forms, to a rapport with nature as an "extension of the body"[12]—appears here as finally complete, but derisively, as a fetish. Paradise lies at the heart of deception.

"Among the first groups of beings with which man had to deal, and which by definition were there to deal with him, were first of all the gods and the spirits of the dead. They, indeed, are the true owners of the things and goods of this world. It was most necessary to perform exchanges with them, and most dangerous not to perform them. But on the other hand, with them it was easier and safer to perform exchanges. Sacrificial destruction has the precise aim of being a donation that must needs be rendered. All forms of the potlatch in Northwest America and Northeast Asia share this theme of destruction."[13]

Two opposite exchange systems: the potlatch, modeled on the sacrifice, and the production of commodities, which presupposes a mercurial, ubiquitous element that can be broken down into parts of uniform value: *abstract labor,* "lacking quality" as a unit of measurement, and money as an "excluded commodity," each mirroring the other. In the potlatch, on the other hand, the incommensurability, the nonexistence of the measuring unit, is recognized, thereby denying that the exchange can ever be equivalent. Whatever is given must be followed by an *excessive* response, signaling a readiness for exchange and unbalancing the scales on the other side. The new response will be a new excess and a new unbalance—and so on, endlessly. It is essential that parity never be acknowledged.

Sacrificial exchange is contradictory because it denies the very principle of exchange, the measuring unit, which is shared by human language and the elements of nature only in the Edenic condition. The myth established the impossible symbolic system, the secret equivalences, each time to be reconstructed, that allowed the exchange to be performed. Thanks to this impossibility, the exchange was precariously redeemed from the sin that marks its origin.

But equivalence has always been present in the sacrifice, corroding it. Theodor Adorno and Max Horkheimer, in *Dialektik der Aufklärung,* singled out the point where sacrifice and the exchange of commodities join: It is sacrificial substitution, the underlying trick of the Enlightenment, that makes it possible to establish the rule of equivalence. From the Enlightenment until the triumph of industry, there has been a linear process of methodical conquest, and today we navigate in the fluid equivalence of everything with everything, and every cipher is transparent: a parody of the Word, *per speculum in aenigmate* [through a glass darkly].

Very often, if we want to find the clearest and most sober explanation of some Western obsession, we have only to look to Aristotle. Thus the *locus classicus* of the implicit condemnation of exchange—corresponding to the passage on the secondary, that is, condemnable, nature of writing in *De interpretatione* (I, 16a, 3)—is in the *Politics* (I, 9, 1257a–1258a), which acknowledges that "all goods have two uses" but that to use them as a value for exchange is "improper" because goods do not exist "for love of exchange." The circulation of commodities thus takes its place in "unnatural chrematistics," which is marked, according to Aristotle, by what for a Greek is the most unforgivable vice: striving toward the unlimited.

Marx resurrects this passage at the beginning of *A Contribution to the Critique of Political Economy,* and the framework of the first section of *Capital* is modeled on it. But exchange had already appeared as a malign, alienating element in his *Auszüge aus Mill* (1844), where there was even the suggestion of a Christ-money equation, in perfect agreement, though from the opposite perspective, with Léon Bloy. In *Auszüge,* the "soul of money" was actually presented as the deceptive hypostasis of an *"outside intermediary,"* which, by interposing itself between men, deprived them of what is their own: "the *activity,* or movement, *of mediation,* the social, *human* act."[14] That the condemnation of exchange is closely linked to the condemnation of appearance and exteriority, that it is even *interchangeable* with them, appears explicitly, however, only in *Capital*: "Things are in themselves and by themselves external *(äusserlich)* to man and therefore alienable *(veräusserlich).*"[15] Here we find an imposing metaphysical premise, as often happens in an analysis that claims only to be historical. It thus suffices to give rise to the fiction of the ego as an enclosed area, with exchange taking place because the world's features have hardened in a deadly lack of relatedness. And is it possible that this does not happen? Combining mythopoetic frenzy and a cold critical acumen, Marx here introduces his utopian model as well, only to thwart it immediately: "For this alienation to be reciprocal, all that is necessary is for men to oppose each other tacitly as private owners of these alienable things and thus precisely as persons independent of each other. Such a relationship of reciprocal isolation does not exist, however, for the members of a natural-spontaneous *(naturwüchsig)* community, whether it takes the form of a patriarchal family, a community in ancient India, or an Inca state."[16] Such *naturwüchsig* communities are clearly considered as a body, where everything belongs and no outside exists, since no *exchange* exists to create the *schism,* through the *lag* between buying and selling that is fomented by "dissolving money." (*Scheidemünze,* usually, is "loose change"; but *scheiden,* "to separate," and *Scheide,* "vagina.") Thus, in one of the most strained passages in *Capital:* "Ancient society denounces it [money] as *Scheidemünze* of its economic and moral order,"[17] and the whole passage merely repeats, with significant changes in tone and arrangement [the two favorite quotations from Shakespeare's *Timon of Athens,* which first introduced the subject, are now put into a footnote] folio 41 of the *Economic and Philosophic Manuscripts,* where money is presented in its pontifical power to loosen and bind ["Can it not perhaps loosen and tighten all bonds?"] and finally as a "universal *means of separation [Schei-dungsmittel],*" culminating in the statement "It is the real *Scheidemünze.*")

Everything circulates *internally.* But the outside appears as soon as the borders of the community are crossed. Then the community presents itself as a *unity* facing another outside unity, and thus in conditions of exchange. And it is here that Marx, in one fell swoop, demolishes in a couple of sentences the utopian image he has just created: "The exchange of commodities begins where communities end, at the points where they enter into contact with outside communities or with members of such communities. But once things have become commodities in relations with the outside, by the same token they become such in the community's internal life. . . . From that moment on, the division is fixed, on one side, the utility of things for immediate needs, and on the other, their utility for exchange."[18] Both for the individual and for the *naturwüchsig* community, the collision with the outside is inevitable, and in that collision the paradise of immediacy is dissolved, destructive exchange is born, and the phantasms of money and commodities begin to spread. And to close the vicious circle of nihilism, the subject that by asserting itself had released these phantasms is annihilated by them. This too had been recognized by Marx as early as the *Auszüge aus Mill*: "With *money,* and that means by total indifference toward both the nature of the material and the personality of the private owner, the total dominion of the alienated thing *over* man became manifest."[19] The liquidation of the autonomous subject, however, occurs not in a brutal and immediately visible way but in a subtle and derisive form, whose triumph Marx sees in the improvement of the banking system—so derisive that the naive followers of Saint-Simon saw in it the sign of its opposite: a return by man to himself, ha-ha! But, observes Marx, "this *return* by man to himself and therefore to other men is only an *appearance,* it is a self-alienation all the *more disgraceful* and *more extreme* insofar as its element is no longer commodity, metal, or paper, but *moral* existence, *social* existence, the *secrets* of the human heart itself." Finally: "It is not that in the credit system money is overcome *(aufgehoben)* in man, but man himself is transformed into *money,* or rather money is *incorporated* into him. *Human individuality,* human *morality,* has itself become a commercial item, a *material* in which money exists."[20] The human body thus becomes an extension of the body of money, mirroring the origin, where nature was an "extension of the body"[21] of man.

The "production of commodities" is thus not only a historical phase but history itself as internally corroded by nihilism, which is primarily the practice of replaceability, algebraic haste, the denial of whatever is incommensurable, and the radical abuse of metaphor. All innocence and blessed unity are negated by the very words that express them, in whose sound, as the seal of equivalence, Robespierre's answer echoes every time, as Hegel noted: "The answer that Robespierre always gave—when they told him that someone had thought or wanted something or said something else— was: *la mort!* Its uniformity is extremely tedious, but it suits everything. You want the jacket: here it is; you want the vest too: it's here; you give a slap: here's the other cheek; you want the little finger: cut it off. I can kill anything, abstract from anything. Obstinacy is thus invincible and in itself can overcome anything. But the supreme thing to overcome would be precisely this freedom, this very death."[22]

"But there is a blasted difference in the first place between barbarians who are fit to be used for anything, and civilized beings who apply themselves to everything," said Marx.[23] The context makes it clear that the "barbarians" are the Russians and the "civilized beings" the Yankees, and his tone anticipated not only a certain kind of macho speech in American movies but also suggested, by its abrupt outburst, that a decisive point was being reached: *abstract work,* work *"sans phrase,"* "without quality," pure negating activity, a category that having crept into the economy, emerges to crack with a diamond point the solid surfaces of all other spheres of life. It is here that Hegelian karma adds something to Adam Smith and David Ricardo, enriching their icy empiricism with a lethal drop of metaphysical poison, the drop that makes it possible to corrode a concrete element unknown to the empirical. Abstract labor means the reduction of any activity to an empty unity, the dissipation of energy involved in any task, apart from any specific difference, that is, from any quality or function, any *meaning.* A huge furnace into which lace, sackcloth, rags, and flags get thrown—anything, so long as it burns—the "productive expenditure of brains, muscles, nerves, human hands":[24] The first inversion of the world of commodities lies in this evaluation of productive labor as *consumption.* The scale of value is shown precisely by the capacity to be burned. It can thus be said that the most appropriate image of abstract labor, as the advanced industrial age has shown, is pure exercise in the void: *l'art pour l'art* as the model for all activity, a basis shared by Stéphane Mallarmé and the assembly line, a mirror image of the "third function of money,"[25] the cycle M-C-C-M [money = commodity = commodity = money], in which money appears as an end in itself and capable of being glorified without restraint in the process of circulation.

This cycle can be reconstructed by following the course of the girls in the park. First phase: production, park. The girls appear as "laughing water," primordial agent of circulation, traces of soma; during their training, they are material operating on material (abstract labor has no subject, it is the work of *manpower*), exercise, abstract labor, the nihilistic practice of form, the elaboration of the body of the commodity, which becomes the "commodity of all commodities," money. Second phase: exchange, theater. The girls are now also persons, their value being the phantasm they offer; their abstract labor, pure exercise, turns out to be *functional,* but in a sense that had not been willed by those who had squandered the energy of the exercise. It could not have been willed, since the exercise, as a model of abstract labor, is *beyond meaning.* The theatrical exhibition causes money to flow into the park, while the "live coin" of the girls enters into circulation in the outside world. The money they have attracted already serves to maintain other female inmates of the park as they too work to transform themselves into money. *Circulus vitiosus dea.*

"Industry establishes as the very principle of its initiatives that any human phenomenon, like any natural phenomenon, is capable of being treated as *exploitable material,* and is therefore *subject* to fluctuations in *value,* as well as to all the *hazards of experience,*"[26] wrote Klossowski. Once they become material, "emblems come back as commodities," Benjamin notes, while our period proves increasingly eager to spread forms on the market, filling with phantasms the scene abandoned by the orders of analogy and symbol—in short, by correspondences. This involves a subtle change in the statute of images. If indeed, in terms of exchange, beings are now primarily phantasms, then phantasms will in their turn enjoy the autonomy of subjects and withdraw themselves from all jurisdiction. This detachment of the thing from the person, which for Freud marked the pathology of fetishism, is now the assumption of every perception and every use of phantasms. Phantasms by now refer to nothing but themselves and their own latent power, which is all the greater insofar as they include in their individual and partial being the totality of the exchange process, just as a single coin expresses the totality of economic circulation. Fetishes thus allow the formation of a new *Adamic language:* "Our objects, in their mutual relations, are the only comprehensible language that we speak to each another. A human language we would not understand, and it would remain ineffective."[27] (Disconcerting things happen: Once it has been proclaimed that fetishes have no power—and after Freud has placed fetishism at the penultimate level of perversions, just above necrophilia, exclaiming in his *Introductory Lectures* "But now enough of these horrors!"—it actually turns out that the signs and beings of the world communicate only in their capacity as fetishes, while consequently fetishism itself appears as the prime guarantee of social exchange: in a word, of normality.)

Among the theorists of *l'art pour l'art,* only Baudelaire understood that the ivory tower should be taken as antiphrasis, as a site for the "universal prostitution of beings," to use the formula that Klossowski has applied to Sade and that Marx, much earlier, had applied to all of industrial society: "Universal prostitution appears as a necessary phase in the social character of personal tendencies, capacities, abilities, and activities."[28] The law of exchange requires a "universal equivalent": the Vedic soma and the *logos* no longer being relevant and usable, they are replaced by the twin couple of "abstract labor" and "excluded commodity," money—and every level of the manifestation, insofar as it is transmitted, becomes one of the various forms of prostitution, the last appearance of the *theologia theatrica* eloquently condemned by Saint Augustine. *"L'être le plus prostitué, c'est l'être par excellence, c'est Dieu"* [the most prostituted being is the being par excellence, God], remarked Baudelaire, and from there the cosmic ladder descends, refracting the divine image down to the bourgeois who sustains it, claiming to buy everything without selling himself, and who would like to withdraw from the constant dispossession suffered by everyone, first of all by God: *exinanivit se* [he emptied himself]. The joke of the reigning order is that this incongruous claim appears to be well founded: "If a poet were to ask the state for the right to keep a bourgeois in his stable, people would be much astonished, while if a bourgeois were to ask for a piece of roasted poet, it would be found completely natural," says Baudelaire in

Mon coeur mis à nu. This may also be the reason why the world does not abound in love; indeed, "love may derive from a generous sentiment: the taste for prostitution. But it is quickly corrupted by the taste for property" (Baudelaire, *Fusées*).

Mine-Haha, this dark novel about money, bodies, phantasms, and chattel, could only have been written within the framework of post-history, a word I happen to use as being just as obvious and just as obscure as pre-history. But let me here try to provide a brief definition for the dictionary:

POST-HISTORY: that portion of history that is enacted in the experimental laboratory of nihilism. Nihilism, of course, has always dwelt in history, but each time it had to get rid of its various orders based on more or less strict and narrow correspondences, analogies, and canons. Once nihilism had inadvertently devoured the last existing forms, Hegel, in the role of funeral director, announced that history was finished. The owl of Minerva took wing, and many believed they were witnessing the triumph of history, which had just disappeared. It was often said, with satisfaction, that all of history was a tireless demolition of idols. Now that the operation was finally complete, it remained only to sell the idols, while taking care that they retained their power of fascination over buyers, even if the regime of uniqueness had been replaced by the indefinite multiplication of images, in obedience to an ever effective principle: Lower the price of everything but make sure that everything has a price. Arthur Rimbaud then opened the grand clearance sale of phantasms like a prestidigitator: "For sale what the Jews have not sold, what nobility and crime have not enjoyed, what the fatal love and the infernal honesty of the masses do not know. . . . For sale priceless Bodies, not belonging to any known race, world, sex, progeny! . . . For sale anarchy for the masses; irrepressible satisfaction for superior amateurs; terrible death for the faithful and lovers! . . . For sale bodies, voices, the tremendous, unquestionable wealth, what will never be sold. The salesmen have not reached the end of the sale! Travelers do not have to render accounts immediately!"[29] Indeed, this sale is still going on.

First post-historical corollary: *The letter is nothing but spirit.* Among the experimental practices that nihilism, an astute rhetorician, has tried to put into operation in its theater, the first and main one is esotericism. A chilling oxymoron has thus been created, one that grips our whole life. Appearance having now been dissolved as referring to another, what one gets is unremitting tautology, the repetition of divine names, a constant exchange of incorruptible mystical commodities, whether they be words, bodies, images, phantasms, or objects. Seen from a distance, this dizzying circulation produces an effect of static hypnosis, a miserable condition of demigods who would like to die but cannot.

Second post-historical corollary: *Common exchange is mystical exchange.* The unit of measure—that is, the capacity of anything to be translated into anything else, equivalence (only the elect are equal), reciprocity— these are esoteric notions, and post-history makes them become the only immediate reality, since it is on them that it bases the circulation of commodities and on such circulation that it models every other exchange. The countless mystical formulas and religious allusions used by Marx, from the *Manuscripts of 1844* to the last parts of *Capital* (to choose at random: "the Grail of gold," "the alchemical retort of circulation," "mystical nature of commodities," "trinitarian formula," "veil of mystical fog" [of the production process], "blinding enigma of the commodity fetish") should be taken literally. Commentators have often avoided them as though they were baroque decoration to be excused, along with Hegelian coquetry, in the name of the sound doctrine they conceal. Yet never was that doctrine so sound and indispensable as in its discovery of the theological dimension of capital.

The theatrical character of post-history, the fact that it is devoid of substance and constantly needs to be absorbed into a phantasmagoria that appeases its insatiable need for fetishes, explains the return to the abandoned stage of all the images of the historical past. Thus, behind the "live coin" of the park dwellers, a throng of other beings appear as well, reflecting the origin of that coin. As "laughing water," we recognize the waves that flow toward Soma in the atmospheric sea, the Apsarases with their rounded breasts and empty eyes, the inexhaustible celestial water nymphs, spontaneously appearing and disappearing in the pond in the park, the pool where the Rig-Veda shows us the beautiful Urvaśī sporting with her water birds. The training of their bodies seeks to make them twin coins, ovoidal cowries, distended and shining, with scalloped edges, like "the right, equal word" of the Dogon, which is woven with another right word. Exchange of twins, said the seventh *nommo*, bisexual ancestor and lord of the word, is the model of equal exchange. It is the twilight of the nymphs, the little *déesses entretenues,* whose fleeting forms Heine and Marx had glimpsed in Christian crypts, still visited by the oldest guardians of the caves, and in the cellars of the Crédit Mobilier. As long as they remain in the park, they experience the joys and rediscover the transparency of a girls' *ghotul,* the "young people's house" of the Muria Indians, the only suitable image of a perfect upbringing that exhausted anthropology has been able to find. "Nihilism is a feeling of happiness," observed Nietzsche, the leading expert. If that sentiment has ever been shown anywhere in its pure state, it is in the park in *Mine-Haha.* But once they leave that sanctuary, they enter the world of unacknowledged and nontransparent nihilism, the one in which we live and whose business it is to inflict on the girls in the park the meanest humiliations while welcoming them as its free citizens.

"An abstract sensuality presupposes an object that contains the possibility of all pleasures," says Marx.[30] Locked inside the park, the girls are intent precisely on turning themselves into that object, following the rules of "reasoned sensuality" that, as Paul Valéry remarked, had been taught by Baudelaire. From time to time, the teacher pays them a visit, his owl-headed cane taps the pavement, and he observes the little girls from behind while tirelessly repeating, "Work is like Brussels lace: The essential is what surrounds the pattern: air, perforation, unjustified absence."

THEATER

LEONORE: Let me just say one thing, Effie. Anyone who appears in public for money no longer belongs to society.[31]

When the girls' initiation in the park nears its end, when the last touches have been applied and the coins have been clipped to make them ready for exchange, the excluded commodity is taken into the theater through underground passageways to offer phantasms to a public hidden behind heavy grating while money pours into the box office. The sacred nuptials of money and bodies are matched on the stage by a playful, irreverent pantomime in the style of Heine, called *The Prince of Mosquitoes,* where the *hieròs gámos* [holy marriage] turns out to be primarily a good excuse to stick girls. In this *bouffonnerie lyrique ou féerique,* plunged *dans une atmosphère anormale et songeuse—dans l'atmosphère des grands jours,* the ultimate goal for which the girls have been raised in their refined stable already appears: mockery and ruin.

In the building with neither doors nor windows, at the borderline between reclusion and the world, where the girls from the park are put on display, the natural history of the theater runs backward: Applause is once again the pulsation of the spectators as the blood of sacrificial animals gushes forth. But then the stage needs to discard such ancient vestiges and take on the characteristics of a commodity: The pantomime of the girls from the park becomes a series of magic-lantern slides, movement on glass, or a collection of dirty pictures leafed through slowly by a dark crowd behind the grating, voyeurs who compose the new, shapeless cloud of Eros around a many-bodied Psyche. Beyond the grating, the world has no contours, only sinister voices. It exults in the darkness; feet shuffle toward the exit.

Apologue of *Mine-Haha*: Whoever has once known the intoxication of being "live coin," an excluded commodity, the commodity of all commodities, and a site of metamorphoses, cannot accept the degradation of again finding herself a person, that is, a woman caught in the pincers of a social order that pretends not to know that it is based on the stimulating fluidity of universal prostitution and insists that that fact remain unspoken. She has, moreover, good reasons: After leaving the park and having experienced that infinite agility and availability, she finds herself again in an unsullied world, which still kills in the name of its good manners and disavows the spectacle of the girls, though it nourishes it secretly all its life. As Hegel observed in one of his notebooks: "People don't go so much anymore to dances, public places, theaters. *On s'assemble en famille; on revient aux moeurs* [They gather together in their families; they return to their habits]. These *moeurs* are the universal boredom of public life, morality."

LEONORE: In the theater, for business reasons, everything is deliberately arranged as though all the spectators were as contemptible and abject as the company of actors.

BAUDELAIRE: Indeed, how often at the theater, on taking a good look at the female spectators in the boxes, have I felt a sly joy at discovering, in the way they majestically offer themselves to the gaze of others, the same rules, barely concealed, that governed the lives of my girls in the park. Just think, *ma chère,* of the soft glow of a Second Empire parterre, but one whose boxes encircle the underground pool of Garnier's Opéra: The *maidens of society,* some serious and grave, others blond and giddy, are reflected in those tiny waves that receive and retransmit the light from their eyes, their jewels, their shoulders, framed by the boxes. They display a precocious bosom with aristocratic nonchalance or an unripe figure with candor, their fans secretly mangled by their teeth, their eyes vague and fixed, no less solemn and theatrical than the spectacle they are pretending to follow. And alongside them, ostentatiously sweeping the floor with its train and the ends of its shawls, with the wide-open eye of the beast that seems to see nothing and examines everything against a boreal background, sometimes pink (to indicate ecstasy in frivolity), sometimes violet (coals being extinguished behind a blue stage curtain), rises the *variegated image of equivocal beauty.* It represents the enclosed savage state of society. The triviality of its life, full of traps and knives, shows through its official decorations, but also through its artificial grandeur, which is linked to a slow movement of the eyes, a certain toss of the head, and a certain way of carrying oneself but goes no further. Or else: curled up on sofas, with their skirts turned up fore and aft to form a double fan, heavy, sullen, obtuse, intemperate, their eyes glazed from brandy, their foreheads round and stubborn, in a hazy and gilded languor of which the indigent classes know nothing—here are *the slaves,* who have nothing of their own, not even the eccentric ornaments of their beauty.

The girls in the park, having arrived on the stage, are also creatures of decoration; they have nothing of their own; they are objects given over to universal pleasure, ready to be stuck by the outsize pins of the *logos* behind the grating as well as by those of the Prince of Mosquitoes, its vicar on the stage. By silent exercises with their harsh discipline, in the White House and red houses, Hidalla's hundreds of companions were being obscurely prepared for this too. The expectation of life, the imminence of disaster, anticipatory tentacles extended beyond the enclosure of the park, dressing for the ball, the party observed in hiding from the darkness at the top of a stairway—it is the aura in which so many heroines of novels lived in those years before meeting Prince Andrey. But here the time has come to say farewell to any possible development, any story: Crystallized in the subtlest animality, with the measured pace of horses, miraculously elastic in their gait, the inmates of the park can only dissolve like shadows swallowed up by the reflectors. Soon thereafter, after they have been thrown into the natural and murderous light of the unknown outside world, threatening faces throw flowers as they pass, spectators throng from all the alleyways, because they have been immolated to something or other, in a pool of water similar to the one where they played games in the park. But we will learn nothing about it, for here Hidalla's story breaks off, as though to suggest that the end is the dull thud of the eighty-four-year-old narratrix falling on the pavement.

HIDALLA: Ultimate image of happiness! To enter the world from a theater box office, while the first spectators are already buying you with their tickets!

On 12 March 1918, around 4:15 in the afternoon, Frank Wedekind was buried in the Waldfriedhof in Munich. A strange, dense crowd had gathered. Representatives of society—men of art, science, and the liberal professions—grouped around the relatives soon found themselves surrounded by swarms of equivocal creatures, for the most part whores with their pimps. The sewers had been opened, and the inhabitants of that realm rushed out to say goodbye to the writer who had once been their loyal and happy guest. Gaudy costumes closed in behind the gentlemen in top hats and frock coats, and as the cortege started, the uninvited mob surged forward, hoping to arrive first at the grave so as to miss no part of the spectacle. The mad stampede reminded one of the onlookers, Kurt Martens, of two lines by Wedekind:

> Happy the man who calm and satisfied
> tramples fresh graves!

Out of that picturesque, unseemly pack emerged a pale youth with long clumsy arms, the writer Heinrich Lautensack, who began giving agitated orders to a cameraman from Berlin who had come to film the scene and telling those present how to behave and in what direction to look. Next he is said to have thrown a wreath of roses in the grave, while shouting words of homage to Wedekind—at that moment, he went out of his mind, to die in the grip of madness a few months later. In the uproar, the nine official speakers could hardly make themselves heard.

4 Enamel Scar

Bois ton sang, Beaumanoire

Dr. Rönne kept going in and out of hospitals, morgues, and literature. He had been living this way for quite a while, proceeding further and further into his first internal emigration. He was an émigré in a doctor's white coat, and later in a Wehrmacht uniform. Rönne's initial gesture was to separate his fate from reality. It was unacceptable that what offered itself as reality should actually be so. A pile of debris, maybe. Material to connect with, even. But the more Rönne connected, the more his separation from all of it grew. A silent eruption was going on. Around his head was a slight whiff of epilepsy.

Dr. Rönne had already appeared in *Ithaka,* a play imbued with medical filthiness that Gottfried Benn published in 1914. But Rönne's identity card shows Brussels, in the early months of 1916, as the place and date of his birth. Benn at the time was a doctor in a hospital for prostitutes and was billeted with his orderly in a requisitioned eleven-room house. He was allowed to go out in civilian clothes, his hours on duty were few, he ignored the inhabitants of the place, and with the war as a pretext he secretly embarked on a mental flight that was never to be interrupted. Very probably, he already knew that "the category in which the cosmos manifests itself is hallucination." Now "life was wavering in a sphere of silence and dismay,"[1] a hallucinatory stasis with fluctuations. Rönne experiences in himself what Benn will later formulate: "The ego is a late state of mind in nature, and fleeting besides."[2] Like Pameelen, another double dating from the months in Brussels, Rönne annotates his own clinical chart: "In this brain something is decomposing that for four centuries has been consid-

78

ered as ego and rightly so; during that period it has sustained the human cosmos in forms transmitted from generation to generation."[3] The process is accompanied by a slight, sinister euphoria. What matters is to render the "basic schizoidness of the human essence"[4] productive and provocative. "Schizoidness" is not a textbook word, freshly coined by Eugen Bleuler, but the seal on every hidden, fading moment. Rönne feels its stamp on his skin in the café or while eating lunch with men who talk about tropical fruits or in the corridors of a hospital. What exists? Those levers, handles, tables, waistcoats, those convinced words, those necks planted like tree trunks—or his invisible delirium, his cold, then burning trance?

> I have devoted various studies in my essays to this theme of absolute prose. I found the first signs of it in Pascal, who speaks of creating beauty through distance, rhythm, and intonation, "through the recurrence of vowels and consonants"—"the oscillating number of beauty," he says once, and "perfection through the order of words."
>
> —*Gottfried Benn,* Doppelleben

To what literary genre does *Gehirne* (Brains) belong? To absolute prose. But what is meant by "absolute prose"? Obviously, something that had burst forth in Lautréamont, in Arthur Rimbaud (*Illuminations,* but also *Une saison en enfer*), in Stéphane Mallarmé *(Divagations),* but they are all still too lyrical; the mocking tone stands out only in Lautréamont and the Rimbaud of *Une saison.* Among his contemporaries, Benn cited Carl Einstein *(Bebuquin)* and André Gide (*Paludes* and nothing else) as producers of absolute prose. As for the surrealists, they were incapable of it. André Breton declared his contempt for art and had too many alexandrines in his ear. For the best examples, look to Saint Petersburg: to Osip Mandelstam (*The Egyptian Stamp* and his prose in general) or Andrey Bely (in his grandiose intentions); or else to a lone woman, Marina Tsvetayeva, when she speaks of her mother and the piano or also of Aleksandr Pushkin. Such is the lineage. It has nothing to do with avant-garde or literary manifestos. Indeed, it has no patience with either. There is only one criterion, and Benn stated it succinctly: "For anyone striving to give expression to his inner self, art is not something relevant to the social sciences but something physical like fingerprints."[5]

Gehirne is a record of drugged writing. An endocrine drug is acting here, secreted by the physiology of a doctor through whose hands many corpses have passed. This drug loosens the connections that make reality feasible. It isolates other connections, which exhibit themselves with mocking clarity to the drugged mind and which to other minds are indecipherable. This nourishes the shifting soil of absolute prose: A space where words are given over to the force of inertia and friction is reduced to a minimum. Images wink at each other, nouns interbreed, and no one knows what they are talking about. Perhaps, a few moments later, even Rönne does not know. He stacks up fragmented figures on the shelves of a café; he puts himself in the shoes of a repulsive gentleman seated at another table. His perceptions are accompanied by overwhelming sarcasm; he rides the crest of a primordial wave. Meanwhile, Rönne tries to respond faultlessly to anyone who speaks to him, and he is pleased that the decomposition going on in his head cannot be noticed from outside.

Rönne's obscurity of mind comes from a compulsion. We believe Benn absolutely when he tells us that "The Birthday" just "happened,"[6] that the "writing totally obeyed a compulsion."[7] We are not dealing with automatic writing as clumsily theorized and practiced by the surrealists. It was the irruption of a twilight state as the average condition (in the statistical sense) of consciousness. He, Rönne, had no need to train, stretch, or goad himself to reach that state. On the contrary, he needed to hold himself back, in order to go on shaking hands with his colleagues, soberly greeting the nurses, and ordering a beer. The drug was flowing in a lethargic and unfathomable sensory apparatus, like water from a faucet left open during the night.

> . . . language that neither wants to (nor can)
> do anything but phosphoresce, incandesce,
> overwhelm, stun. It celebrates itself, it drags what
> is human into its subtle but also powerful organ-
> ism, it becomes monologue, indeed monomania.
> —*Gottfried Benn, Letter to Wellershoff,*
> *22 November 1950*

Weary of all avant-gardes and formalisms, we take a dim view of these words, since we have heard so many others like them. "Writing that refers to nothing but itself"—how many times have we heard that? But what looks similar can also be immensely distant. That "phosphoresce," which for Benn was the result of long sojourns on the other side of the river Acheron, can never become a pedantic prescription. The literature that celebrates itself and only itself and has cut all its moorings is precisely the one that derives in minute detail from that psychical darkness, that silent cavern where at intervals the style phosphoresces like an ignis fatuus. Many have brandished this literary thyrsus, but there have been very few bacchants. And today almost all of them are dead. Benn takes leave of Wellershoff: "But I would be happy if I've succeeded in showing you that it's not just a question of style and language, but of problems of substance."[8]

> . . . a sacrilegious azure . . .
> —*Gottfried Benn,* Englisches Café

The azure sky is in Benn from the start. But it is the azure of someone who traveled very little, whose knowledge of other languages was poor, whose idea of delight was to read a detective story in English. Even Nietzsche, after all, took a few walks around Santa Margherita. Benn's biographical landscape instead is dirty snow, with a few wooden hulks sticking up in it. It is Berlin around the end of the war, the scene that greets Benn's final representative, the Ptolemean who emerges from his beauty parlor. This is no Club Med divined by the poet. "Azure" is a vision of devastation that invades any bystander, an intensity that relates to nothing, a cutting mental irruption. This azure is sacrilegious, a gash, an enamel scar.

> He found this significant and ominous: perhaps
> metaphor was already an attempt to escape, a
> kind of illusion and a lack of fidelity.
>   —*Gottfried Benn, "Der Geburtstag"*

When Rönne was a doctor in a bordello and had reached the age of thirty, he began to reap the stylistic consequences of the earth tremors being produced in him, glacial and carboniferous, the friction of continental plates. Metaphor lay always to hand, like a jimmy for a burglar, if the only possibility for relief was offered by a chronic "attempt to escape." And the "lack of fidelity" sounded like a rousing virtue for someone who, like Rönne, felt oppressed by sincere and truthful citizens, purveyors of public opinion. "The Conquest" and "The Journey" are variations of an archetype that is the polestar for the modern: the strolling of the schizophrenic, introduced by Georg Büchner in *Lenz,* doused with metropolitan poison by Baudelaire, unraveled with amiable despair in Robert Walser. To stroll in an unknown city, among hostile Belgians armored in their language, to sit for hours in a café, to end up for no particular reason in sordid neighborhoods, and finally to walk around in a greenhouse—this is all it takes to be sucked back into metamorphosis, the ceaseless billowing of figures, which can also be terrifying. "By now the formless was spreading, and the monstrous lay in wait."[9] Strolling and escaping now coincided.

One of Benn's peculiarities was a supreme sense of exhaustion. "I suddenly felt a profound exhaustion and a poison in my limbs."[10] My father always suffered from fatigue, his daughter Nele was to say. It is an exhaustion that comes from above and crushes like a giant hand. The frequency of such verbs as "waver," "fluctuate," and so on also pays homage to expressionist conventions. But what conveys Benn's tone is the backwash in the blood, the crouching vampirism in the breath, a cosmic gasping.

> Those who love strophes also love catastrophes;
> whoever is for statues must also be for ruins.
>   —*Gottfried Benn,* Drei alte Männer

The Rönne stories are not always *beautiful.* They are sometimes dull, sometimes overloaded; at times images are not set free or are set too free, while bits and pieces of poetry remain trapped by the harsh laws of prose. But what does it matter? There is, after all, a throb in every line, a hammering at the temples, a fever that dries up the throat, and one cannot say why. There will be time for beauty later, maybe the next line, maybe some forty years later, amid venereal disease and Wehrmacht uniforms, in multiple internal emigrations, and always with a poker face. But it had all been made possible by that "unprecedented" year when "Rönne, the physician, the flagellant of individual things"[11] was born in Brussels, a year governed by a feeling of landslide, of forever wandering about while losing one's footing. Catastrophe first, then strophes.

It should be noted that Rönne is *not* a "born artist," even if at the end he "perceives art."[12] What happens in him is not a literary apprenticeship but a slippage of geological strata. He witnesses something, or rather, undergoes it, and there he sinks. And as he sinks, for a moment he would still like to be one of those steely and obtuse gentlemen who toss down a glass at the officers' club and accompany it with a quip. That way it would be easier to survive. The solution will come later, in a perennial "double life." One day Rönne, or Benn, will open a medical practice, treating venereal and skin diseases. And he will write a few perfect poems, six or eight by his own count. This is how poets are: "petit bourgeois, born with a particular impulse, half for volcanic action and half for apathy."[13]

> If I must be precise, my happy moments were all connected with crime: adultery, drunkenness, infidelity, hatred of parents, falsity, double standard of morality, and a sentence by Hamsun came to my mind: There is only one love, the stolen kind—among the truest words in human history.
>
> —*Gottfried Benn,* Die Stimme hinter dem Vorhang

A breath of criminality blows throughout *Gehirne,* striking the stagnant air of the cemetery behind the pastor's house, the house where Benn was born; it blows as well through Nietzsche and "as statistics prove, more than 50 percent of Germany's great men."[14] There is the cruel Lutheran dictate of Benn's father, forbidding the son to administer morphine to his mother in her tortured death throes, since suffering comes from the Lord and we must accept it as such; there is the nest of mice embedded in the diaphragm of a girl drowned among the reeds. The doctor's hand grazes them. Without having to move a step, Benn falls into extremes, and his words are tinged with that magic that Nietzsche had evoked: the magic of the extreme, the eye of Venus.

> . . . down with truth
> —*Gottfried Benn,* Lebensweg eines
> Intellektualisten

Benn's daughter Nele had written from Denmark to ask him a question like a good Nordic girl: God? Benn got up his nerve, and remembered having written, "God is a bad stylistic principle."[15] But then he added, "To believe already puts me outside of God, that is to say the universe, and affirms that in general I would be something. But I'm really nothing, it's just that something runs through me whose provenance and direction have always seemed veiled to me and every day more veiled."[16] No one, not even Nietzsche, knew so well as Benn how to mock the Germans. But reading these overly simple words to a daughter who wants answers from her daddy, we cannot help thinking of a few other great Germans— Eckhart, Hölderlin, Nietzsche.

Benn was forever overturning categories in the minds of many of his readers. How can one be regressive and classical at the same time? How can one be algae or a jellyfish and at the same time the capital of a column? How can one obey the fluctuations of a primordial lymph and at the same time establish the rigid rule of form? Fearful as it may be, one can manage to follow Benn on one of the two paths, but how to do so on both? And yet, unless one follows him on both paths, one loses him. Benn escapes: He becomes a brute nostalgic for the primordial or else a wan defender of form. To read Benn, one must see the algae on the capital and the capital in the algae.

> Words, words—nouns! They have only to
> spread their wings and millennia drop from
> their flight.
> —*Gottfried Benn,* Epilog und lyrisches Ich

Benn read everything and collected names in his notebooks. Later he rediscovered them, isolated and radiant. "Phaeacians," "megaliths," "Lerna," "Astarte," "Geta," even "olive" (as in "The Birthday") or "theogonies"— for a Romance-language reader, it is hard to grasp the force with which these sounds collide with the knots of Germanic consonants. But for Benn, and for the antennae with which he constantly probed words, they were almost the whole vital tension. Had that been taken away from him, he could even imagine having spent his life selling cigarettes behind a counter.

> . . . a quick look, just leafing through some-
> times produces a slight intoxication.
> —*Gottfried Benn,* Doppelleben

Whoever reads Benn's prose, from the Rönne stories to *Novel of the Phenotype,* is struck by a volley of verbal splinters, mostly nouns, and often composite nouns, hybrids invented on the spur of the moment. They are not readable in linear sequence, but arrange themselves in constellations. And then the prose appears, a prose like the segments of an orange. Aware that *Novel of the Phenotype* was "markedly incomprehensible,"[17] Benn once politely mentioned the circumstances in which those words arose. It was during the war, in the Landsberg barracks, and he had happened on an art book, *The Beauty of the Female Body,* reproductions of famous paintings from all periods. Benn leafed through it, and from that perusal his prose was born: "Always new details, which otherwise would have had to be assembled with effort and annotated and might never have been found."[18] And now instead: "Venuses, Ariadnes, Galateas rise from their cushions under arches, gather fruits, veil their mourning, drop violets, convey a dream."[19] There are doves, dogs, boats, conches, swans, hares, shrubs. Then begins "the process, which may last half an hour."[20] And it is deposited on a page. But here is the secret: Keep turning the pages, do not even let your eyes stop.

> There is the motto of an old French family, the
> Beaumanoires, which is basically the motto of
> all artists: *"Bois ton sang, Beaumanoire"*—drink
> your blood, Beaumanoire: which is to say, for
> the artist, if you suffer, do as best you can, you
> are your sole redemption and your god; if you're
> thirsty, you must drink your blood, drink your
> blood, Beaumanoire!
> —*Gottfried Benn,* Totenrede für Klabund

5 On the Fundamentals of the Coca-Cola Bottle

On receiving the news of Martin Heidegger's death, Italian cultural critics, with rare exceptions, were quick to offer new proof of a certain persistent poverty. For a few days, newspapers and magazines treated us to a succession of canned obituaries, thoughtful exhortations, and academic litanies. There was talk of negative and positive existentialism (the latter a comical subspecies on which Italy has a monopoly), of Heidegger's adherence to Nazism, and of Jean-Paul Sartre and Juliette Gréco as notable examples of the philosopher's influence; nor were allusions lacking to a certain obsolete quality in Heidegger as far as present-day problems are concerned. One seemed to be witnessing a series of dutiful and hasty farewell gestures to a glorious old figure who had always been secretly hated and whose exploits people had trouble remembering.

So it came as a real surprise when an article by Massimo Cacciari, fresh and vigorous in its approach, appeared in the magazine *Rinascita*. Not only did Cacciari not apply to Heidegger the stupid rigmarole ("irrationalistic alignment . . . objectively reactionary . . . decadence . . . exponent of the monopolistic bourgeoisie") to which we have been inured for decades by our vaguely Marxist culture ("an increasingly misleading expression," as Cacciari correctly observes), but he also recognized these stupidities for what they were and swept them away with a gesture of impatient contempt, along with their even more disgusting secular Enlightenment equivalents ("lack of faith in man . . . mystical attitude . . . disintegration of values"). Once this salutary disinfestation has been carried out, and we find ourselves in the void—that exhilarating void, the one place where thought can operate—we may finally begin to commemorate Heidegger while rediscovering the shadow of his thought projected all around us. For even before we get to the Pastures of Being, Heidegger's thought can and should lead us to an understanding of the metaphysical fundamentals of a Coca-Cola bottle.

But there is another controversial image of Heidegger, one much stronger than that raised by the inadequate objections always raised against him in Italy. More than by any other, this image has been put forth by the one adversary who could measure up to Heidegger in a Germany ultimately forsaken by philosophy: Theodor W. Adorno. In a little book, admittedly not one of his best, Adorno furiously attacked Heidegger as the incarnation of the "jargon of authenticity." What is this jargon? In the cultural pages of conservative German newspapers and the inaugural lectures of Nazis hiding out in universities, in appeals to sound German customs and the praise of ecstatic mountain climbing, in the condemnation of foreign words and the recourse to "dialogue," "hierarchies," and the "spirit," all threatened by mass society, Adorno's unfailing ear detected dire words and expressions that had their origin somewhere in the romantic tradition and were now wandering adrift, like pernicious messengers and revenants, in the Germany of Bonn: "Sacral without sacral substance, frozen emanations, the clichés of the jargon of authenticity are the waste products of aura."

Thus, behind the terrorism of Heidegger's philosophical language, Adorno, like a shrewd dog sniffing for truffles, detected those treasures of profound banality that had nourished Germany since the Biedermeier years in the first half of the nineteenth century, protected the rise of Nazism, and created a pedestal for Konrad Adenauer and that still inspire the slogans of the German Christian Democrats. In Adorno's view, Heidegger in the end was to blame for having concocted a complex speculative plot to justify the acceptance of the norm. And we know that for critical theory, to whose tradition Adorno belongs, the worst disgrace of thinking is to renounce Marxian "criticism of what exists."

All this would no doubt be praiseworthy were it not fundamentally false. Not that the "jargon of authenticity" is not alive and well, often in a sinister way, in Heidegger's writings. But to take it as a key to everything is no less a blunder than the blatant error committed by those seeking to demolish the great composer Richard Wagner on the basis of the unmitigated rubbish he sometimes uttered. Despite all the alluring mythology usually associated with Heidegger's person—the forest hut, the paths in the fields, the "interrupted paths"—his fearful philosophical machine is operated by something quite different from that Teutonic bigotry that crops up at times in some of his writings. In each of Heidegger's phases, from that of *Sein und Zeit* to that of his last oracular fragments, we feel that the game is upheld by a cold, lucid, implacable power, quintessence of the modern: The monumental nihilism that has guided Western thought since its origins toward a glorious self-destruction here celebrates its twilight of the gods.

Like a Tibetan monk endlessly spinning his prayer wheel, Heidegger, with prodigious virtuosity, goes over and over the whole history of thought from the Greeks to Nietzsche, dropping down into abandoned gorges and irrevocably twisting the meanings of accepted terms. The history of metaphysics, a history that is a destiny, has never attained such terrifying clarity as in Heidegger's analyses. It is, to be sure, a clarity gained at the price of much violence and injustice; it is a destiny retouched by a masterful cosmetician so that its line leads directly to the threshold of Heidegger's hut in the Black Forest. There he would like to take it by the hand and carefully guide it beyond itself, over "slender little bridges" to the "overcoming of metaphysics."

But even those who, with constant suspicion, follow this trail of the destiny of metaphysics must admit that it involves an original and illuminating design. No one has succeeded in reconstructing with such compelling exactitude the cage within which Western thought has fatally operated from Plato to our own day, repeatedly doomed to call itself into question until all its possibilities are exhausted. This limit, Heidegger states, may be said to have been reached with Nietzsche, last thinker in metaphysics and its closing sign, who evoked that devastating and intoxicating "will to will" that governs us today. (The subtle revenge inflicted by Heidegger at this point is clear: He sends the most elusive philosopher of the West back to the garden of Armida,[1] from which he had always tried to escape; this is already a good example of Heidegger's strong-arm tactics.)

What happens to thought after Nietzsche? Here I must return to the fundamentals of the Coca-Cola bottle, which I mentioned at the beginning. Besides being a fascinating interpreter of classical philosophical texts, as well as a surprising contriver of strings of verbal associations, Heidegger was an indispensable guide to the present. To verify this, one need only turn to two of his essays: "The Question Concerning Technology" and "Overcoming of Metaphysics."[2] How many congresses, how many vexed reflections on the evils and blessings of technology we have had to put up with throughout the twentieth century! How many vacuous disputes between "scientists" and "humanists"! How many recommendations of different ways of using technology! As though any of it actually depended on our will! When technology has already set its stamp on our will! Technology, to all intents and purposes, means metaphysics, Heidegger suggests. Having run off the tracks of history, the West synchronically relives the destiny of metaphysics in the eloquent silence of its own operation. It is impossible to account for the Coca-Cola bottle without going back to Plato's *Ideas.* It is impossible to speak of the Coca-Cola bottle as a thing without explaining that it could only appear in a world that "has already destroyed things as things."

All this may seem abstruse. But it is an attempt to approach the supreme abstruseness of what surrounds us. If very few in our midst feel the need for metaphysics (a word now almost always used in a derogatory sense), it is because everything is *already* metaphysics. And—ultimate joke!—philosophy has now become primarily a useful fact. Useful for what? For *Ge-Stell.* I will skip the usual ironic remarks about Heidegger's linguistic acrobatics and abuses and merely specify that this word, ordinarily used in the sense of "scaffolding" as well as "bookshelf," becomes in the late Heidegger the black sun around which he arranges, in eccentric harmony, compounds of the verb *stellen* (to put), from the *vorstellen* (to represent) of classical metaphysics to the *bestellen* (to order, in the commercial sense) that is heard every day in the business world. And what, finally, is *Ge-Stell*? *Ge-Stell* indicates above all the appearance of all that exists (and therefore including man) as availability, material to be used, exploited. Man becomes "the most important raw material," capable of being ravished ad libitum, and is *employed* as such. In a vein of metaphysical irony, it then turns out that the employee is the figure corresponding in every sense to this state of the world. And so—and it may come as a surprise to many—only Heidegger could have come up with a definition of Hitler as first among employees. And it is significant how the obscure *Ge-Stell* accords perfectly with the analyses of the visionary Marx in the first book of *Capital,* which depicts the world as a "warehouse of commodities," a place of total availability and exchange.

In considering further variations on *Ge-Stell,* we see that they also throw light on Heidegger's foremost enemy, Adorno. Adorno's dialectic of the Enlightenment is superimposed, in its crucial features, on the destiny of nihilism as *recounted* by Heidegger in his *Nietzsche* and in many of his later writings. Thus, Adorno's theories on industry and on the culture industry find a natural place among the many applications of *Ge-Stell.*

How do these collisions and coincidences among hostile thinkers happen? Because beyond all the obvious things that make them mutually incompatible, they are united by something much deeper, allowing us to pass from one to the other as from one knot to another in the same network (of secret agents?): the fact that they drive nihilism to its most radical forms while trying at the same time to look at it *from outside,* an enigmatic and fleeting outside that Heidegger called the "overcoming of metaphysics," Adorno called "utopia," and Marx highlighted as the end of prehistory. Nihilism is the great funnel of Western thought. The closer one gets to its mouth, the more the incompatible elements are forced to mix. This may produce a sense of vertigo. But without that vertigo, thought is now impossible.

6 The Perpetual War

"Hardly anyone could venture to write an introduction for *The Last Days of Mankind*. It would be both arrogant and superfluous. The introduction is carried inside by everyone born in this century and doomed to live in it." Thus wrote Elias Canetti, who for nine years had "let every spoken and written word [by Karl Kraus] take effect on me: for five years without resistance, for four with growing criticism."[1] What follows is *not* an introduction but a cluster of occasional notes that have sprouted around some of the joints in that majestic and monstrous construction known as *The Last Days of Mankind*.

Kraus's fundamental experience was acoustic, and it was constantly repeated. Like Hildegarde von Bingen, Angela da Foligno, and many anonymous schizophrenics, he heard voices, but his voices were all the more alarming since they had bodies, circulated in the streets of Vienna, seated themselves in cafés, and even put on affable smiles. The inflections beat on him like waves; their deadly horde provided the most faithful company for his "threefold solitude: that of the coffeehouse where he is alone with his enemy, of the nocturnal room where he is alone with his demon, of the lecture hall where he is alone with his work."[2] There, behind a reading desk on a bare stage, Kraus himself became the voice-that-catches-all-voices, while in the darkness other unknown beings were transformed into the Wild Hunt of legend: "Imagine the army of the Wild Hunt in a concert hall, trapped, locked up, and forced to sit still, and then repeatedly summoned to its true nature." There was a vibration in his voice that sent a quiver through the audience: "Chairs and people seemed to yield under this quivering; I wouldn't have been surprised if the chairs had bent."³ These sequences of scorching and magical electric shocks were repeated more than seven hundred times, very often in Vienna. And according to eyewitnesses, the Viennese readings were the most memorable. For Kraus needed *that* arena, *that* air, for his hallucinations. Like all true demons, he was bound to a small terrestrial circle, drawn by an invisible pair of compasses. From that soil he derived his powers, and to that soil he returned them.

Kraus's first public reading in Vienna took place on 3 May 1910. The program offered three perfect texts for performance: the uncharitable but playful *Heine und die Folgen* (where Kraus claimed to be setting up for once and for all a watershed in the literature of decadence), *Die chinesische Mauer,* and *Die Welt der Platake:* essays at once visionary and frivolous—if Monsieur le Bourreau will, for the moment, allow such a thing. Thus they manage to bring together the erotic back room of a Chinatown laundry with the imminent eruption of the planet, all of it then confirmed by the erratic appearance of advertising posters. This, then, was Kraus: an essayist barely arrived at that ripeness that is all and ready to extend the tentacles of an omnivorous and already "armored"⁴ idiom, with its sparkling combinations of syntax, to the new enormities and trifles offered to him every day—and Kraus asked nothing more—by the *Neue Freie Presse.*

But that was simply his last cover before unveiling the more demoniac substance, more dangerous to touch, of his words. That moment would come a few years later, the day he began to give public readings from his "tragedy in five acts," *The Last Days of Mankind.* Outside, there was still the war, and in the darkness of the hall, this tiny man, with "a face so mobile that it couldn't be pinpointed, penetrating and exotic, like the face of an animal, but a new, a different face, an unfamiliar one,"⁵ *rehearsed* the war. He rehearsed it as though it were a creaking old play in a provincial theater, *while* the war was going on. This man, pursued from the start by acoustical hallucinations and believing from the start, with the consistency of an ancient Chinese, that the most evil facts ensued directly from scraps of conversations he had overheard on the streets of Vienna, had finally succeeded, by the most prodigious coup de théâtre of his life, in reversing the situation. And this awesome event, which eluded everyone and hung over everyone, found its hallucinatory replica *while* it was happening, its acoustical facsimile, at a reading desk on the bare stage of a theater in Vienna. Or rather, from there a voice was raised that called the facts into existence, just as the facts had aroused the voice. And once the war was over, he was to go on adding new scenes to that proliferating text, which had started to grow along with the war and now ended by expanding until it reached a length unsuitable for any theater, but the only suitable and ultimately adequate length for the voice-that-catches-all-voices, for his shamanic gift, which had allowed him to capture *all* possible prisoners in his net of words, from newsboys to foppish officers, from the famous journalist Alice Schalek to old Biach, from patriotic housewives to court chamberlains, from shopkeepers and poets to the two emperors.

If we keep clearly in mind this incongruous image of a shaman wearing a starched collar and little oval spectacles, we can see how fully *The Last Days of Mankind* departs from every literary genre. It is not an early example of "documentary theater" or "epic theater" or "political theater" or "theater of the absurd," to cite the paltry labels that people have sought to apply to this work (and it is not hard to apply them, at the cost, of course, of losing the essential), but a *magical practice.* A remote and chilling magic, in which breath and blood mingle, in which every name is already bewitched and expression is given over, without any modesty or restraint, to the "whim of the surroundings," as Kraus himself once called it with fierce understatement, adding, "It is its flood and throng of names and manners, voices and faces, apparitions and memories, quotations and posters, newspapers and rumors, rubbish and circumstances that accidentally gives me the signal for attack—and every letter of the alphabet can become a sign of fate."[6]

Kraus demonstrates that a new astral body, composed of fragments of sentences, the shells of roving images, and splinters of accents, has formed in the world. It covers the earth like a motionless hood. And every movement of language is first of all a gasping effort to breathe under that mantle while trying in the end to rend it. For some years, this new leaden sky had covered up a reality that had been making heedless headway through the streets of Vienna. Kraus had already been intent on showing that those phantoms out of humorous gazettes, when closely examined, revealed hellish features and turned out to be so many attendants of disaster. But now the background of these minor facts had been uncovered, like the wings of a stage suddenly lit up by floodlights, and it was slaughter. To write *The Last Days of Mankind,* Kraus had almost no need to enlarge or alter his perspective, as far his local chronicles were concerned. He gathered his usual materials and let fly against a new backdrop. The "wall of fire" on which his hallucinations were projected in the silence of his room ("The experiences I need, I have them before me on the wall of fire I see from my desk")[7] had merely become a "barrier of flames," the backdrop of any theater of war. There his loquacious characters now appeared, along with countless soldiers "fallen for the resumption of tourism."[8] There appeared their shadows, to be ever more swiftly devoured, until the "barrier of flames" became a cosmic stage curtain enveloping the blazing planet.

The Last Days of Mankind has only one literary precedent, one that Kraus could not have known and that we ourselves can scarcely know, since part of the material is still unpublished: the "second part" of Flaubert's *Bouvard et Pécuchet,* known as the *copie,* that mass of *quotations,* collected in eight bound volumes, each comprising about three hundred sheets, which reposes today in the Municipal Library in Rouen. It is the *peacetime* equivalent of what the 792 pages of *The Last Days of Mankind,* about half of which consist of quotations, were in *wartime.* The two texts could be seamlessly joined, and the whole thing would form that Great Hybrid within which we live and where every distinction between wartime and peacetime has become a joke. Even though all agree that *war* is ever more inconceivable, the slaughter only increases.

The epiphany that dazzled Kraus is the same one that had made Flaubert's last years compulsive and feverish: the prodigious eruption of *la bêtise* [stupidity] as the beginning of a new era, an era paved and cemented with it once any kind of alkahest or universal solvent had disappeared. This appalling event, from whose light most people averted their eyes, was obsessively followed and properly recorded primarily by three writers: Flaubert, Kraus, and finally, Léon Bloy. To them we gratefully turn as to the pioneers of a new science, the only one wherein we can follow the treacherous waverings of that uninterrupted experiment-without-experimenter that is the world's recent history.

If one were to choose the symbolic and juridical act marking the beginning of this "glorious era" of experiment, it would not be so much some overworked episode of the French Revolution as a simple and effective bureaucratic invention that came somewhat later, one that the Convention had already introduced as a "blood tax" but that Bonaparte, by the law of 28 Floréal of the year X (28 May 1802), ratified as the normal method for army recruitment: compulsory conscription. Since then, humanity has become more and more obviously "human material," as the walk-ons with their placards in *The Last Days of Mankind* proudly and tirelessly repeat. Just when humanity was proclaiming the reign of the subject at the top of its lungs, it was getting ready to count its members as so many items available for the operations of an ulterior subject, which was then society itself.

We ourselves are now a manageable entity, one that may even survive for a long time in the stillness of the warehouse but that must expect at any moment to be called upon to help redress the balance of slaughter—and no longer because we are basically the private property of a prince but because humanity (which is obviously still Western), having attained its full rights, has nothing to look forward to but to let itself be molded crudely by society and even thrown on the scrap heap at the end.

Throughout the nineteenth century, this new truth seeps slowly (what else is Benjamin Constant's *De l'esprit de conquête et de l'usurpation* about?) and sluggishly into perception and declares itself in reality. But the moment in which it emerges in all its oppressive pomp is 1914. Then, in a few months, the first thing to go to pieces once and for all, is that conception of European equilibrium that since the Peace of Westphalia, that is, for a little less than three centuries, had been the impossible dream of those who still thought that to engage in politics meant to *control* something. But this is almost a modest corollary to the most important theorem demonstrated by the war: that the murderous impulse of events would seem to be autonomous, or else guided by an invisible experimenter who surprises and mocks the very leaders who are convinced they caused these events. Now everything goes *beyond* all expectations and intentions and yet obeys a consistency of its own while acting directly on the bodies and souls of the victims. It is too late to contain an enterprise that is already preparing new surprises, and no war can be allowed to end without laying the foundations for the concentration camps that will bloom in the next one. War is, in short, a spirit of industry wholly devoid of ideological prejudices: Lenin's goatee or Wilhelm II's curled mustaches are all the same to it, and above all useful. Thus we come to the age that hangs perpetually under the sign of these "last days of mankind," which are endless, and also to the culmination of that peculiar phenomenon by which the more complex events become, the more irrelevant do those claiming to guide them turn out to be. The Great Politician of the new age puts a little plaster Napoleon on the mantelpiece and locks himself in his office to work on a crossword puzzle. But there are always a few squares he cannot fill. Meanwhile, the continuity of life is assured by lazily shifting the massacres from one square to another on the planet.

It is Stupidity that envelops these brutal happenings in a protective cloud: There was a time when its necessity would have been called structural. If the cracks that open between events did not get filled by wads of stock phrases; if laboratory schizoidism were not concealed by the conviction of doing Good, and a Good that keeps steadily improving; if the devastating rationale did not contain the incarnation of Common Sense; if . . . —the machine would jam, and the great age of experiment would fall into a sudden, dull silence. The buzz of Public Opinion helps to prevent it. This is the unsurpassed psychical fuel that now drives life forward. As Kraus once remarked, "'Life goes on.' More than is lawful."[9]

In addition to being the worldwide proclamation of the fatal news that had already been circulating for some time throughout Europe, to giving us entry into a world where the further we advance the less we know, and finally to welcoming the seeds of chaos that had long been lurking on the threshold of our psychical and social life, the war of 1914–18 signified the pulverizing of experience. Strictly speaking, all that can be said of that event is contained in a sentence of Walter Benjamin's: "A generation that had still gone to school in a public carriage found itself under the open sky in a landscape where nothing but the clouds remained unchanged, and in the middle, at the center of a field of forces where explosions and devastating currents clashed, was the tiny, fragile body of man." Anything that goes beyond this sentence is in a way pointless and redundant. But the fact, hostile and opaque, that results from it still remains before us: that men returned from the front "struck dumb, not richer but poorer in communicable experience."[10] All the psychological forces were set against that realization, for had it been accepted, the whole war would have had to end, destroying the zeal that emerged because no one was able to recognize the "bloodthirsty look" of peace, especially on that Viennese innkeeper's face where "mildness reigns."[11] At first, young Germans had been allowed to depart for the "tempests of steel" as described by Ernst Jünger: "Having grown up in a period of security, we all felt a desire for the unusual, for great danger. And so the war seized on us like drunkenness. We left for the front under a rain of flowers, in an air intoxicated with roses and blood. The war was supposed to offer us, finally, great, strong, solemn things."[12] Thomas Mann's attitude, though more fearful and mean-spirited, was not much different: He hoped that war meant the repudiation of the laxities of peace and a restoration of the Germanic essence, which had been trampled on by malign commercial nations. They expected a grander experience, and they witnessed the disintegration of experience. Today "experience" can only refer to a past. Otherwise it is synonymous with "horror."

As Jünger himself was to observe ten years later, in 1930, the real experience of the war would turn out to be not far from factory work, from the "precise work rhythm of a turbine fueled by blood."[13] He thereby introduced the category that designates the secret aspect of the availability of "human material": total mobilization. Under the sign of this category, the final assimilation of peace and war was in place as preparation for a chronic civil war as a future possibility. Having left for the front with the ardor of a young Germanic warrior, Jünger in the end thus specified with admirable detachment the peculiar sense in which the war of 1914–18 seemed "different from other wars whose history has been handed down to us." In that "great catastrophe," first of all, "the genius of war had been permeated with the spirit of progress." And the first fruit of that amorous encounter had been the rapid absorption of the "image of war as an armed action into the vaster image of a gigantic working process." Not only did the war *serve* industry, but the war itself was already an advanced form of industry. War based on total mobilization was "an act by means of which the current of modern life, with its whole vast network of ramifications, is channeled, thanks to a single move on the command dial, into the great current of wartime energy." And so what the young warriors, who went to the front dreaming of aristocratic tournaments, found there was primarily "the democracy of death."[14]

Kraus never theorized about the war or, strictly speaking, about anything else. Ensnared at every moment by his voices, he completely lacked speculative detachment. During the war, these voices multiplied and splintered, but—and this was his most astonishing feat—"There was not *one* voice that he did not hear, he was possessed with every specific timbre of the war and rendered it compellingly."[15] But behind these shamanic journeys lay concealed from the start, clear and steadfast, those same two implications later to be formulated by such dissimilar writers as Benjamin and Jünger: on the one hand, the pulverizing of experience; on the other, total mobilization as the main procedure of the new era. And to arrive at this conclusion, Kraus never needed to abandon himself to the "air intoxicated with roses and blood."

What is the most terrible sentence, the faithful echo of horror, in *The Last Days of Mankind*? "Clusters form." These two little words discreetly accompany us in the stage directions from the very first page, the second line to be exact. They swell like poisonous clouds for hundreds of pages and strike us at the end, when their *unique* significance is finally revealed in scene 4, 29,[16] where they are spoken by the Faultfinder to designate the throng of bystanders who want to have their picture taken alongside the corpse of the hanged Battisti, while the jovial hangman looks on. Groups are not an expression of democratic spontaneity. Their origin is much older. Groups always form around a corpse. When there is no corpse, that empty place evokes the many corpses that have been there and the many yet to appear. It is the last rite that holds civil society together. The group is a "crowd crystal."[17] Those who form it obey a calling, suddenly revealing their adherence to a vast sect: devotees of an officially innocuous, essentially persecutory power: Opinion. They throng together and jostle each other without realizing it; they all converge toward one point, which is the empty circle at the center of the group. There, as René Girard has pointed out, they were once able to see the mangled body of the victim of the original lynching.

Respect for Kraus as a modern exponent of satire that "is not only critical and negative but in the highest sense becomes the guardian of values"[18] has kept many from accurately perceiving the nature of his work, and especially of *The Last Days of Mankind.* The title is well known, the text much less so. If Kraus had filled 792 pages just to say that war is a bad thing—as many have believed and insist on believing—he would have been not the author of his play but one of the characters flayed in it. In the café, among friends, in the office or restaurant, there is no harm in speaking out against the "madness of war." And how many people have we seen going into raptures over that dreadful peace dove that Picasso presented to Stalin? Kraus said something quite different: He said that peace is founded on slaughter and that war is the charity ball at which humanity stages what it normally does, but does not like to talk about, so that the public will get excited and make enough small offerings to allow the slaughter to continue. Unlike many, Kraus did not depict the horrors of the war. He only brought the news that peace in the end was impossible:

OPTIMIST: But all wars have ended with peace.

FAULTFINDER: Not this one. This one has not taken place on the surface of life. . . . no, it has raged inside life itself. The front has been extended to the whole country. And there it will stay. And this changed life, if there still is life, will be accompanied by the old spiritual condition. The world is perishing and won't know it. Everything was yesterday and will be forgotten; no one will see today or be afraid of tomorrow. They will forget that the war was lost, forget they began it, forget they fought it. That is why the war won't end.[19]

The "last days of mankind" are the first days of the world of perpetual war.

The most effective of Kraus's magical practices is quotation ("putting my times between quotation marks").[20] But we are not dealing with a declaration of principle, ready to be carried away by a burst of supposedly autonomous creativity. Kraus is never autonomous, not even in relation to the posters he glimpses in the street. When at the very outset of *Last Days,* he warns that here "the rawest inventions are quotations,"[21] we must once again take him literally. Indeed—except for the marvelous typographical utterances that flow from the Faultfinder's mouth (and they are farewell gestures of insult by the *character* Kraus toward the world in whose company he perishes) and except for the portions in verse, which serve to extend the limits of an enormous range of sound at whose extremes stand Goethe and Offenbach—Kraus tampered as little as possible with the raw materials offered to him from time to time by the world scene. Whereas perhaps one-sixth of Georg Büchner's *Danton's Death*—the only play that can be called political in a sense similar to Kraus's—consists of quotations, the quoted texts in *Last Days* make up almost half of the whole. To give a few concrete examples of what might seem to be the most unlikely scenes: scene 2, 19 (Schalek with the laughing Serbian women) repeats the situation and some quips from an article by Schalek herself; scene 3, 19 (in the mosque) is derived, again by extracting small blocks of words, from an article in the *Süddeutsche Monatshefte*; scene 3, 20 (Alfred Kerr's "Rumanian song") reproduces *word for word* the poem published by Kerr under the pseudonym "Gottlieb" in *Der Tag*; scene 3, 21 (the doctor who warns against smoking) is taken from a letter by Professor Molenaar of Darmstadt that had been printed in *Die Fackel*; scene 3, 31 (letter to Otto Ernst) is composed of quotations from letters by Ernst's enthusiastic readers; scene 3, 33 (Schalek speaks) is woven entirely out of quotations from a news report by Schalek, quoted more fully in *Die Fackel*; in scene 4, 7, the psychiatrist's grandiose speech on the food situation in Germany orchestrates topics presented dryly in a bulletin from the Wolff Agency; in scene 4, 22, the contents and price of the "Hero's Pillow" are repeated verbatim from an advertisement; in scene 4, 25, remarks by Paul von Hindenburg and Erich Ludendorff are mostly taken from an interview with them by the journalist Paul Goldmann; scene 4, 37 (Wilhelm II and his men at General Headquarters) is based on testimony by Rear Admiral Persius, which Kraus had found in his book on the war at sea. And one could go on and on. Finally, even the Faultfinder's speeches are woven out of quotations from Kraus. Aphorisms, bits from essays written in peacetime, articles from *Die Fackel* published while he was writing *Last Days*—all this is swept into that ultimate vortex of words whereby Kraus presents himself just as he does the other historical characters, that is, as a picturesque and raving solitary in the picturesque Vienna of the war, who is dubbed the "Fackelkraus" and pointed out in the street by the members of factious groups. But at the same time, since his name is hidden behind the figure of a comic character (the Faultfinder), his words are a voice that no longer belongs to him and that guarantees the life of this nonstop spectacle. Their function is like that of the blade used by Chuang-tzu's perfect butcher, who for nineteen years used the same knife to quarter thousands of oxen; the blade never lost its edge, "because I let it go through only where it can"—in the imperceptible empty interstices. And Prince Wen-hui answers the butcher: "Thank you, you have just taught me how to prolong one's life, by using it only for what does not consume it."[22]

Exactly a year and a month after the assassination in Sarajevo, Kraus, in three days, wrote the "Prelude" to *Last Days* and conceived the plan of the work. The first months of war had been a period of paralysis and silence for him. And he gave the reasons for this silence in the pulsing words of the speech "In dieser grossen Zeit,"[23] where he even alluded to the growing din of voices in his room, "whether they come from animals, from children, or only from mortars," but stopped short with the injunction: "If anyone has something to say, let him step forward and shut up!"[24] For ten months thereafter, only one slim issue of *Die Fackel* would be published, in February. But for Kraus, this silence, as would later be the case on the advent of Hitler, was the dark side of a monstrous discourse about to burst out: "Everything Kraus wrote is like that: a silence turned inside out, a silence that catches the storm of events in its black folds, billows, its livid lining turned outward."[25] Once Kraus's tension had reached that state of mimetic and judicial fever that for him was the necessary condition for writing, he threw himself into his most reckless enterprise and succeeded: "The world war entered completely into *The Last Days of Mankind,* with no solace and no respect, no embellishment, no sweetening, and above all, this is the most important point, without ever getting accustomed to it."[26] He announces it in a splendid letter to his beloved Sidonie Nádherný on 29 July 1915, a letter that might stand as an epigraph for the whole work:

> I've seen too many sad things in these days, and yet they have given birth to a new job—a job that ends each time at six in the morning, just when I smell the victims rotting under my window. I'll tell you what sort of job it is, of which I've finished writing a first section in three days and three nights, but first let me give you an idea of my state of mind from this page in my diary (which I already meant to send you):

> 26 July
>
> Now, while from my desk I can hear the daily, inevitable, and awful cry—Extra! Extra!—which will henceforth afflict the human ear for all time, now I have spent an hour in Thierfehd [a Swiss village where Kraus had been with Sidonie]. And nothing, nothing has changed! No idea, whether thought, spoken, or shouted, would be loud enough, no prayer fervent enough to pierce this material. So to *show* this impotence, won't I have to disclose everything that I *can't* do just now—and at least do something: expose myself? What else is there to do?
>
> This road will have to be taken, even if it goes on too long, as long as the road to China is still open. I'll choke on what ought to be shouted, so as not to choke some other way. I'm not sure anymore of my nerves in the street. But it would be better if all this were to happen according to a precise plan, and also that it be dedicated to that person for whom I live, and I'd no longer care to live if *she* thought that to keep silent threatened her *own* human dignity, to

the point where I can no longer stand to witness events in silence, or rather words that have erased humanity's memory for all of cosmic time. There is a person without whom nothing can happen, because everything must happen for her. . . .

This state of fatigue has still released a spark, and it has given birth to the plan for a work that, should it ever appear, would certainly be equivalent to exposing myself in the most total fashion. The first *act,* the prelude to the whole, is finished and could even stand by itself. But where to send it? Switzerland, where we took refuge with our dear little automobile, fails us in this. Maybe it will be of some help to us later; or otherwise America.

Anyway, whatever may or may not happen at this point, I now feel freer.[27]

Thus *The Last Days of Mankind* was born.

Kraus implies that the "last days of mankind" are unending and tend to become a chronic condition in which one can survive with tranquillity. The war that Kraus described was an eruption of the peace that he had just finished describing, and the next peace would be an eruption of that war he was describing, until a new war would turn out to be an eruption of the previous peace. But Kraus was not to see that war. This very new age in which we live would descend from it, to repeat the mechanism of the former age and moreover, to aim to make tranquillity and slaughter coexist, now no longer separated in time but only in space—and a very elastic space, besides. At times the distance is measured in continents, at times in neighborhoods, as in Beirut.

A perceptive reading of *The Last Days of Mankind* would be fatally damaging to Bertolt Brecht. Such a reading is long overdue. Having drawn for decades on the rich storehouse of that text and having derived from it most of the formal devices that were to make his theater's fortune (from montage to the scrambling of levels, from cabaret parody to the use of raw material), Brecht would find himself forced to accept a direct comparison, and this would crush him. Kraus abandons himself to the force of language without restraint, like one possessed, without any ulterior motive of social pedagogy, and he achieves almost unbearable heights of comedy and terror: I mention only the appearances of Schalek (the *"true heroine of this glorious era,*"[28] who puts any Mutter Courage in the shade) or of old Biach (no death is more epic than his, when he gurgles and chokes on sentences from the newspaper, whereupon, in retaliation, "groups form" around his corpse in scene 5, 9), or the invincible, sugary ravings of the feuilletonist Hans Müller (scene 1, 25), or the scene with the patriotic housewives (scene 2, 18), or the tormented intimate dialogue of the Schwarz-Gelber couple (scene 2, 33), or the exhortation to tourism uttered by the schoolmaster (scene 1, 9), or the meek and bloody ravings of Franz Josef (scene 4, 31), or the Prussian von Dreckwitz's vigorous and sportive bloodbath spirit (scene 2, 14), or the choral delirium, as of a domestic slaughterhouse, in the final scene of the last act. Brecht, like a good German, instead of putting "art at the service of the shopkeeper," puts it at the service of the Cause, which is not always better. Didacticism in itself is already a disaster for form, but most of all this captious and blackmailing didacticism, this attempt at the aesthetic transfiguration of Sovietism, ends by arousing a certain disgust. In the course of time, the same thing may happen with Brecht as happened with Voltaire: a complete chemical separation of texts. On the one hand, many of his poems will be read as being by the greatest Chinese poet of the century; on the other, there will be an increasing tendency to forget his misused theater. Like Voltaire's tragedies, which everyone used to know and today no one dares read, Brecht's plays belong in great part to those literary creations that marry for love the mediocre side of their period's intellectuality and sink with it to the bottom.

The hagiographic literature on Kraus—from Leopold Liegler's book, the first authorized study, to the products of a few zealous campus dwellers who in recent years have started browsing on "the Austrian Mind"[29]— offers the most convenient and immediate arguments against him. According to the image of Kraus that emerges from this apologetic mosaic, we would have on our hands a human being exclusively endowed with fine sentiments, prone to all the proper indignation, vaguely nostalgic for a purer and more noble past, fond of women and animals, and encased in his ideas as in a coat of mail. All of which would lead one to suspect the worst. But fortunately the image is false. Meanwhile, if we want to grant Kraus the highest honor, that of being "the greatest German satirist, the only one in the literature of this language whom one has the right to name next to Aristophanes, Juvenal, Quevedo, Swift, and Gogol," by the same token we will have to recognize that he shares with these writers "a very definite kind of substance, which I would simply call 'murderous.'"[30] And Canetti's curt remark should be enough to deter us from the image of a humanitarian hero. As for his relation to the past, one can fully concur with what Benjamin observed with subtle irony: "It is his program to reverse the development of bourgeois-capitalist affairs to a condition that was never theirs."[31] But things change in the face of existing realities, and one need only read once the "tragic couplets" of Franz Josef (scene 4, 31) or the forlorn judgment on him (with its marvelous beginning: "He was merely a pedant and not a tyrant, merely cold and not ferocious. . . . He was a tireless worker, and among various death sentences he also signed one that struck down humanity")[32] to understand that Kraus was the first and only writer to bury, without hesitation, without tears, and with perfect knowledge of the Habsburg "demon," the whole glorious history of that monarchy that "for reasons of prestige . . . must long have wanted to commit suicide."[33] He was really not the right person for the kind of operation that in stock-market jargon is called a recovery in values.

In his long essay on Kraus, Benjamin quotes a single but decisive passage from *The Last Days of Mankind:* "Kraus portrayed himself as hopelessly subjugated to the demon; in the pandemonium of the age he reserved for himself the most melancholy place in the icy wilderness lit by reflected flames. There he stands on the *Last Day of Mankind*—the 'grumbler' [that is, Faultfinder] who has described the preceding days."[34] The passage from Kraus follows: "I have taken the tragedy, which is divided into the scenes of decaying humanity, on myself, so that it might be heard by the spirit who takes pity on the victims, even though he may have renounced for all time his connection with a human ear. May he receive the keynote of this age, the echo of my bloodstained madness, through which I share the guilt for these noises."[35] These are the lines in which Kraus, more lucidly than anywhere else in his work, acknowledged his involvement in the evil he was skewering. Not only is reality here tinged by black magic, but so is the language that hurls itself at that reality. To grasp this infernal connection, one must venture all the way to that archaic and demonic nucleus that Benjamin was the first to perceive in Kraus: "The dark background from which his image detaches itself is not formed by his contemporaries, but is the primeval world or the world of the demon." Thus, again we approach obsessive voices, and the voice-that-catches-all-voices:

"His passion for imitating them [his fellow men] is at the same time the expression of and the struggle against this implication, and also the cause and the result of that ever-watchful guilty conscience in which the demon has his habitat." Finally, with an elegant wave of his hand, Benjamin presents us with the genealogy of the satirical writer: "The satirist is the figure in whom the cannibal was received into civilization."[36] Benjamin's words echo Canetti's about the "murderous substance" in which all great satirists communicate. And they also echo a late sentence by Kraus, who in a few words describes his work of gloomy exorcism, where from the start he had not been spared contagion: "Night after night, for twenty-six years, I laugh when the raw material of my time gets ready to pass into my mold."[37]

The subtitle *Tragedy in Five Acts* should be understood primarily in its rhetorical function as antiphrasis. Just as the single acts do not have the necessary requirements to be such, since each would last at least a whole night, so the word "tragedy" hangs suspended like a neoclassical relic over the heads of hundreds of characters, all of them unfit to be called tragic. As for the dialogues between the Faultfinder and the Optimist, which perform the function of the chorus in Greek tragedy—and perhaps no text in modern literature achieves the fiery eloquence of scenes 4, 29 and 5, 54— they do no more than suggest that tradition. The Faultfinder, of course, is Kraus himself, who subjects the war to the acid test of words, but he is also a little Viennese figure alongside the others, an eccentric whom they have all seen grow up and who now, behind a lectern, recites his works like a maniac. "They can say what they like . . . but what a writer!"[38] observes one of his anonymous Viennese listeners, and with this the judge with the flaming sword is cut down to size and becomes no bigger than all the other little Viennese figures. "There have been periods when causal thinking was a fine thing, the mark of a small clique of discerning people; today it's dishwater, every newspaper reader offers us the fundamentals of his *Weltanschauung* and his rheumatism; today what we must put up with is the juxtaposition of things, and to give expression to it has become our most suitable and substantial task."[39] So, amid the rubble of a later war, wrote Gottfried Benn, one of those great writers whom Kraus did not care to understand. And yet in *Last Days,* Kraus was acting in the sense of that sentence. Antiquated as he was in some of his tastes, and suspicious of the modern, he was nevertheless devastating in drawing the ultimate formal consequences from the situation around him. Instead of abandoning himself to expressionist pathos, which tries to compensate for the impossibility of tragedy by the immediacy of pain, Kraus set up the only theatrical structure suited to the case: a theater of repetition and aimless chatter, in which atrocities go forever hand in hand with futility, a perennial juxtaposition of everything with everything else, which allows for no development, where every direction is equally legitimate, and one is not even given the satisfaction of seeing a finger pointed on the stage at those responsible.

> OPTIMIST: Do you really think the world war was decided on by a handful of wicked men?
>
> FAULTFINDER: No, they're only the instruments of the demon who brought us to ruin, and with us Christian civilization. But we'd better take it out on them, since we can't catch the demon who branded us.[40]

Kraus is careful to bypass any question of responsibility, which can always be conveniently attributed to reactionary intrigue or to the intrinsic malevolence of capitalism. These last facts may not be in doubt, but they are still secondary to the "abysmal void" of Foreign Minister Poldi Berchtold's face as he appears, smartly dressed and charming, in a photograph on which Kraus comments. This is "the void into which we have all been flung and that has swallowed us up."[41] Because it has not cared to pay attention to these little things and has treated such words as paradoxes and not as sober observations, a society devoted to Good Causes, with its moist eye and ever thoughtful brow, has gone on accumulating "correct analyses" in the face of the century's successive atrocities, while a greater consideration of physiognomy, tone of voice, gestures, and minutiae of style would have spared it from making such an enormous contribution to the legacy of stupidity in our time. Thus, before Nazism existed, even only as a name, Kraus wrote the most precise description of Nazism to appear in the German language. And not because he was informed in advance about the iniquities that would be committed by Hitler and the big industrialists. All he had to do was to hear the voices and look at the faces in the street twenty years before.

Behind idle questions of responsibility, Kraus found something much more distressing: the certainty of general irresponsibility, the now ritual impossibility of achieving that knowledge of guilt that is the very soil of tragic events. The world that Kraus *rehearses* before our eyes is "a world

that fights wars for which no one can be held responsible." And this because never before had it been so obvious, as in August 1914, that no one,
among all those clearly and thoroughly responsible, had any idea what he
was doing: "None of them was fully aware. Austria can't help it! She just
let herself be encouraged by Germany to drag Germany into the war. And
Germany drove Austria to wage this war that she didn't want."[42] The
Viennese "I can't help it" here takes on a cosmic dimension, like the
posters of the Gersthof innkeeper Wolf. That sentence contains the most
despairing condemnation, one that reverses the Gospel saying "Father,
forgive them; for they know not what they do" (Luke 23:34). For Kraus,
no one is more loathsome than those who did not know what they were
doing: They now rank first among the unforgivable. And since our whole
world, in peace and war, is an experiment in which no one knows *what*
the experiment is about or *where* it is heading (not only that, but—and
this is the worst—people *deny* not knowing), it is subject to the same
condemnation.

And so nothing was left but the comical, a category elastic enough to
absorb the parade of catastrophes. Indeed, this is what sticks in one's mind
after reading *Last Days:* first a sense of oppression, the feeling of a progressive loss of breath; then a progressive exhilaration, as gradually the circular
and demented nature of the action emerges, along with scenes of frightful
comedy, like the one between the court councillor Schwarz-Gelber and his
consort, *née* Bardach, at the end of the second act. None of the great play-
wrights of the twentieth century has conceived anything comparable. And
perhaps only Ernst Lubitsch could have filmed it properly.

But I said that this comedy is frightful. Behind its hundreds of voices,
each riveted by its slightest nuances, we can hear Kraus's unique and compulsive voice. This is the demon who sits beside us and goads us each time
to inescapable, automatic laughter, which has the sound of dry leaves.
Thus the actual ending of *Last Days* should only be listened to, and it
overflows the text. It can be found on a recording,[43] where Kraus reads the
true introduction to what happened *after* "the last days of mankind"; its
title: "Advertisement for Tours of Hell." The subject is a brochure that
spares us nothing in offering a program of visits to the battlefield of
Verdun "at the reduced price of 117 francs." Kraus printed it in full on a
single folding spread in *Die Fackel*,[44] and he used to read it in public. The
text is divided into two main sections. The first gives the reasons for this

touristic initiative. With the scrupulous pedantry of someone who insists on showing that his offer is well worth 117 francs, the anonymous author explains why Verdun deserves to be included in the pantheon of the picturesque: "In this small area, where more than a million, indeed perhaps a million and a half men gave their lives, there is not a single square centimeter of surface that has not been blasted by grenades." This makes Verdun "the battlefield par excellence" and therefore "an image of terror and horror of unprecedented grandeur." But in the details of the tour and the satisfactions it offers, a sort of psalmody begins in which each versicle begins with a verb addressed to the customer:

> *Depart* by the evening express train, second class, from Basel. . . . *Stay* overnight in a first-class hotel, service and tips included. . . . *Enjoy* an ample breakfast in the morning. . . . *Cross* the destroyed villages in the fortified zone of Vaux with their giant cemeteries with hundreds of thousands of dead. . . . *Visit* the Ossuaire (charnel house) of Thiaumont, where the remains of unknown casualties continue to be collected and stored. . . . *Visit* the Tranchée des Baïonnettes or des Ensevelis. . . . *Skirt* the Ravin de la Mort. . . . *Enjoy* lunch at Verdun's best hotel, with wine and coffee, tip included. . . . *Return* in the afternoon through the horribly devastated Haudiaumont zone. . . . *Dine* at our hotel in Metz, with wine and coffee, tip included. . . . *Everything included in the price of 117 francs, with lavish hospitality in first-class hotels.*

Kraus reads in a solemn and persuasive voice, as though slowly extracting a salesman's high-quality samples from a suitcase. Then comes a page in his text where the psalmody of verbs is resumed and transformed into a volley of raging syllables. The voice lacerates and paralyzes; its violence sweeps everything away, like an elephant in a Hindu village. The decisive sentence is hidden in the middle of the psalmody: "*Understand* that this goal was worth the trouble of making this trip, and this trip was worth the trouble of fighting the world war."[45] For this is the motto of our world: *"Everything included."*

II
Exegesis

7 The Forty-nine Steps

By nature, Walter Benjamin was just the opposite of a philosopher: He was an exegete. The shameless boast of the individual who says "*I think such-and-such*" seemed basically foreign to him. Instead, from the beginning, we see in him the disguised determination of the exegete, the gesture of hiding behind piles of material to be commented on. We know that his dream was to disappear, at the height of his work, behind an insuperable flow of quotations. And so far I have not mentioned the premise that constitutes the first and crucial transgression of such a commentator: to relinquish the sacred text with hypocritical modesty, but at the same time to treat any other text or object of discussion with the same devotion and care traditionally required by the sacred text. One has no hesitation in saying that nothing essential changes in Benjamin from the clandestine theology of his early writings to the Marxism of his last years, except that the vice of the commentator becomes increasingly perverse, urging him toward ever more refractory material, as he himself reveals in a rare and marvelous moment of confession in a letter to Max Rychner in 1931: "I've never been able to study and think except in the theological sense, if I may put it that way, that is, in accordance with the Talmudic doctrine of the forty-nine steps of meaning in every passage in the Torah. Now, my experience tells me that the most worn-out Marxist *platitude* holds more hierarchies of meaning than everyday bourgeois profundity, which always has only one meaning, namely apology." Certainly those Marxists who, born to adore Georg Lukács, now struggle to come to grips with Benjamin are not equipped to face such meaningful stairways. Were they capable of ascending even the first steps of his work, they would already have dismissed him as an example of the most superstitious depravity.

The pompous and mournful triumphal arch that introduces Benjamin's work is *Der Ursprung des deutschen Trauerspiels,* or *The Origin of German Sorrowful Plays,* to translate literally the ambiguous title of the study that Benjamin, with a touch of pure romantic irony, was bold enough to offer as part of his application for a university teaching post. The irony, as one might expect, was not understood, and the post was denied him; indeed, this is a book likely to throw anyone, not just professors, into confusion and dismay. It can be read on at least three levels: as the most important study ever written on the rich theatrical literature of seventeenth-century Germany; next, as a dissertation on the history of allegory, in which Benjamin, with perfect instinct, bases his arguments primarily on the early iconological analyses by the Giehlow-Warburg-Panofsky-Saxl school (that is, the most knowing eyes in this century to read the images of our past); and finally, secretly and in a play of mirrors, as allegory in action in Benjamin's thought, which here justifies his own predilection for the allegorical form. But how did Benjamin come by this form? Let us try to tell it as a kind of imaginary biography.

Picture Benjamin as a cabalist shipwrecked in the vision of a nature wholly entangled, to its ruin, in the chain of sin, a nature that no longer offers illuminating letters, written on things, such as only Adam might have read, but a Babelic tangle of signs, a text forever corrupt. Having abandoned the Scriptures and clandestinely emerged from the ghetto, he joins a group of the most radical romantics a few centuries later, keeping quiet about his origin and observing to himself, with a hidden smile, how these youngsters go wild in their disorderly search for certain themes and notions long familiar to him from the Cabala. What attracts him in the romantics is rather the lightness with which they move amid the sinews of form, their capacity to dismiss any consistent totality, as though they too had recognized the disfigured character of nature. But Benjamin soon observes in them an ever clearer tendency to exalt the powers of the symbolic, to seek a language of images implicit in things. The saturnine cabalist incognito accordingly turns his back, slightly disgusted by these foolish ambitions, and retires to a spent crater in the shelter of buttresses built with heaps of books: the seventeenth century. There, under the *"Soleil noir de la Mélancholie"* [black sun of melancholy], his grandiose meditation is finally fulfilled; there Benjamin meets a dark Beatrice, allegory, so often misunderstood by her romantic companions, and discovers in her the only device proportionate to the abrupt, maimed, and perennially forlorn essence of history as a natural process and of nature as the history of the chain of sin. And this is precisely because of the violent arbitrariness of the allegorical connection between the image and its meaning, which reveals the unbridgeable distance between the two orders, similar, Benjamin suggests, to the example of alphabetic writing, the first brutal imposition of meaning on a letter that does not want to accept it. In short, for the very reasons that drove Goethe to reject allegory and devote himself instead to the blessed immediacy and totality of the symbol, Benjamin reclaims it, because only in allegory can one recognize what classicism was never able to grasp: "the *facies hippocratica* of history as an unrelenting primordial landscape." There is no sharp distinction between symbol and allegory, since allegory is the symbolic itself in disarray, dead from hypertrophy. But this decomposition of the symbol liberates a vast power, the cold algebraic meaning, and it is this that makes it possible to decree conventions with sovereign will and insist that anything can stand for anything else. "Seventeenth-century allegory is not the convention of expression but the expression of convention": This is likewise the basis of the myth of writing, a perennial feast of death, given over to the "sensual pleasure with which the meaning rules, like a grim sultan, over the harem of things." Uninhibited allegory, now remote from any living order of meaning, the pure compulsion to marshal images and repeatedly construct their meaning through distorted combinations, above all causes the images themselves to overflow. Just as objects obsessively invade the stage of the baroque theater until they become the true protagonists, so pictures erupt like threats in the emblem books, to celebrate the growing gap between image and meaning. Who, opening Andrea Alciati's *Emblemata* and seeing an amputated hand with an eye on the palm, planted in the middle of the sky over a rural landscape, would ever think of prudence, as the text for the emblem requires? Instead, he will recognize that a human body has been mutilated, a silent allusion to the state of nature as rubble and an unconscious establishment of the fragment as the prevailing aesthetic category. By the accumulation of these materials, the stage is being set for the modern. The history of that time prefigures the real history of today: These images, which then emerged into the world like wild beasts from their cages, are still at large. Kafka described them: "Leopards break into the temple and empty the sacrificial vessels; this is repeated time and again; in the end it can be foreseen and becomes part of the ceremony." In allegory, a writer is the witness of this scene.

8 The Superior Man and the Absolute Cocotte

Having haunted so many restless youngsters in the first thirty years of the twentieth century and having then been interred among those books known to have once been important, though no one can say why, Otto Weininger's *Sex and Character* has just been reissued. And one can already foresee that although it will excite the unseemly enthusiasm (after all, it's *so* Middle European!) of a few rare zealots, most people will greet it with a flicker of impatience, if not indignation, and ask, "What? After three quarters of a century, do we still have to put up with this arrogant and suicidal young man? This student who went out of his way to bad-mouth women, homosexuals, and Jews?" Agreed, but does today's sorry official culture really have any reason to look down its nose at him?

The true anti-Semite says, "Besides, some of my best friends are Jews." The true enemy of women says, "Besides, she's a nice girl." The true homophobe says, "Besides, I like them." Weininger is just the opposite of these people. First of all, he himself was Jewish; second, it was precisely his atrocious remarks about women that aided Karl Kraus, that most eloquent worshipper of woman, in putting the law to shame when it sought with impunity to condemn a number of Viennese *filles de joie*; third, what Weininger wrote about homosexuality is an early, clumsy effort to approach a subject about which modern thought has never been able even to rise above clumsiness.

So one begins to suspect that the whole story is a bit more complicated, ambiguous, and misleading. I will try to tell it for what it *also* is: an erotico-philosophical feuilleton. Believe it or not, there was once a time when the "problem of sex" actually existed, and was not merely fodder for statistics, sociologists, marriage counselors, and liberators of humanity.

For three generations, from the midnineteenth century on, any hint of sex gave rise to excruciating spasms and cast a pall over everything. Then, as always, sensitive young people indulged in masturbation, but in the heroic certainty that they were courting madness and death.

Indeed, according to what was then accepted doctrine, the spinal cord would supposedly turn rapidly into pulp and trickle down the backbone. And when Strindberg, in *Son of a Servant,* revealed that this was one of many deceptions practiced on him as a child, it was a gesture of unheard-of audacity. There were also, as Frank Wedekind described, epidemics of suicide among high school students overwhelmed by erotic fantasies and guilt. And the whole world kept piling libido on every knickknack: All of Art Nouveau can be seen as an attempt to eroticize industry, the beginning of the mass production of objects (winding flights of stairs, untrustworthy door handles . . .) that Weininger's amoral, insatiable woman might continually relate to in her increasing boredom with the ever present and inept man of the law, so stupid and so convinced of being the custodian of the spirit. And it is even plausible that abstract art, whether pre-*Informel* (as in Schmithals) or absolute decoration (as in Gustav Klimt), was born of an excess of erotic tension: The chromatic blur serves primarily to cover or envelop in a vibrant veneer scenes too indecent to be shown.

It was amid these quicksands that Otto Weininger was born in Vienna in 1880. He was one of those fatal individuals (fatal especially to themselves) who cannot say anything without carrying it to its "ultimate conclusions." Like many others, he had the vice of the Absolute, and with a neophyte's energy he went looking for it where people at that time supposed it to be: in science. But for a shrewd eye like his, it was precisely science that presented an image of distressing uncertainty behind its positivist arrogance: The most subtle theorists, like Ernst Mach, had reduced the ego to an *anteroom* through which impressions flowed. The nihilistic sword of the new epistemology drove consciousness into the "sea of sensations" and transformed it into a "bundle" of chance psychic aggregations. The subject, proud and positive, discovered itself to be a patchwork, a "kaleidoscope" that "reduces everything to a hodgepodge of elements," "renders everything meaningless and without foundation," and "destroys the possibility of starting from a fixed point for thought." In the end it destroys "the concept of truth."

Behind these agonizing results, one glimpses the impassive sneer of

David Hume. But who was it who championed the unity of the subject against Hume's corrosive acids? The great Immanuel Kant, and the whole of nineteenth-century German culture was a continual gesture of homage and betrayal toward him as the last bearer of the law. Weininger therefore turned to Kant as to an unassailable rock in the "hodgepodge" of elements. Had he been an ordinary spirit, his path would have been laid out: a chair in philosophy and a lifetime of sober research as a neo-Kantian thinker, of which there were quite a few in the Germany of those years. But Weininger had an aberrant originality and followed his own phantasms rather than common sense. And his mind was equally violently obsessed by ethics and by eros. Thus he had the utter effrontery to launch himself on a hitherto unheard-of project: to marry epistemology and sexuality by squeezing Kant, "the superior man," and Lulu, "the absolute cocotte," into the same bed. As might have been foreseen, the two of them sprang out of that bed with mutual repugnance (perhaps Kant's famous *Realrepugnanz?*).

From this incident emerged *Sex and Character,* first a graduate thesis, then a heavy tome, and finally a contagious best-seller until the late 1920s. But Weininger was not around to witness this last phase: He had fired a bullet into his heart a few months after the book's publication in 1903. He was twenty-three years old. The reasons for his suicide can be divined from the illuminating fragments collected as *On Last Things* and published posthumously. Weininger, who had invested his book with the fanatical necessity of being *the* truth, had come to a growing realization that his creation was a grandiose failure and above all that the *person* Otto Weininger was not the spotless and perfectly conscious subject he had thought; rather, he had increasingly come to resemble woman's proxy, the criminal. Judge Daniel Paul Schreber, caught in a similar conflict, had found a way out in paranoiac delusion.

The Kantian Otto Weininger chose suicide: "The *decent* man proceeds by himself toward death, if he realizes that he has become definitely wicked." So how should one read *Sex and Character*? Certainly not as a scientific treatise. That would be to fall into the error of which Weininger himself was a victim, in order to derive the mean satisfaction of smiling superciliously at these sometimes hilarious pages, pure fin de siècle grotesqueness, in which he lashes out at women, Jews, and homosexuals. No, *Sex and Character* is a desperate, subtle confession, both lucid and raving, that stages an intermezzo in the "tragedy of consciousness." And precisely *for theatrical reasons,* Weininger had to give it the seal of scientific solemnity, to formulate it in that grave and cumbersome language that is nevertheless continually shaken by a tremor, the first sign of a psychical tempest, the omnipresent threat of eros.

The hidden point from which the whole book proliferates is the specter of the androgyne. The bisexuality marvelously depicted by Plato, the cabalists, Jakob Böhme, and books of alchemy, all the way to Honoré de Balzac's *Séraphita,* and now a lost and elusive chimera, resurfaces by murky underground channels in young Weininger, as it also did, and by no less murky channels, in the slightly older Wilhelm Fliess and Sigmund Freud. Having stated the obvious fact that masculine and feminine traits coexist in every person but carrying it—as though obsessed—to its "ultimate conclusions," Weininger ended by noting that bisexuality necessarily led to an incurable and baleful split in the subject. On one side is man, something, affirmation, the heir of Kant's transcendental subject, reduced to a policeman ever on the alert, his will vainly tense, in danger of losing his identity and damaging the law, which in his coercive vacuity he represents. On the other is woman, nothing, negation, this amoral and irresponsible creature, this Lulu who has no ego (and yet is sovereign), who tells lies out of biological necessity and copulates continually with everything around her.

This outrageously comical comparison was not *invented* by Weininger, as his undiscerning critics have always insisted, but *transcribed* by him. The text from which he transcribed it was none other than the clandestine system of thought that governed (and still governs) our civilization. Weininger sketched that oppressive cage in the darkness and made it recognizable. Thinking the cage's founding assumptions through to their "ultimate conclusions" caused it to creak. Or rather, Weininger himself tried to get out of the cage but could not, precisely because of his "scientific" and Kantian assumptions. Outside the cage, he might truly have begun that "research on principles" (masculine and feminine) promised by the book's subtitle. And there he would have encountered alchemical and mythological symbolism to serve as a guide. Instead, Weininger's involuntary grotesqueness rages just when he is fumbling to emerge from his cage.

Once he had finished writing *Sex and Character,* Weininger seems to have realized that his whole system did nothing but *describe a hallucination* produced by fear of the void and its troubling synonym Woman:

"And this is also the explanation of man's deepest *fear: fear of the woman,* that is, *fear in the face of the absence of meaning*: that is, *fear before the seductive abyss of the void.*" For if *"woman is man's sin,"* as Weininger observes at the end of his Kantian "deduction of femininity," his whole book could no longer claim to have described woman as a real being, but woman as a perpetual hallucination of sin. And this is no small feat: He may not have written a scientific work, but he was surely a faithful and clairvoyant chronicler of the specters of his civilization. His error, once again, was the one that Karl Kraus is said to have pointed out in Strindberg: "Strindberg's truth: The order of the world is threatened by the feminine. Strindberg's error: The order of the world is threatened by woman."

The "cultural world," in its ever renewed respectability, has not been exactly generous toward that valuable error known as *Sex and Character*: when the book appeared, because it had too much success, was read too avidly by young girls, and therefore could not be taken seriously; today, because it is offered as a period piece, for the grotesqueness scattered throughout it and for the pompous incongruity of the scientific apparatus that goes with it. Very few people have actually acknowledged a debt of gratitude to this book. And those who did were writers who were indeed horrified by the "cultural world": Kraus, Strindberg, Wittgenstein.

9 The Ordeal of Impossible Words

The sound of the banalities generally uttered about Simone Weil can already be heard in these few words by Simone de Beauvoir: "A great famine had just struck China, and they told me that Simone Weil broke down and wept on hearing the news. Those tears, more than her philosophic gift, made me feel respect for her." This sentence illustrates a reaction that is still with us today: One pronounces Simone Weil's name and is immediately surrounded by contrite faces. Rising to the occasion, someone says he respects her because even though she was an unskilled intellectual and graduate of the Ecole Normale Supérieure, she took a job in a Renault factory; another ups the ante of admiration because she joined in many trade-union struggles; someone else recalls the war in Spain; another vouches for her piety and alludes thoughtfully to her lasting reluctance to be baptized; and some estimable and obtuse layman will also stand ready to call her a "saint of our time."

I think nothing would have annoyed Simone Weil more than to see herself reduced to an upholder of good causes, one of those sanctimonious and undiscriminating people who plunge into every good deed of the moment. Those who speak of her this way would really like to evade and ignore her, since they are incapable of "paying attention to her soul," as one of Hugo von Hofmannsthal's characters demanded.

Unlike Simone de Beauvoir, we will not be content with a few sobs over China. By now it has been settled beyond any doubt that crying about the world's disasters is no more significant than a certificate of good conduct. Let us look instead at what is really intimidating in Simone Weil, which Beauvoir clumsily calls her "philosophic gift": her thought. Let us finally open her books, especially her truly secret books, those

Cahiers written in the overly clear handwriting of a model schoolgirl between 1940 and 1943, the year Weil died in London of exhaustion and tuberculosis, at the age of thirty-four.

What sort of mind emerges from these books? Certainly not one suitable to be considered in the usual histories of modern philosophy, and not even one capable of feeding those encyclopedias that are all the more dismal the more they claim to bulge with ideas. No, Simone Weil was not an academic philosopher, nor was she one of those tiresome, long-winded pundits who continue to hold the stage today. We need only read a few of her pages to realize that we are in the presence of something of which many may even have lost all recollection: a mind both transparent and hard as a diamond, a mind stubbornly focused on a slim bundle of words. And among them we recognize almost all the *impossible* words: those words so old, so immediate, but also so abused and threadbare that many people avoid saying them and circumvent them out of fear and shame. Those who do so are sensitive, enervated, and cultured. For Simone Weil, it would not have been possible. She continued to fix her gaze directly on *those* words, the same ones, moreover, that we find woven into the few inexhaustible texts to which she always returned: the Upanishads, the Bhagavad Gita, the pre-Socratics, Plato, Sophocles, the Gospels: "Love," "necessity," "good," "desire," "justice," *"malheur,"* "beauty," "limit," "sacrifice," "emptiness."

Weil was well aware that these words are likewise ordeals: Those who utter them are made to pass through the fire. Those who are able to utter them, because they know what they refer to, emerge unscathed. But almost nobody emerges unscathed. In the mouths of almost everybody, such words are mangled corpses. Under Simone Weil's pen, they return to being what they are: mysterious crystals. To observe these crystals *with attention,* one must at least be a mathematician of the soul. And that is what Simone Weil was.

It is customary to distinguish two periods in Weil's brief life: one of "social commitment" until 1938, the other of "mystical conversion" lasting until her death. These embarrassing definitions belong in a biographical dictionary. The truth is that Weil was always one thing only: a gnostic. When in the early years, they called her "the Red Virgin" and she was inciting the stonebreakers of Le Puy to revolt, when she irritated Leon Trotsky with her unassailable objections, when she participated in the struggle against Franco during the Spanish Civil War (and Georges Bataille made fun of her in the character of Lazare in *Bleu du ciel*), Simone Weil was already what she would later discover herself to be. "Very few are the spirits to whom it is given to discover that things and beings exist," she once wrote to Joë Bousquet. And in her writings, we feel from the beginning, with the articles calling for immediate political action, that truly for her, "things and beings exist."

Of course, in that first militant period, the whole vertiginous network of connections and resonances, from algebra to the zodiac, that we find later in the *Cahiers* had not yet formed in Weil. And yet there is already an impressive distance, as far as lucidity is concerned, between Weil and her most renowned contemporaries. Think of all the Oxford dandies, poets from the Latin Quarter, and German exiles who discovered "social commitment" and even the "proletarian cause" in the early 1930s! But Simone Weil was the only one capable of *simultaneously* following the oppressed to the point of working with them on the assembly line, and recognizing that the very country the oppressed looked to as their liberator was actually the most abusive mutation of oppression. In examining the socialist world, Weil did not fall into any of those traps into which almost all intellectuals of the time threw themselves, quite content to feel that they were on the side of history. She did not need to wait for the proofs, the documents, that so many others with sluggish reflexes were still waiting for half a century later. The lucidity of her mind was enough for her, and when Trotsky, with glum amiability, teased her about her drastic ideas, she once replied, in connection with the words "revolutionary" and "counterrevolutionary," that "if one wanted to seek the truth, it was necessary to set limits to that terminology." Sublime understatement.

I have spoken of "crystals" and of "attention." Today, when the beaches of the world lie strewn with huge ideological carcasses, to encounter Weil's writings may be the equivalent, to use the categories of *Mount Analogue* by René Daumal (one of the few writers akin to her, as well as a friend), of finding a *peradam,* that strange "curved crystal," difficult and dangerous to procure, that is "the sole substance, the sole material body in which the guides of Mount Analogue recognize a value." In this world of analogy, "it is the sole guarantee of every coin, as gold is for us," and also the only source of "incontestable authority." To find it, one need only have a clear mind and that particular clairvoyance of sight that Weil called simply "attention." But she also remembered that "true attention is a state so difficult for man, a state so violent that any personal disturbance in sensibility is enough to prevent it." And the same word allowed her to offer the most elementary, but in the end persuasive, definition of culture: "What is culture? The formation of attention."

10 A Report on Readers of

Schreber

Daniel Paul Schreber's *Memoirs* were published in 1903 by the firm of Oswald Mutze in Leipzig.[1] This edition, printed at the author's expense, is hard to come by today, the family having apparently bought up and destroyed most of the existing copies.[2] The book did not, however, wholly escape the notice of psychiatrists. That same year, 1903, a review of it appeared in the *Allgemeine Zeitschrift für Psychiatrie,* followed by another in 1904 in the *Deutsche Zeitschrift für Nervenheilkunde.* The first reviewer, C. Pelman, set out to distinguish Schreber's *Memoirs* from the mass of those "more or less voluminous works by our ex-patients in which they make loud, public accusations claiming to have been denied their freedom and put the blame on criminal doctors."[3] Pelman, with a gesture of ironic detachment, dismisses at the outset any similarity to these "dubious literary products," pointing out that Schreber's book has "only one thing in common" with them, "namely, the fact of having been written by a mental patient, while in all other respects it towers high above them" (p. 657). Indeed, Schreber's primary concern could not be said to express personal resentment; but rather, he "offer[ed] his person to the judgment of experts as an object of scientific observation" (p. 658). Having thus given his approval to Schreber's worthy purpose, Pelman provides a quick and extremely vague summary of the *Memoirs.* He shows greater interest, however, in the court proceedings whereby Schreber eventually regained his freedom, and in particular he concedes that the judge's judicial battle with the authorities was no confrontation between "two ordinary adversaries," since the dispute can be said to have occurred "on an equal level." Finally, Pelman concluded, "For these reasons I would be sorry if the book were removed from circulation . . . because it deserves a better fate.

That Schreber is sane is not something that will be accepted by any thinking person. But one must surely recognize that here is a man both intellectually gifted and worthy of respect for his feelings" (p. 659).

The second review, signed by one R. Pfeiffer, deserves to be quoted in full for its lack of perception:

> The author, a typical paranoiac, introduces his book with a brief open letter
> to Professor Flechsig, followed by 350 pages describing in detail his deliri-
> ous systematized ideas, in which medical experts will find nothing new.
> What is more interesting is the verbatim reproduction in the documents of
> the trial proceedings and the court's reasons for deciding to lift the ban on
> Schreber, despite the persistence of his delirious ideas. There is no reason to
> fear a wide circulation of this book among the lay public, although it
> might, despite the obvious situation of the facts, create confusion.[4]

One of these two reviews very probably attracted the attention of the young Swiss psychiatrist Carl Gustav Jung, then an intern at the Burghölzli hospital. Or perhaps he encountered Schreber's *Memoirs* among the new works issued by the same publisher who, a year before, had brought out his own first book, *Psychologie und Pathologie sogenannter okkulter Phänomene*. Be that as it may, we find Jung already citing Schreber's *Memoirs* in 1907, in his *Psychologie der Dementia praecox* [The Psychology of Dementia Praecox].[5] We know the fundamental importance of this work in Jung's development: It marks, among other things, an early declaration of principle with respect to Freud. Indeed, in the preface, dated July 1906—three months after beginning his correspondence with Freud, to whom he had presented a copy of his *Assoziationstudien*—Jung is anxious above all to explain how much he is "indebted to the brilliant discoveries of Freud" (p. 3), and after specifying that no criticism of Freud makes sense except *within* psychoanalysis, he mentions for the first time certain reservations of his own, especially his resistance to placing sexuality "so predominantly in the foreground" or granting it "the psychological universality which Freud, it seems, postulates" (p. 4). These ominous words manifest a difference of perspective that was to be practically wiped out in the next few years, only to reappear later in a much more radical form at the time of Jung's break with Freud. In *The Psychology of Dementia Praecox,* the references to Schreber's *Memoirs* serve primarily to illustrate certain characteristics of the illness being treated, and there is no attempt at interpretation. The first interpretative essay on Schreber's *Memoirs* is thus the one by Freud, written in the autumn of 1910.

Before examining its theses, I would like to review a few aspects of its complicated prior history. The problem of paranoia had already come up for Freud in the early years of psychoanalysis, as attested by the many times he mentions the subject in his letters to Wilhelm Fliess in the years 1895–96 and especially by the farsighted "Draft H," enclosed with a letter of 24 January 1895 and devoted to a first theoretical formulation of paranoia. Here paranoia is traced back to the various pathological modes of defense already singled out by Freud—namely, hysteria, obsessive neurosis, and states of hallucinatory confusion—and at the same time differentiated from them; the draft for the first time, among other things, employs the term "projection" (later treated further in "Draft K"). The much less drastic public explanation of this theory appeared the following year, in Freud's *Weitere Bemerkungen über die Abwehrneuropsychosen,* whose third section is devoted to the "Analysis of a Case of Chronic Paranoia." Here, for the first time in the German language, Freud uses the term "psychoanalysis," referring specifically to the case of the paranoiac female patient who was sent to him by Josef Breuer and who is the subject of the study. In this rapid analysis, Freud's aim is once again to show how "paranoia, or groups of cases belonging to it, is also a defence-psychosis; that is to say, that it results from the repression of painful memories, as do hysteria and obsessions, and that the form of the symptoms is determined by the content of the repressed memory."[6] Freud does not, however, risk establishing a theory of paranoia on this basis and specifies that his analysis is limited to "some such conclusion as this: this case is a defence-psychosis and in the category of paranoia there are probably others like it" (p. 170). In fact, this caution conceals his already clear ambition to provide an exhaustive interpretation of the entire paranoiac pathology, and some of the terms that recur in the course of this analysis, for example "projection," will also remain fundamental in successive formulations of the theory. What Freud instead abandons entirely is the theory of a specific sexual trauma, with the discovery in 1897 "that there is no 'indication of reality' in the unconscious, so that it is impossible to distinguish between truth and emotionally-charged fiction."[7] Finally, in a letter to Fliess in 1899, Freud goes a step further in his theory of paranoia, coming to consider it "a surge forward of the auto-erotic tendency, a regression to a former state" (letter 125; p. 304).

After this letter, more than ten years pass during which Freud makes almost no mention of paranoia in his published works. He continues, however, to wrestle with the many problems raised by it, as is apparent in his letters to Jung, who, in *The Psychology of Dementia Praecox,* had already discussed the case of the paranoiac woman presented by Freud in 1896. Jung recognized it as "extremely important for psychopathology,"[8] and in the end he offered a criticism that touches the truly delicate spot in Freud's study: "The 'hysterical' mechanisms he uncovered suffice to explain the origin of hysteria, but why then does *dementia praecox* arise?" (p. 35). As early as the first months of his correspondence with Jung, Freud raises the question of paranoia, and in a letter of 6 December 1906 he states openly, "I have still formed no definite opinion on the dividing line between dementia praecox and paranoia. . . . But my experience in this field is meager."[9] Freud will come back to this second statement several times, almost with a feeling of inferiority with respect to Jung, who had numerous patients suffering from paranoia and dementia praecox in the Burghölzli clinic. And it is significant that Freud's great study of paranoia, the paper on Schreber, is the only one of his great cases to be based solely on a text. After his first meeting with Freud, in Vienna in March 1907, Jung wrote to him, obviously commenting on conversations they had had during his visit, "*Autoerotism* as the essence of Dementia praecox strikes me more and more as a momentous deepening of our knowledge" (p. 25)— and here we see the reemergence of the theme mentioned in the letter to Fliess in 1899. Even in the early exchanges, we observe differences in terminology between Freud and Jung when they are dealing with paranoia and dementia praecox. Common to both, however, is their impatience with the ambiguous term "dementia praecox," which, in fact, was to be replaced by the fatal word "schizophrenia" only after the publication in 1911 of Eugen Bleuler's important treatise *Dementia praecox, oder Gruppe der Schizophrenien.* In April 1907, Freud sends Jung the outline of a paper, "A Few Theoretical Remarks on Paranoia." This is the first time that Freud, in a gesture of paternal trust, asks Jung's opinion of a manuscript. In these fundamental notes, he states, among other things, "The sexual instinct is originally autoerotic," "In paranoia the libido is withdrawn from the object," and "Projection . . . is a variety of repression, in which an image becomes conscious as perception" (pp. 39–40). Jung reacts to this manuscript with oblique criticisms. He shows it to Bleuler, who tells him he will use it in his major study on dementia praecox. The observation added by Jung, in his letter of 13 May 1907, is supremely comical and illuminating for the history of psychiatry: "He [Bleuler] doesn't want to say autoerotism (for reasons we all know) [that is, prudery], but prefers 'autism' or 'ipsism.' I have already got accustomed to 'autoerotism.'" (pp. 44–45).

Meanwhile, Jung relentlessly continues to feed Freud interesting cases of dementia praecox encountered in his clinical practice. In June 1907, Freud singles out among them the case of a paranoiac with "homosexual experiences," and this is the first time that homosexuality appears in connection with paranoia. In a letter of 17 February 1908, however, Freud suggests to Jung for the first time a possible theoretical connection between homosexuality and paranoia:

> I have been in contact with a few paranoia cases in my practice and can tell you a secret. . . . I have regularly encountered a detachment of libido from a homosexual component which until then had been normally and moderately cathected. . . . My old analysis (1896) also showed that the pathological process began with the patient's estrangement from her husband's *sisters.* My one-time friend Fliess developed a dreadful case of paranoia after throwing off his affection for me, which was undoubtedly considerable. I owe this idea to him, i.e., to his behaviour. One must try to learn something from every experience.[10]

In this letter, Freud throws a sudden light on the obscure basis and complex personal connections that mark his theory of paranoia. It turns out here to be linked in its central element—the role of homosexuality—with the most serious, passionate, and painful psychological experience in Freud's life: his friendship with Fliess and its breakup. Clearly, Jung grasps at once the importance of what Freud revealed to him, and he replies three days later with a ploy that takes on an all too obvious meaning in light of what occurs between them a few years later: "The reference to Fliess—surely not accidental—and your relationship with him impels me to ask you to let me enjoy your friendship not as one between equals but as that of father and son" (p. 122). The solid basis is thereby laid for a difficult and emotional relationship, one that will also be broken in due course. During 1908 the copious exchange of ideas on paranoia between Freud and Jung continues, as does a correspondence between Freud and Sándor Ferenczi, with whom Freud succeeds in working out a crucial hypothesis: "What we regard as the manifestations of their disorder [paranoia] . . . is their attempt to cure themselves" (letter to Jung, 26 December 1908; p. 191).

The year 1909, marked by Jung's second visit to Vienna in March and by the trip of both men to America for the Clark Conference in the summer, was to charge the relationship between Freud and Jung with ever more ambiguity and ambivalence. Meanwhile, Jung discovers myth as his favored material for analysis, and Freud, for the time being, shares his enthusiasm. At the beginning of 1910, they are making preparations for the Nuremberg Congress, and Jung seems increasingly aggressive in presenting his ideas. In the important letter of 11 February 1910, in which he describes himself as "sitting so precariously on the fence between the Dionysian and the Apollinian," Jung emphatically states, "Religion can be replaced only by religion."[11] While the favorite pupil speaks of "the Walpurgis Nights of my unconscious" (p. 296), the master does not insist on their differences and proves accommodating, albeit worried. The Nuremberg Congress is held at the end of March. When it is over, Freud and Jung spend a day together at Rothenburg, and it was probably on this occasion that Jung first spoke to Freud about Schreber. There is, however, already a first indirect reference to Schreber in Jung's letter of 17 April (p. 307), and from then on until the end of the correspondence there are numerous such references. Freud seems in particular to have playfully absorbed various expressions from the *Memoirs,* such as "miracled," "basic language," and "nervous conjunction" (this last appears often in the correspondence with Karl Abraham as well). In a letter of 22 April, Freud refers explicitly to "the wonderful Schreber," whose book he has set aside for the holidays, and he observes that the man "ought to have been made a professor of psychiatry and director of a mental hospital" (p. 311).

During the summer of 1910, after a particularly exhausting year, Freud went to Holland for a rest and from there left in September for a long-desired trip to Italy, accompanied by Ferenczi. The journey coincided with a moment of intense self-absorption on Freud's part, when he found himself confronting a new obstacle in his self-analysis. Once again it was a question of Fliess *and* paranoia. Ferenczi kept pestering Freud with questions precisely about paranoia, a subject he himself was involved with for the moment, and Freud must frequently have been loath to respond, for once he was back in Vienna, he felt the need to justify himself to Ferenczi in a revealing letter that includes these words: "Not only have you noticed that I no *longer* have any need for that full opening of my personality, but you have also understood it and correctly returned to its traumatic cause. . . . This need has been extinguished in me since Fliess's case, with the overcoming of which you just saw me occupied. A piece of homosexual investment has been withdrawn and used for the enlargement of my own ego. I succeeded where the paranoiac fails."[12]

Freud had taken Schreber's *Memoirs* with him on the trip to Italy, and he read about half the book, but with the feeling that he had already grasped its secret. Back in Vienna, he immediately announced to Jung, without mentioning Schreber, that he was preparing an article on paranoia. But Jung understood what was going on and promptly replied, on 29 September, "I was touched and overjoyed to learn how much you appreciate the greatness of Schreber's mind and the liberating ἱεροὶ λόγοι of the basic language." Further on in the same letter, Jung demonstrated that behind Schreber he had glimpsed the whole mythological and religious background with which he was concerned at that moment: "The Manichaeans (Schreber's godfathers?) hit on the idea that a number of demons or 'archons' were crucified on, or affixed to, the vault of heaven and were the *fathers of human beings.*"[13] Freud replied, "I share your enthusiasm for Schreber; it is a kind of revelation. I plan to introduce 'basic language' as a serious technical term. . . . After another reading I may be able to resolve all the intriguing fantasies; I didn't quite succeed the first time. . . . I wish you luck with your immersion in mythology" (p. 358). Freud worked on the Schreber case from then until mid-December. On the sixteenth, he wrote to Abraham and Ferenczi that he had finished his paper. A few days earlier, he had announced to Jung that he would bring the manuscript with him to Munich, adding, "I am not pleased with it, but it is for others to judge. . . . I shall have to leave other parts of my speculation on paranoia for a later paper" (p. 377). And on 18 December he repeated, "The piece is formally imperfect, fleetingly improvised. I had neither time nor strength to do more. Still, there are a few good things in it, and it contains the boldest thrust at + + + [sexual] psychiatry since your *Dem. Pr.* I am unable to judge its objective worth as was possible with earlier papers, because in working on it I have had to fight off complexes within myself (Fliess)" (pp. 379–80). Nothing could be clearer: Once again the ghost of Fliess looms behind Judge Schreber. Freud's paper was published in 1911, in an issue of the *Jahrbuch* that marks the great watershed in the history of psychoanalysis. Indeed, it also contained the first part of Jung's new book, *Wandlungen und Symbole der Libido,* which made it clear that the pupil, now turned rebel, had taken a quite different path. Meanwhile, on 28 March 1911, Jung's young and talented disciple Johann Jakob Honegger Jr. committed suicide; in Nuremberg he had presented a paper on paranoia that anticipated with remarkable lucidity the ideas that Jung would later express on the subject.[14] On 14 April, Schreber died in the Dösen psychiatric clinic, near Leipzig, unaware that his *Memoirs* had become the basis for the theory of paranoia that would dominate the century, and without Freud knowing of his death.

Freud's paper on Schreber consists of three parts and a postscript. The first part follows the course of the judge's illness as described in the *Memoirs.* Freud gives an extremely partial summary, picking out from Schreber's tangled account only what may be useful for the interpretation he later offers. Almost entirely lacking, for example, is any reference to the political aspects of the judge's delusions, to the "compulsion to think," or to transformations of the "basic language."

The second part of Freud's paper is entitled "Attempts at Interpretation." After a rapid methodological preamble, the crux of the theory appears: "The study of a number of cases of delusions of persecution have led me as well as other investigators to the view that the relation between the patient and his persecutor can be reduced to quite a simple formula."[15] This formula says, "The person who is now hated and feared as a persecutor was at one time loved and honoured" (p. 424). In Schreber's case, this person is obviously Dr. Paul Emil Flechsig. And here comes the homosexuality: "The exciting cause of his illness, then, was an outburst of homosexual libido; the object of this libido was probably from the very first his physician, Flechsig; and his struggles against this libidinal impulse produced the conflict which gave rise to the pathological phenomenon" (p. 426). Having revealed this enormity, Freud pauses for a moment to ask himself, "Is it not an act of irresponsible levity, an indiscretion and a calumny to charge a man of such high ethical standing as the former Senatspräsident Schreber with homosexuality?" Having overcome this grave doubt, which says much about the caution required at the time by even the least cautious of psychoanalysts, Freud goes into detail about the relationship with Flechsig, discerning behind his figure those of Schreber's father, whose qualities as an authoritarian pedagogue lead

Freud to find him particularly suited to the role; his dead brother; and finally the God in the *Memoirs* and his representative, the sun. These transformations seem to Freud to be connected to the theme of the Double, which he mentions, however, only in passing. Finally, at the end of the chapter, Freud analyzes the problem of the motivation for the outbreak of the conflict, which must be related to "some privation in real life" (p. 442), and he suggests that this privation might have been Schreber's lack of progeny: "Dr. Schreber may have formed a phantasy that if he had been a woman he would have managed the business of having children more successfully; and he may thus have found his way back into the feminine attitude towards his father which he had exhibited in the earliest years of his childhood" (p. 443).

The third section, "On the Mechanism of Paranoia," contains more complex theoretical considerations. Here the starting point is the observation that what has gone before is insufficient to establish the "distinctive character of paranoia," which must be sought by entering into the "mechanism by which the symptoms are formed."[16] Meanwhile, a brief genetic digression allows Freud to single out "the weak spot in their [the paranoiacs'] development," which "is to be looked for somewhere between the stages of auto-erotism, narcissism and homosexuality" (p. 448), and he adds that a "similar disposition would have to be assigned to patients suffering from Kraepelin's dementia praecox or (as Bleuler has named it) *schizophrenia*" (p. 448). At this point, Freud begins to analyze the transformation, under the pressure of various pathological impulses, of the proposition "I *love* him" into "I *hate* him," as part of persecution mania or in other forms such as erotomania, paranoiac jealousy, and alcoholic delusions of jealousy. It is this portion of Freud's paper that has perhaps had the most influence on subsequent psychoanalytic literature, because of the extreme subtlety and flexibility of the transformations suggested and the vast range of pathologies to which they can be related.

As for the formation of symptoms of paranoia, Freud singles out as the most striking characteristic the process of *projection,* which he defines as follows: "An internal perception is suppressed, and, instead, its content, after undergoing a certain degree of distortion, enters consciousness in the form of an external perception."[17] And Freud promises to take up this crucial theme again in some future study, but this was not to happen. With the passage on projection, all the fundamental elements in the paper have been presented, and Freud goes on to a final, intricate orchestration of his themes, stressing first the three phases of repression in paranoia and then problems connected with the "detachment of the libido," a phenomenon peculiar to paranoia but not unique to it. At the end of this section, various differences with Jung on the subject of dementia praecox—differences that had already cropped up several times in their correspondence—reappear in disguised form. Having thus arrived at the end of his analysis, Freud feels the need—and this is clearly significant—to state that his theory of paranoia was formed *prior* to reading Schreber's *Memoirs*: "I can nevertheless call a friend and fellow-specialist to witness that I had developed my theory of paranoia before I became acquainted with the contents of Schreber's book. It remains for the future to decide whether there is more delusion in my theory than I should like to admit, or whether there is more truth in Schreber's delusion than other people are as yet prepared to believe" (pp. 465–66). And this surprising, penultimate sentence is the real end of Freud's paper on Schreber.

Then there is the postscript, two and a half pages of fundamental significance in the history of psychoanalysis. Freud read them at the Weimar Congress (21–22 September 1911, the last public occasion on which Freud and Jung seem to have been officially united). Here Freud's attitude seems almost to be one of mild self-defense: having begun by recalling that in analyzing the Schreber case, "I purposely restricted myself to a minimum of interpretation,"[18] Freud recognizes that a wealth of other material can be extracted from the *Memoirs* and cites in this connection the references to Schreber in Jung's *Wandlungen und Symbole der Libido* and in an article by Sabina Spielrein. He then turns to the subject of the *sun* as offering new *mythological* interpretations, mentions totemism for the first time, and in the last paragraph takes up, again for the first time in his work, the theme of mythology in general, with words that were to have considerable resonance:

> This short postscript to my analysis of a paranoid patient may serve to show that Jung had excellent grounds for his assertion that the mythopoeic forces of mankind are not extinct, but that to this very day they give rise in the neuroses to the same psychological products as in the remotest past ages. I should like to take up a suggestion that I myself made some time ago, and add that the same holds good of the forces that work for the formation of religions. And I am of the opinion that the time will soon be ripe for us to make an extension of a principle of which the truth has long been recognized by psycho-analysts, and to complete what has hitherto had only an individual and ontogenetic application by the addition of its anthropological

and phylogenetically conceived counterpart. "In dreams and in neuroses," so our principle has run, "we come once more upon the *child* and the peculiarities which characterize his modes of thought and his emotional life." "And we come upon the *savage* too," thus we may complete our proposition, "upon the *primitive* man, as he stands revealed to us in the light of the researches of archaeology and of ethnology." (pp. 469–70)

With this tribute, Freud also said farewell to his favorite pupil Jung and at the same time announced *Totem und Tabu.*

Jung, for his part, reacted badly to Freud's paper on Schreber. In a letter of 11 December 1911, rather resentful in tone, he referred to a point in the paper where Freud speaks of the paranoiac's "loss of . . . libidinal interest"[19] in the world:

> As for the libido problem, I must confess that your remark in the Schreber analysis . . . has set up booming reverberations. This remark, or rather the doubt expressed therein, has resuscitated all the difficulties that have beset me throughout the years in my attempt to apply the libido theory to Dem. praec. The loss of the reality function in D. pr. cannot be reduced to repression of libido (defined as sexual hunger). Not by me, at any rate.[20]

The tone, the moment, the context of these words make them look like an explicit declaration of war and the recognition of a now unavoidable split. The Freud-Jung relationship had begun with discussions of dementia praecox, and it collapsed with them, along with the ridiculous name of the disorder. We are left with schizophrenia.

Jung's different view of libido appeared more clearly than ever in the second part of *Wandlungen und Symbole der Libido,* first published in the *Jahrbuch* of 1912 and issued later in the same year along with the first part in a book. There are other references in it to Schreber's *Memoirs,* and still more appear in the revised version published by Jung in 1952 under the title *Symbole der Wandlung.* Here Jung states explicitly, among other things, that Freud's analysis of the Schreber case is "very unsatisfactory," and in a footnote he claims to have drawn Freud's attention to the *Memoirs.* Otherwise the references are illustrative, and the *Memoirs* are considered on a par with all the other mythological, poetic, mystical, and psychopathological subjects discussed in the book.

In any case, in 1914, two years after their break, Jung attacked Freud in connection with the Schreber case in his long supplement to his 1908 lec-

ture "Der Inhalt der Psychose" [The Content of the Psychoses], which
Freud at the time had liked. In these pages, Jung gives what has remained
a classic explanation of the methodological differences between reductive
interpretation (that of Freud) and amplifying interpretation (that of Jung
himself), here called "constructive."[21] The Schreber case, according to
Jung, can be said to reveal in a striking fashion the insufficiency of the
first method, which permits the analyst to complete only "one half of the
work" (p. 186), while leaving quite open the question of the *purpose* and
dynamics of the delusion, to which Jung thought he himself had already
provided a first answer in *Wandlungen und Symbole der Libido*.

In 1911, the same year in which Freud's paper on Schreber appeared, Sabina
Spielrein published an article on a case of schizophrenia in which she referred to the *Memoirs*. Of Russian origin, a pupil of Jung in Zurich and
involved with him in an ambiguous love affair, and much esteemed by
Freud, Spielrein is one of the most interesting and least studied among the
pioneers of psychoanalysis. The dates of her birth and death (1886?–after
1934) are still uncertain. Alexander Grinstein lists thirty of her psychoanalytic contributions from 1911 to 1931. Finally, we know that Spielrein
was Jean Piaget's training analyst and that in 1923 she returned to the
Soviet Union, where she disseminated Freudian doctrine and taught
in Rostov until 1933, when psychoanalysis was banned. In the above-
mentioned article, Spielrein analyzed the case of a schizophrenic woman
that presents some analogies with Schreber's story: for instance, the fear of
"Catholicization" as a "conversion to sexuality"; the influence of the psychiatrist Auguste Forel on the patient, similar to Flechsig's on Schreber;
and the mythological delusion, which Spielrein subtly traces. Moreover, in
the "Final Considerations" of the paper, we find Freud's basic statements
in his postscript to the Schreber case anticipated almost to the letter: "The
parallel with the mythological way of thinking goes back to a particular
affinity of the dream mechanism with archaic thought. I was much struck
by this during the analysis of this patient. If Freud and Jung have established a parallel between neurotic and dream phenomena and schizophrenia, I think I am able to add an essential element to their conception
by proposing that all this be considered in relation to its phylogeny."[22]

In a review of the Schreber case in 1912, Bleuler, despite all his doubts and
hesitations, openly acknowledged the enormous importance of Freud's

paper: "This brief sixty-page essay contains a huge wealth of thought. It is not to be read but studied."[23] This acknowledgment is followed by various objections that Bleuler had been brooding over for years, but he wholly accepts the crux of the theory, that is, the connection between paranoia and homosexuality. With this review, the first phase of the history of the Schreber case becomes somehow crystallized. Freud, for his part, will come back time and again over the years to questions connected with his paper on Schreber,[24] but it will always be to find confirmation for the ideas formulated in it. As for his followers, a sort of holy terror has seemed to surround Schreber's name for decades. The theory of paranoia is obviously accepted, but no one dares to take a closer look—though the master himself had suggested it!—at other aspects of the *Memoirs*.

On 6 July 1928, the *Literarische Welt* published a piece by Walter Benjamin entitled "Books by Mental Patients" and subtitled "From My Collection." Benjamin tells of finding one of the rare copies of Schreber's *Memoirs* in a small antique bookstore in Bern in 1918. He does not recall whether at the time he had already read Freud's essay. But never mind: "I was highly fascinated at once."[25] Schreber's *Memoirs* occupied a central place in Benjamin's precious "pathological library," along with a book by the nineteenth-century doctor C. F. A. Schmidt: "If the world of delusion, like that of knowledge, also had its four faculties, the works of Schreber and Schmidt would be a compendium of its theology and philosophy" (p. 617). In an elegant digression, Benjamin then gives his readers a fleeting report on the themes and language of the *Memoirs,* concluding with a passage in which casual journalism yields to the tone of a great essayist: "There is something daunting about the existence of such works. As long as we feel accustomed to consider the sphere of writing as, despite everything, superior and protected, the appearance of madness, which insinuates itself stealthily as never before, is all the more terrifying. How has it succeeded in penetrating? How has it been able to get past the guards of this hundred-gated Thebes, the city of books?" (p. 618).

So far, the one great attempt outside of psychoanalytic circles to interpret Schreber's *Memoirs* is by Elias Canetti. Here, too, it is interesting to note how he came to read them. In August 1939, Canetti was living in London, in the studio of the sculptor Anna Mahler, daughter of the composer. "Among her books, which I knew well, I noticed one that was new to me:

Schreber's *Memoirs*. I opened it and immediately saw that I'd find it very interesting. I didn't know where it had come from and I didn't even connect it with Freud, whose work I had not yet read."[26] The book was there by chance, having been left behind by a doctor who had lived in the studio and had emigrated to America. Canetti asked Mahler if he might take it with him, but he did not get around to reading it until May 1949. It was a disturbing experience, one that inspired him to write the two chapters on Schreber in *Crowds and Power*. A note from 1949 testifies to the book's immediate effect:

> What things I have found here [in Schreber's book]! Support for some of the ideas that have been haunting me for years: for instance, the insoluble link between paranoia and power. His entire system is the description of a struggle for power, with God Himself as his real antagonist. Schreber long imagined he was the only surviving human being in the world; all the others were the souls of dead people and God in multiple incarnations. The illusion that a man is or would like to be the only one, the only one among corpses, is decisive for the psychology of both the paranoiac and the extreme practitioner of power. . . . But Schreber also had in him the complete ideology of National Socialism as a delusion. . . . This study of paranoia has its dangers. After just a few hours, I am seized with a tormenting feeling of being locked in, and the more convincing the system of madness, the stronger my fear.[27]

It is clear from these words, and from the whole passage, that Schreber appeared to Canetti to be a little like the sovereign inhabitant of the last room in that huge waxworks museum of power called *Crowds and Power*. And it is just in that position, right before the epilogue, that Canetti placed his retelling of the Schreber case in the book that for decades occupied his life. The technique is narrative, as required by Canetti's particular method—he also tried it successfully on Franz Kafka's *Letters to Felice* and Speer's *Memoirs*—of thinking while narrating, a method that makes the reader realize he is being led to an inevitable interpretation of the facts when he thought he was simply listening to a recounting of them.

Canetti deals first of all with the paranoiac's *"sense of position"*: It is always a position of cosmic importance, which allows the paranoiac to speak of constellations "as though they were bus-stops just round the corner."[28] And here the connection with the powerful figure already appears: "By the very nature of power, the same must be true of the ruler. His sense of his own position is in no way different from that of the paranoiac" (p. 436). The second point touched on by Canetti concerns the *crowd,* as it appears in the myriad souls surrounding Schreber. The third point is the obsession with *conspiracies,* equally essential for the paranoiac and the ruler. Thus the structure of Schreber's delusion in relation to political power has already been outlined:

> Disguised as one of the old conceptions of the universe which pre-supposed the existence of spirits, his delusion is in fact a precise model of *political* power, power which feeds on the crowd and derives its substance from it. An attempt at a conceptual analysis of power can only blur the clarity of Schreber's vision. This contains all the real elements of the situation: the strong and lasting attraction exercised over the individuals who are to form a crowd; the ambiguous attitude of these individuals; their subjection through being reduced in size; the way they are taken into the man who in his own person, in his *body,* represents political power; the fact that his greatness must continually *renew* itself in this way; and final-ly, a very important point not so far mentioned, the sense of catastrophe which is linked with it, of danger to the world order arising from its sud-den and rapid increase and unexpected magnetism. (p. 441)

As we see, many of the themes patiently developed by Canetti in his great work can be found concentrated, and greatly intensified, in Schreber's vicissitudes, if we look at them in terms of power. And Canetti will cer-tainly be the last to let go of such a theme, since his story-meditation fol-lows this line, avoiding any possible distraction; he is similar in this to Freud, who treated Schreber's text from an equal and opposite bias. Canetti's method allows him to arrive at some of his most important aphoristic conclusions: "To be the last man to remain alive is the deepest urge of every real seeker after power."[29] "No-one has a sharper eye for the attributes of the crowd than the paranoiac or the despot who—as will perhaps be more readily admitted now—are one and the same" (p. 447). "Paranoia is an *illness of power* in the most literal sense of the words" (p. 448). And at the end of the first part of Canetti's treatment, the image of Hitler and Nazism appears, operating "in a rather cruder and less liter-ate form" (p. 447) than Schreber's delusion.

In the second part, after having established a firm link between para-noia and power, Canetti goes on to give a kind of descriptive picture of the paranoiac, still as seen through Schreber. The psychological analysis is prodigiously acute here, and it points from the start in quite other directions than Freud: "[There was] a well-known attempt to find the origin of his particular illness, and of paranoia in general, in repressed homosexuality. There could scarcely, however, be a greater mistake. Paranoia may be occasioned by anything; the essence of each case is the *structure* of the delusional world and the way it is *peopled*."[30] In the analysis of this structure, many themes already treated by Canetti reappear by contrast: Here the accent is on rigidity, on the petrification of the paranoiac's world, as opposed to the world of metamorphosis, to which a splendid section of Canetti's book is devoted. In Schreber, this rigidity is manifested primarily in his "mania for finding causal relations" (p. 452), and in verbal obsession. On this point Canetti achieves some of his best characterizations: "Perhaps the most marked trend in paranoia is that towards a complete seizing of the world through words, as though language were a fist and the world lay in it" (p. 452). At the close of this second section, Canetti restates with even greater clarity his theme of the relation between paranoia and power: "In this, too, the paranoiac is the exact image of the ruler. The only difference between them lies in their position in the world. In their inner structure they are identical. . . . It is difficult to resist the suspicion that behind paranoia, as behind all power, lies the same profound urge: the desire to get other men out of the way so as to be the only one; or, in the milder, and indeed often admitted, form, to get others to help him *become* the only one" (p. 462).

The apathy of psychoanalysis toward Schreber gradually breaks down after the end of World War II. Very little stands out from prior years except for two articles by W. J. Spring and R. P. Knight, dating from 1939 and 1940 respectively.[31] In the appendix to a lecture delivered in 1946 to the British Psycho-Analytical Society, Melanie Klein refers to the analysis of the Schreber case as containing "a wealth of material which is very relevant to my topic,"[32] which is then a rapid sketch of the "paranoid-schizoid position" in relation to various processes of splitting. Among the various quotations from Schreber in Freud's paper, Klein especially singles out those concerning the *division* of souls (for example, Flechsig's), a process she understands as "a projection of Schreber's feeling that his ego was split" (p. 23). On this and other points, Klein suggests corrections and amplifications of Freud's theory but concludes, however, that "Freud's approach to the problem of schizophrenia and paranoia has proved of fundamental importance. His Schreber paper . . . opened up the possibility of understanding psychosis and the processes underlying it" (p. 24).

In 1949, the American psychoanalyst Maurits Katan began publishing a number of short articles on Schreber,[33] later to be recycled in his detailed analysis of 1959.[34] These contributions established almost a model text that keeps reappearing today: a prudent variation on the themes in Freud's paper and the extrapolation of a few details from the *Memoirs* to lend them new importance, but without raising doubts about the fundamentals of Freud's analysis or carrying it to more far-reaching conclusions. Articles by A. C. Carr, R. Waelder, J. Nydes, P. M. Kitay, R. B. White, and H. F. Searles all belong to this kind of text, naturally with notable differences of position.[35] The last two authors are primarily concerned to stress the importance in Schreber of the mother complex as well, a theme later taken up in an interesting paper by R. Stoller, which deals in general with the problem of bisexuality in Freud.[36] The most obvious sign of the renewed interest of official psychoanalysis in the Schreber case appeared in 1962, when a symposium was held in Atlantic City, New Jersey, on *Reinterpretations of the Schreber Case: Freud's Theory of Paranoia.*

Until 1955, most discussions of the Schreber case continued to be confined to Freud's paper, there having been no new edition of the *Memoirs* in German or any other language. It was therefore an extremely useful, indeed pioneering, event when an English translation, amply annotated and edited by Ida Macalpine and Richard A. Hunter, was published in that year.[37] In their introduction, the two authors first outline the history of the Schreber case and of the notion of paranoia in the evolution of psychiatry, showing the many and curious fluctuations and uncertainties that have marked it from the beginning. This highly·useful historical introduction is paired with a theoretical discussion at the end of the volume in which the authors, with daring sincerity, denounce the inadequacy of Freudian theory. The alternate theory they proposed is, however, extremely weak, and as such has been the target of Jacques Lacan's cruel mockery.[38] For Macalpine and Hunter, the crucial element in Schreber's paranoia can be said to be his "fantasies of pregenital procreation,"[39] provoked by his frustrated wish to have children. Thus the whole axis of Freudian interpretation is shifted, without bearing much fruit. In particular, the mythological and anthropological examples that the authors come up with are quite meager and random, especially when compared with the enormous possibilities along these lines to be found in Schreber's *Memoirs.*

Papers began appearing after 1950 providing new information about Schreber's life and family, thus fulfilling a wish expressed by Freud forty years earlier. The first moves in this direction were by W. G. Niederland and F. Baumeyer,[40] who from the beginning offered highly interesting data that have become the basis for all studies of Schreber in the context of his family. The figure who particularly emerges from these articles is the father, Daniel Gottlieb Moritz Schreber, an enlightened and sadistic pedagogue who for the whole nineteenth century had, and in an underground way still has, an enormous influence in Germany as a champion of hygiene, gymnastics, and a narrowly moralistic upbringing. For many years, the most documented work on him was the dissertation by Alfons Ritter, a young Nazi who venerated the elder Schreber and inscribed this apothegm at the beginning of his book: "The path to the renewal of the German essence and German strength necessarily leads to a profession of faith in blood and soil."[41] The elder Schreber seemed to him, with some justification, to be a precursor of such a "renewal."

Niederland's and Baumeyer's studies were able to explain some hitherto mysterious details in Schreber's *Memoirs* by reconnecting them with facts in his life. In addition, in the Arnsdorf clinic, where he was the director from 1946 to 1949, Baumeyer unearthed some clinical files relating to Schreber, files that had come from the archive of the Sonnenstein nursing home. These documents were printed in the most recent German edition of Schreber's *Memoirs,* accompanied by Baumeyer's commentary.[42] They are especially important because they contain a number of statements by Schreber that are not in the *Memoirs,* including the famous sentence *"Die Sonne ist eine Hure"* ("The sun is a whore"), on which Lacan shrewdly commented.[43]

Once the figure of Schreber's father had been recalled from oblivion with such surprising results, research was extended to previous generations of this remarkable family of scientists and jurists. An excellent article published in *Scilicet* documents the recurrence, in various forms, of certain moralistic obsessions in the judge's forebears, thereby casting a glaring light on an admittedly heavy karma.[44] Finally, the most brilliant work, one that more or less sums up these first investigations of Schreber's family, is M. Schatzman's book.[45] It is characterized by a generous defense, in the manner of R. D. Laing, of Schreber's rights to his delusion in light of the oppression he suffered in childhood, an oppression that Schatzman finds *transformed* at various points in the *Memoirs*. It would be hard to deny, for example, that some of the "miracles" recounted by the judge correspond perfectly to certain orthopedic torture machines invented by his father. But one must say that this time, too, the judge eludes reduction: Those details from the *Memoirs* that can be traced back to his terrible relationship with his father are only one area of his delusions, which continue to develop and proliferate in other directions, about which not much has so far been said. Besides, it is odd that the numerous investigations of the elder Schreber have not been matched by an equal interest in the historical figure of Dr. Flechsig, who might hold just as many surprises in store. Only one article, by Niederland, deals with some aspects of the real relationship between Schreber and Flechsig.[46] Might it not be because father Freud, in his paper, did not encourage any research on the life and works of his colleague Flechsig?

In France, the study of Schreber is linked primarily with Lacan, who in 1955–56 had already conducted a seminar on the Schreber case. In 1959, his long essay "D'une question préliminaire à tout traitement possible de la psychose" [On a Question Preliminary to Any Possible Treatment of Psychosis], appeared in the fourth issue of *Psychanalyse,* repeating much material from the prior seminar. Dedicated, with a certain macabre solemnity, to the *genius loci* of the Sainte-Anne psychiatric hospital, this essay is clearly central in Lacan's work and is the only one in the psychoanalytical sphere to differ radically from Freud's. Since it raises highly complicated questions that would take us too far from the judge, I will limit myself to a few points in a convoluted argument. "Half a century of Freudianism applied to psychosis leaves its problem still to be rethought, in other words, at the *status quo ante*": Lacan begins his discussion with this ruthless and long-awaited declaration of failure, all the more significant coming from the lips of a psychoanalyst who had made his debut many years before with a paper entitled "De la psychose paranoïaque dans ses rapports avec la personnalité" [On Paranoiac Psychosis in Its Connection to Personality]. And a few lines later, speaking of the "long metaphysical coction of science in the School" and of the "smell of burnt fat" that betrays the "age-old practice in the said cooking of the preparation of brains"[47] he triumphantly puts us on a level with Schreber, something that previous psychoanalysts had avoided doing. Above all, Lacan seems moved—like Freud, who had even recognized in a passage of the *Memoirs* a ghostly anticipation of the theory of libido[48]—by a justifiable admiration for the judge, combined with a furious scorn for his post-Freud readers. The chief target for this fury is "Mme Macalpine," separated for the occasion, rather churlishly, from her coauthor, Hunter. As for Freud ("Towards Freud" and "With Freud" are the titles of the first and third sections of the essay), Lacan here reinterprets his fundamental texts in minute detail, and they take him in many centrifugal directions before returning him in the fourth section *"du côté de Schreber,"* but not until he has casually let drop a sentence indicative of the theoretical shift now underway: "Homosexuality, supposedly a determinant of paranoiac psychosis, is really a symptom articulated in its process."[49] And there are primarily two categorical quarries that Lacan will bring back from this raid: *Verwerfung* (foreclosure) and the Name-of-the-Father, who represents the symbolic father of *Totem und Tabu,* the Law, the Dead Father. These categories will finally come together in the densest formulation given by Lacan of the mechanism of psychosis:

> For the psychosis to be triggered off, the Name-of-the-Father, *verworfen,* foreclosed, that is to say, never having attained the place of the Other, must be called into symbolic opposition to the subject.
>
> It is the lack of the Name-of-the-Father in that place which, by the hole it opens up in the signified, sets off the cascade of reshapings of the signifier from which the increasing disaster of the imaginary proceeds, to the point at which the level is reached at which signifier and signified are stabilized in the delusional metaphor.[50]

Various papers on Schreber and allusions to him derive in varying degrees from Lacan's teachings following the publication of *Ecrits* in France, in particular those by G. Rosolato, O. Mannoni, and M. Mannoni.[51] An acclimatization of Lacan (with Jacques Derrida in the background) in Germany through Schreber occurs in S. M. Weber's long introduction to the Ullstein edition of the *Memoirs.*[52] Finally, I should like to mention two books, born in the same climate, that are not only important in themselves but indicative of a certain change of perspective as regards the judge, who by now often appears in them as the banner of an argument always threatening to be unfurled: *Anti-Oedipus* by Gilles Deleuze and Félix Guattari and *System and Structure* by Anthony Wilden. In the fascinating, seemingly frenzied, and crypto-academic structure of *Anti-Oedipus,* the judge's name pops up several times, invoked along with Antonin Artaud, Lewis Carroll, and Samuel Beckett among the patron saints of the revolt against the Oedipal triangle. Though without undertaking a detailed analysis of Schreber's *Memoirs,* Deleuze and Guattari are particularly anxious to counter any compulsory Freudian interpretation of the book, and they raise a serious rhetorical question against it: "How does one dare reduce to the paternal theme a delirium so rich, so differentiated, so 'divine' as the Judge's"?[53] Indeed, if Freud, in his paper on Schreber, felt the need to apologize for the "monotony of the solutions provided by psychoanalysis,"[54] the result of the supposed monotony of sexuality, it means that he too realized the disproportion in this case between the material to be interpreted and the outcome of the interpretation. "From the enormous political, social, and historical content of Schreber's delirium, *not one word is retained,* as though the libido did not bother itself with such things. Freud invokes only a sexual argument, which consists in bringing about the union of sexuality and the familial complex, and a mythological argument, which consists in positing the adequation of the productive force of the unconscious and the 'edifying forces of myths and religions.'"[55] If Schreber's role as a character in *Anti-Oedipus* thus seems clear, a permanent challenge to the history of psychoanalysis and in a way to our whole history, what still remains vague is just how Deleuze and Guattari propose to interpret the *Memoirs,* especially when one thinks of their attempts to draw a line, always a difficult task, between paranoiacs (a little too similar to Bad Guys) and schizophrenics (a little too similar to Good Guys) without analyzing, except occasionally, any passages from the judge's *Memoirs.*

Another critical acclimatization of Lacan and Derrida, within an Anglo-Saxon context set forth by Bateson, Laing, and MacKay, in addition to Marx and Fanon, appears in Anthony Wilden's essay. Here too Schreber's reasons can celebrate their victory over the reason of psychoanalysis. Wilden, after an acute review of Lacan's interpretation, goes on to present Schreber as a cultural hero hostile to the prevailing phallocentrism and thus wrongly assigned to the repressed homosexuality suggested by Freud. After observing that "the chief merit of Freud's interpretation lies not in its faithfulness to the text, but its *aesthetic* simplicity,"[56] and after criticizing Lacan's different phallocentric position, Wilden continues with a lively analysis of what Schreber, in his *Memoirs,* "is metacommunicating about the Manicheistic ideology of his culture, without being entirely capable of defining that metacommunication" (pp. 295–96). This partial incapacity does not, however, keep Wilden from recognizing that as a "social philosopher" and "psychologist-philosopher" (p. 295), Schreber provides an interpretation of himself that "transcends Freud's either/or 'homosexual' bias, Lacan's digitalized 'linguistic' bias, and Macalpine and Hunter's oppositional theory of 'sex identity'" (p. 298). For Wilden, the crucial point in Schreber's vision is the wish for emasculation—as transformation into a woman—which should, however, be connected not with homosexuality or the terror of castration but with a lucid wish to *recover the body,* to reacquire the condition of sensual pleasure, while abandoning the cage of obsessive dichotomies that govern our society. In this sense, writes Wilden, "Schreber deserves a place among the great mystics and the great utopian socialist philosophers" (p. 301). And with this generous posthumous recognition of Judge Schreber's qualities, I conclude this rapid journey through the twentieth-century psyche.[57]

II Accompaniment to the Reading of Stirner

Only a few years after its publication, Max Stirner's *Der Einzige und sein Eigentum*[1] had become "infamous."[2] In a way it still is: Just as we would search histories of literature in vain for a comprehensive treatment of certain great pornographic writings, so we will find nothing adequate about Stirner in histories of philosophy. And yet *Der Einzige* had and still has a great many readers, scattered all over the world and differing in level, quality, culture, and intentions. The most faithful, the ones who have constantly felt attracted to Stirner, are autodidacts and maniacs. Academics are less sure about the book, for they seem to fear a loss in status should they take an interest in Stirner. As Ettore Zoccoli had already observed in reference to "Germanic culture" (but his words can be applied to culture in general):

> Intellectual Germany, before lending an ear to a thinker's words, requires him to give proof and confirmation that before developing his ideas, he has not ignored the facts; that before thinking with his own mind, he has taken account of the thought of others; that, in short, before speaking out, he has deeply and calmly studied the book of science and life.
>
> Max Stirner in no way satisfied these requirements of Germanic culture. He was a solitary. He wrote only one book, in which facts are implied and hasty syntheses abound, abstract statements wholly exclude empirical investigation, and metaphysics wins out over historical reality.[3]

Dusting off these sentences from the turn of the century, one can see why Stirner is still held in suspicion. In his favor, however, is the fact that in

The German Ideology, Marx and Engels subjected *Der Einzige* to a criticism "as voluminous as the book itself," as Engels himself admitted.[4] So we need not hesitate to consider Stirner to be worth citing. The notes that follow, a fragment of an "annotated bibliography," seek to offer some justification for anyone wishing to read *Der Einzige* today.

PUBLICATION OF *DER EINZIGE*

On 1 October 1844, the teacher Johann Caspar Schmidt, the thirty-eight-year-old son of a flute carver, born in Bayreuth, left Madame Gropius's Lehr- und Erziehungs Anstalt für höhere Töchter, a private school for girls from good families, located at 4 Köllnischer Fischmarkt, Berlin. He had taught there since 1839. During the same month, the Leipzig publisher Otto Wigand, a leader in the political and philosophical radicalism of the period (he had published Arnold Ruge and Ludwig Feuerbach, as well as Lorenz von Stein's *Socialismus und Communismus des heutigen Frankreichs,* which already spoke of "class struggle" and which had made Mikhail Bakunin dream of factions and uprisings in the forbidden land of revolutions), published *Der Einzige und sein Eigentum* in an edition of one thousand copies. It was Schmidt's first book, and he called himself Stirner, as he already had in various articles appearing in newspapers and magazines over the previous three years. The date on the book's title page, however, was 1845.

On 26 October, Wigand submitted a copy of the book to the authorities of the Königlich-Sächsische Kreis-Direktion. Two days later, *Der Einzige* was banned because "not only in individual passages in this work are God, Christ, the Church, and religion in general treated with the most disrespectful blasphemy, but also the whole social order, the state, and the government are defined as things that ought no longer to exist, while lying, perjury, murder, and suicide are justified, and the right to ownership is denied." But on 2 November, Minister von Falkenstein allowed the book back into circulation. It could certainly not be said, he wrote, that reasons were lacking for the ban, "for in individual passages in this book not only is everything sacred to religion and the Church disparaged, but there even seems to be an attempt to undermine the religious and moral foundations of all social life, and to replace them with a system of the crudest egoism." Nevertheless the minister thought it more appropriate to lift the ban: "This book, both for its size (491 ottavo pages) and its language and tone, will not be able to make a harmful impression on persons among whom it might circulate. On the contrary, leaving aside whatever the author's true intentions may be, it seems likely to show in the harshest light the consequences not only of the philosophy here under discussion but also of the one applied by the author himself, thus revealing to what lamentable results it leads and the point where humanity would arrive were this philosophy to be introduced into practical life, a possibility moreover that is here assumed. One reads this book in large part as though it were ironical and loudly refuted itself." That is, beyond the "question of *juridical* grounds" for the ban, which the minister acknowledged, that of its "utility and real necessity in relation to the public weal" needed to be considered, and here there were doubts. Minister von Arnim disagreed and had the book banned on 7 November, although it continued to circulate freely outside Prussia. The Prussian High Council for Censorship was to decide on 26 August 1845 to confirm the ban definitely, since the book turned "most decidedly against religion and morality in general, against every social and political order," while furnishing the "justification for any crime."[5]

LETTERS ABOUT *DER EINZIGE*

Der Einzige had hardly been printed and the first review of it published when three letters about it by renowned writers and correspondents crossed one another in the mails. Engels to Marx, Feuerbach to his brother, Ruge to the publisher Fröbel: three immediate and almost feverish reactions to reading the book. And for different reasons, each of the writers confesses, albeit timorously, a certain enthusiasm for it. As the years pass, the destinies of the three writers increasingly diverge. But on one thing they will all be unwittingly in agreement: condemning Stirner and, above all, keeping silent about him.

Engels, in Barmen, letter of 19 November to Marx in Paris

You will have heard about Stirner's book *Der Einzige und sein Eigentum*, if you haven't already received it. Wigand sent me the page proofs, which I took with me to Cologne and then left with Hess. The principle of the noble Stirner—you know, that Schmidt from Berlin who wrote about the *Mystères de Paris* in Buhl's magazine—is Bentham's egoism, except in his case it is developed more consequentially in one sense, less consequentially in another. More consequentially because St[irner] places the individual as atheist above God or even as an ultimate entity, while Bentham still leaves God above everything in some cloudy distance, in short because St[irner] stands on the shoulders of German idealism, as an idealist fallen into materialism and empiricism, while Bentham is a simple empiricist. St[irner] is less consequential since he would like to avoid the reconstruction of society dissolved into atoms, as promoted by B[entham], but he doesn't succeed. This egoism is nothing but the essence of today's society made conscious, the last thing today's society can say against us, the whetted edge of every theory stirring within the current stupidity. But this is just why the thing is important, more important than the way Hess, for example, sees it. We shouldn't put it aside, but take advantage of it precisely as a perfect expression of the current lunacy and, *by overturning it,* continue to build on it. This egoism is so driven to the extreme, so crazy and at the same time so conscious of itself, that in its one-sidedness it can't hold up for a single moment, but must immediately collapse into communism.

But once the one-sidedness is defeated, condemned in the name of the total and the all-sided, Engels thought there was a substantial grain of truth to be found in *Der Einzige:*

> And here it's true in any case that we must first of all make a thing egoistically our own, before we can do something for it—that therefore in this sense, even apart from eventual material hopes, we are communists out of egoism too, and out of egoism we want to be *men,* not simple individuals. Or to put it another way: St[irner] is right to reject Feuerbach's "man," at least the one in *The Essence of Christianity*; F[euerbach]'s "man" is derived from God, F[euerbach] has arrived at "man" from God, and so "man" is crowned with a theological halo of abstraction. The true path for arriving at "man" is the opposite one. We must start with the ego, the empirical, corporeal individual, not to remain attached to it, as happens with St[irner], but to lift ourselves from there to "man."

A few lines later, Engels goes so far as to demand a further whetting of Stirner's egoism: "But if the flesh-and-blood individual is the true base, the true starting point for our 'man,' then obviously egoism—naturally not *only* Stirner's egoism of the intellect, but also the *egoism of the heart*— is the starting point for our love for mankind, otherwise it remains suspended in midair." And as usual, it is that very air that irritates Engels. His impatience with all "theoretical chatter" grows. Stirner appears as its last and most bewitching offspring: "Stirner's book shows once again how deeply rooted abstraction is in the Berlin essence. Among the *Freien* [Free Ones], St[irner] is obviously the one with the most talent, independence, and precision, but with all that he too turns his somersaults from idealistic abstraction to the materialistic kind without arriving at anything."[6] Each of these judgments should be kept in mind while reading the furious attack on Stirner in *The German Ideology,* where he is presented as "the most feeble and boorish member of that philosophical confraternity [the *Freien* group]."[7]

Feuerbach, letter to his brother, late 1844

Feuerbach's first impression is that *Der Einzige* is a work of "extreme intelligence and brilliance" and that it has "the truth of egoism—however eccentric, one-sided, and untrue—on its side." Feuerbach goes on to say that Stirner's attack on anthropology (that is, on himself) is based on a misunderstanding. For the rest, he considers him "the freest and most talented writer I have ever known."[8] So at first Feuerbach thought of answering Stirner in a light and friendly manner in an open letter that would begin: "'Inexpressible' and 'incomparable,' kind egoist: Like your writing itself, your judgment on me is truly 'incomparable' and 'unique.'" But caution and suspicion soon got the upper hand: In another letter to his brother, on 13 December, Feuerbach already suggests that "Stirner's attacks betray a certain vanity, as though he wanted to make a name for himself at the expense of mine." Finally, in the review he later wrote of *Der Einzige,* Feuerbach seems to be intimidated and chiefly concerned to protect himself. He does not care to make concessions to Stirner and defends the honor of his own doctrine. Then silence. In 1861, in a letter to Julius Duboc, he recalls that old controversy as having been settled for once and for all.[9]

Ruge, letters of November and December 1844 to the publisher Fröbel

Ruge's first mention of Stirner appears in a note sent in November from Paris, reporting that Heinrich Heine's poems and Stirner's *Der Einzige* are "the two most important publishing events of recent times." The audacities of the *"Deutsch-französischen Jahrbücher"* (meaning Marx) now seem "largely outdated." Ruge, at first a friend and defender of Marx and then his bitter enemy, combines praise for Stirner with gibes at Marx in another letter to Fröbel a few days later (6 December). Or rather, for the first time he *uses* Stirner as a stick with which to beat Marx:

> Marx professes communism, but he is a fanatic of egoism, and with a conscience even less apparent than Bauer's. Hypocritical egoism and the urge to play the genius, his posing as Christ, his rabbinism, priest and human victims (guillotine) reappear in the foreground. Atheist and communist fanaticism is still, in reality, the Christian kind. Sneering and gnashing his teeth, Marx, a new Babeuf, would send all those who stand in his way to slaughter. He *imagines* these festivities, since he cannot *observe* them. Fanatical egoism is loaded with sin and guilt, while egoism that is able freely to acknowledge itself as such is the pure kind, which does not live like a vampire on the blood of man, with the excuse of understanding him to be a "heretic," "inhuman monster," "publisher," "shopkeeper," "capitalist," "bourgeois" . . . and so on. A mean person's egoism is mean; a fanatic's is hypocritical, false, and eager for blood, an honest man's is honest. For *each* wants and should want himself, and to the extent that each *truly* wants this, the abuses of power are balanced. I have praised Stirner's (Schmidt's) book to you.

Later, in a letter to his mother on 17 December, Ruge again comments on Stirner:

> The book by Max Stirner (Schmidt), whom Ludwig may also know (he used to come in the evening to the Walburg tavern and sat in front of us), makes a strange impression. Many parts are absolutely masterful, and the whole effect can only be liberating. It is the first readable philosophy book to appear in Germany, and one might say that it marks the appearance of the first man entirely devoid of pedantry and old-fashioned attitudes, indeed entirely self-assured, were it not that his own fixation, which is that of uniqueness, makes him much less self-assured. Anyway it has given me great joy to see that disintegration has now reached this total form, whereby no one can swear with impunity on anything.[10]

But in this case too, enthusiasm for Stirner does not last long. In 1847, Ruge enthusiastically approves Kuno Fischer's violent attack on Stirner and the "modern sophists," and this marks the beginning of the habit of branding *Der Einzige* an infamous book. And when Stirner publishes his reply, Ruge promptly suggests to Fischer, "It would certainly be a good idea for you to answer Stirner with a letter and trip him up once more over his basic stupidity. These people get furious when someone shows them their lack of genius and wit, for in the end it all comes down to the fact that they are geniuses and other people are asses. . . . They confuse *theological* movement with *philosophical* movement or, in other words, the praxis of will with the praxis of freedom."[11]

FIRST REVIEWERS

The first mention of *Der Einzige* in the press appears in a brief item from Berlin in the *Mannheimer Abendzeitung* (12 November 1844). After identifying Stirner as a "close friend" of Bruno Bauer, the anonymous journalist goes on to explain that *Der Einzige* is nevertheless an all-out attack on the "outlook of 'humanitarian liberalism'" (namely, Bauer's). But what strikes the reviewer particularly is Stirner's excessiveness: "With this book the neo-Hegelian tendency is pushed to its extreme: the freedom of the subjective spirit is here sought in the individual's total lack of restraint, in every man's singularity, in egoism." Frightened as he is, the writer is still attracted to Stirner: "Even if this principle, as here presented, is still too one-sided and untenable, it is nevertheless based on true and correct intuitions, and if sifted properly, may turn out to be fruitful." This first reviewer was expecting a thrill from *Der Einzige,* and he got it. These were the culminating years of "critical criticism," criticism that "took no prisoners."[12] It seemed natural to expect something that made one say "this goes too far" while putting to rout all previous attacks as being too timid and cautious. And here it was. The last phase in the "process of decomposition of absolute spirit"[13] was being carried out. Having fired a few skyrockets, starting in 1842, with his short essays (the most important one, "The False Principle of Our Education," appeared in the *Rheinische Zeitung,* the paper to which Marx also contributed, and of which by an ominous coincidence he became editor-in-chief two days after Stirner had published his last article in it), the silent, aloof Stirner now came forward with a massive work that made only one claim: that of burying philosophy in general.

The first long, systematic reviews of *Der Einzige* came, in order of prestige, from Feuerbach,[14] Moses Hess,[15] and the Prussian officer and future general, Franz Szeliga.[16]

Stirner replied to them with an essay restating the ideas of *Der Einzige* and making them, if possible, even less tolerable.[17] The same thing happened two years later, when the renowned historian of philosophy Kuno Fischer vehemently attacked Stirner's book. The author's response (signed G. Edward) was again harsh and sarcastic.[18]

After *Der Einzige,* Stirner's public activity seems to come unraveled and virtually disappears. He publishes translations of Jean-Baptiste Say and Adam Smith, which were supposed to be accompanied by his own commentary. But in the first he reserves his comments for the second, and in the second the comments are unaccountably missing. In 1848, for the *Journal des österreichischen Lloyds,* he writes a series of terse political news reports, punctuated here and there by esoteric allusions, but he leaves them unsigned. Even the two volumes of the *Geschichte der Reaktion,* published in Berlin in 1852, conceal behind the inviting title a work of compilation, an anthology with a vague outline, in which Stirner appears mockingly in a few hidden lines. One can say that after *Der Einzige* and the two replies to his first critics, Stirner declared silence and, moreover, maintained it. And meanwhile, the world declared it on him. When Stirner died—because, it was said, a fly had infected a carbuncle that had erupted on his neck (the same kind of painful boil that for years tormented Marx on the anus while he was writing *Capital*)—only a few friends attended his funeral and few newspapers reported it. It was June 1856.

BERLIN

To understand the atmosphere of Berlin in the 1840s, that peculiar mixture of Absolute Spirit and shopkeeper mentality, stale respectability and noble aspirations, bigoted deference and "critical" anger, which Marx (impatient to emerge from it as from the ultimate ghetto) found so exasperating, there is not much use in following the writings of the various Young Hegelians close to Stirner, from the two Bauers to Feuerbach himself, except to note how little aware they all were of the realities of life. Every editorial hack in Paris around 1830 was somehow forced to be better informed. This naïveté greatly intensifies the clash that Stirner, by accepting the language of the whole idealist tradition in order to besmirch it, manages to produce between the sublime and the ridiculous.

But there is a still very lively book that tells us about the city at that moment—from its waiters and flaneurs to its police informers, bankers, whores, and artisans—and from a perspective well suited to its troubled spirit. It is Dronke's *Berlin,* in which Stirner makes a fleeting appearance:

The author re-evokes the disorderly scene of Stirner's wedding, with friends playing cards, the betrothed couple forgetting the rings, and Bruno Bauer saving the day by producing two brass ones from his purse. Such irreverence had made the city tremble. And it is Dronke who uses the word *Übermensch* in connection with Stirner and his friends: "Since they stand 'above' life, life will pursue its goal as best it can, paying no heed to the 'whims' of philosophical supermen."[19]

It was a fortuitous matching of Stirner with a word waiting to explode. Nor is this the only time such a thing happened: One of the first appearances of the term *Nihilismus* in Germany, following those in Jean Paul and Jacobi that Martin Heidegger pointed out, occurs in a note in connection with *Der Einzige* in Karl Rosenkranz's philosophical diary.[20]

THE GERMAN IDEOLOGY

To many people today, Stirner's name rings a bell only because Marx and Engels speak of him in *The German Ideology.* And indeed, to read *Der Einzige* side by side with the comments of Marx and Engels is still a mandatory ascetic exercise for all good readers of Stirner (and of Marx).

The text of *The German Ideology* had an extremely tortuous history. It begins with Engels's letter to Marx of 19 November 1844, devoted to an enthusiastic examination of *Der Einzige*—too enthusiastic and too ready to find acceptable and usable elements in the book. Marx, who with his usual political foresight had seen Stirner as the enemy from the beginning, must have answered Engels sharply. But unfortunately the letter has been lost. In reply, in January 1845, Engels makes amends by beating a retreat. A few months later, on returning from a summer trip to England, Marx and Engels decide to settle accounts with the Young Hegelians among whom they had come of age. A first reckoning, *The Holy Family,* had already appeared a few months earlier, but this new book, *The German Ideology,* was clearly centered on *one* adversary: Max Stirner. Its criticism of *Der Einzige* takes up 320 dense pages in the *Marx Engels Werke.* Stirner's statements are singled out line by line, attacked, and mauled. And the stratagems of this procedure will disclose not so much Stirner's secrets as those of Marx and Engels in one of their phases of irreversible transformation, the one in which Marx invents Marxism as a lingua franca. This shapeless manuscript is the laboratory from which every future International will emerge, especially the Third, even though *The German Ideology* teems with anti-Soviet sentiments.

Having finished their destructive book, which became the pattern for all future rooting out of petit bourgeois anarchists and individualists (meaning, with slight variations according to the moment, almost all human manifestations), Marx and Engels tried for several months to get the text published. But after arduous negotiations, funds eventually ran out. There were other figures in urgent need of destruction, Pierre Proudhon in particular (and Marx would ask Engels's permission to draw on various themes in *The German Ideology* for *The Poverty of Philosophy*). And so *The German Ideology* was stored away in the great attic of Marx's unpublished works, to be exposed to the "gnawing criticism of the mice," which damaged many pages. Marx did not seem to mind: As he was to note in the introduction to *A Contribution to the Critique of Political Economy* (1859), the manuscript had already fulfilled its main purpose, that of "clearing up the question to ourselves" on the part of its two authors. And that clarification had been both too drastic and too deep-seated to be made public.

Engels, too, though he wavered from time to time, must have thought something similar. In 1883, he proposed to Eduard Bernstein that the manuscript of *The German Ideology* be published in installments as a supplement in *Der Sozialdemokrat,* and he called the text "the most insolent thing that has ever been written in the German language."[21] But he quickly gave up the idea because, according to Bernstein, he feared the text would offend certain right-wing Social Democrats.[22] As for Stirner, Engels was to give vent to a final illuminating judgment on him, explaining in retrospect the political reasons for *The German Ideology* in quite different and much more convincing terms than those set forth by Marx and himself in their text: "Stirner has experienced a rebirth through Bakunin, who moreover was also in Berlin at that time and was seated in front of me, with four or five other Russians, at Werder's course on logic (it was 1842–1843). Proudhon's innocuous, and only etymological, anarchy (that is, absence of a state authority) would never have led to the anarchist doctrines of today if Bakunin had not poured into them a good dose of Stirnerian 'rebellion.' As a result, anarchists have likewise become 'egoists,' such egoists that you can't find two of them able to get along with each other."[23] This is the private counterpoint to the brief public allusion to Stirner that Engels had made the previous year: "And at the end came Stirner, the prophet of present-day anarchism—Bakunin took a lot from him—and over sovereign 'self-awareness' he erected his sovereign unique 'I.'"[24]

The *Antistirner,* as the book attacking Stirner that bursts from the framework of *The German Ideology* might rightly be called, was in the end published after the deaths of both Marx and Engels. In 1903–4, Bernstein came out with a partial edition of it under the title *Der "Heilige Max."* Until then, it had not been known that Stirner was the adversary Marx and Engels had spent hundreds of pages reviling. This helps to explain why various socialist theorists and scholars in the 1890s still continued to show an obvious sympathy for Stirner.[25]

THE PROFESSOR

So far, *Der Einzige* had found readers only among enlightened left-wing intellectuals, including Hegelian ancestors of every sort of well-meaning radicalism, solicitous for Humanity, Freedom, Progress, and so on. As confirmation there is the reply—forceful, but "between civilized people"—that the worthy Friedmund, son of Bettina von Arnim, attempted to make to Stirner (in an article that many attributed to his mother).[26] Anyway, Marx and Engels had also abused Stirner, while still pretending to place him inside the circle of well-meaning Good Guys (Feuerbach, Bruno Bauer, et al.). The criminal aspect of the book was excused as a somewhat daring outburst. They kept silent about the sudden fits of brutality that disrupt the continuity of the text. But the age of the "sense of history" was impending, and it was to squeeze philosophy into the mold of the history of philosophy, striking out that extreme aspect belonging to thinking itself that would be revived only with Nietzsche's "magic of the extreme." The revenge carried out by the "sense of history" on Stirner initially took the exemplary name of Kuno Fischer. As the admirable Fritz Mauthner remarks, "It is already proof of Stirner's importance that a man born old, born his Excellency, like Professor Kuno Fischer should come a cropper with him, as he would with Schopenhauer and in the end with Nietzsche."[27]

Even before Fischer began publishing his historical manual of modern philosophy, whose purpose was to set in order the threatening swirl of thought of previous decades, a pamphlet attacking Stirner had already announced his intention to remove any indecent intruder from that gradual, carefully evolving ascent that the history of thought *ought* to be if it really wished to culminate, as it had demonstrated, in the incompatible marriage of Hegel and Darwin. And yet Fischer still treated Stirner's case with a certain respect. His essay, undoubtedly agile in its execution, is read today primarily because certain expressions have over time assumed an esoteric significance of which Fischer does not seem to have been aware. I will cite only these: Fischer sees Stirner's book as an attempt at a coup d'état: "The sophistic autonomy of the subject against the hierarchical autonomy of thought—what else is this if not a change of dynasty, a July Revolution of thought?"[28] As for "sophistry," it seems to him to be the "supreme enemy" of thought, the "diabolical principle belonging to it" (p. 277), and therefore a shadow that cannot be eliminated and now threatens to swallow the very body of thought. Hegel's philosophy, that "pantheon of all systems" (p. 280), had produced its own sophistic double, like an allergic reaction that was now pursuing and transfixing thought in every one of its recesses: "It is the reaction of the *random subject* against the free subject, of the *nonphilosophical* personality against the *philosophical* one, of *brutality* against *culture*" (p. 280). The "struggle against culture," a creature hatched by the didactic century par excellence, was thus about to raise its ugly little head in the assembly of minds: Here, already, was the specter of the Tuileries in flames, which would give Nietzsche nightmares (and Fischer was writing on the threshold of '48)! Fischer was the first, albeit cautiously, to sniff the barbarism in Stirner.

Not only that, but he spotted its origin in the highest and most subtle articulation attained by thought: that perennial babble between Substance and Subject that had been deposited in novelistic form in Hegel's *Phenomenology of Mind*. Stirner's demon operated by crushing that "dialectical difference," so that "the subject, and precisely that individual, atomistic one, became the destiny of substance," abandoning itself to "its own enjoyment in the destruction of all the powers of substance, all prevailing thoughts,"[29] and transforming itself into *"pure negativity."* (Let us too abandon ourselves to savoring everything these expressions can be said to have exuded.) For history, Stirner would have nothing to offer but the "text of a headstone" (p. 281). What Hegel had foretold was therefore not the *mysterium coniunctionis* between Subject and Substance but the destructive work of purity: "Pure self-awareness is in truth the annihilation of substance" (p. 286). Now a movement begins "from nothing to nothing, with no points of support" (p. 287).

These quotations all refer to Stirner but are taken from the first part of Fischer's pamphlet, which is devoted as well to the usual and more noble purveyors of the warning signs of disaster (Feuerbach, the Bauers, and so on). When he comes to deal directly with *Der Einzige,* Fischer's argument turns banal, while at the same time aiming to debase the phantom of Stirner and expel it from philosophy. But even here presentiments are not lacking: "To shatter men egoistically into brutal atoms simply means, in truth, to seek *a sheepdog* for them [here it is Hitler who begins to loom, still euphemistically], and whoever starts beating others with a stick will know very well that the *gendarme* is not far away."[30] In his prolix explanation of *Der Einzige,* Fischer dwells primarily on the subject's new face, unveiled by Stirner's "monomania": "Sophistry [read: Stirner] has named the crude, brutal individual as successor to the spirit" (p. 309). The historian would like to maintain to the last a superior irony in the face of this degenerate thinking. But in the end it does not hold up: The sinister laughter that Stirner attributes to the ego exasperates him, and then he cannot resist a deprecation that betrays his solemn vacuity: "Laughter is an act that in general is only possible for the spirit; only the complete, *rational* subject, identical with the essence of the world, can really *laugh;* laughter is the dissolution of egoism and the upheaval of the individual; with it one is irrevocably consigned to the world of spirits" (p. 311). With this truly excessive claim that one can laugh only from an academic chair, Fischer slammed the door of the boarding school behind the teacher Max Stirner, who, henceforth considered unworthy to mingle with philosophers in the café, was consigned to debtors' prison, among criminals, swindlers, and other ragged specimens of life and the spirit. And yet his laughter has never ceased.

Stirner's reply to Fischer is the final coda of words to come from the circle around *Der Einzige.* It appeared in *Die Epigonen* and was signed "G. Edward," but there is little doubt that the author was Stirner himself. The tone is slightly resentful, less free than in previous replies. Here Stirner employs the usual technique, already used by Fischer as well, of juxtaposing quotations in order to demonstrate their incongruence. It is a technique without luster in this case, though Stirner once again shows admirable skill in his passages of direct and brutal sarcasm. There is not much to point to in these pages, except a few essential lines, Stirner's credo and true farewell:

> I wish only to be myself; I despise nature, men, and their laws, human so-
> ciety and its love, and break off every general relation with it, even that of
> language. To all the claims of your duty, to all the designations of your cate-
> gorical judgment, I oppose the "ataraxia" of my ego; and I already make a
> concession by making use of language; I am the "unspeakable"; "I only
> show myself." And do I not perhaps have, with the terrorism of my ego,
> which rejects everything human, as much reason as you with your humani-
> tarian terrorism, which immediately marks me as an "inhuman monster"
> if I commit something against your catechism, if I do not let myself be
> disturbed in my enjoyment of myself?[31]

Fischer must have taken these words as confirmation of his adversary's lack of decency. The proposal to consign him to the dregs of humanity shines through his counterreply. He speaks of the "Saint Vitus dance of a sophist whose every movement betrays absurdity and every leap stupidity."[32] With pointer in hand, Fischer distinguishes (ah, the inexhaustible repeti-tiveness of the West!) between the "laws of ethical liberty" and the "law-less will that dissolves the limits of spiritual self-determination in the empty zero of their abstract dialectics." There is no point asking on which side Stirner stands, and Fischer adds that he himself finds it "barbaric to consider spiritual forms with such mortal fear" (p. 153), as Stirner indeed does. Here the warning purpose of Fischer's pamphlet is clear: To attack Stirner means to defend oneself from the "reaction, not of doctrinaires, but of wicked, uncouth, brutal subjects against the principles of liberty and their fulfillment in science, art, and politics" (p. 154). The adversary's change of category, from philosopher to criminal, is here made plain. Fischer seems to want to apologize for having suggested that Stirner in some way belonged to history, albeit the history of heresy: "I do not gen-erally speak of heretics, and if I did, I would not grant a man like Stirner the honor of considering him in this historical category" (p. 154). The im-ages, as always more revealing than the concepts, verge rapidly toward the savage: "The apparent strength of these pirates [Stirner and the so-called sophists] lies in quite another sphere than thought, they behave toward their premises as do *predatory states with civilized states*" (p. 156). Con-fronted with this *"barbarous dogmatism,"* one must say it "has nothing in common with the name of philosophy and criticism" (p. 156). And now finally comes the decree of expulsion: "It has been said that Stirner would be the end point of German philosophy. . . . I would say that Stirner stands *at the corner (an der Ecke)* of German philosophy," accompanied by the final donnish witticism: the play on words between "to stand at the corner" *(an der Ecke stehen)* and the one who stands at the corner (*der Eckensteher,* meaning "corner boy"). Thus Fischer ends his subtle polemics by calling Stirner a "street loafer." Actually it would have been simpler to begin that way. But by now it seemed clear that the philosopher of the down-and-out was merely a philosophizing bum. Better to forget about him, and they did so for forty years.

STIRNER IN RUSSIA

Russia is the country where Stirner found the most sympathetic soil for his ideas. The most mutually antagonistic figures of the 1840s reacted to *Der Einzige* promptly and with fervor: Vissarion Belinsky, Aleksey Khomyakov, Bakunin, Fyodor Dostoyevsky, Aleksandr Herzen (who with impassioned eloquence takes up Stirnerian themes in *From the Other Shore,* though he does not mention Stirner by name until 1858). When one thinks of the eagerness with which all German philosophical texts were read in those years,[33] and if one also remembers that this was just when the nihilist cloud was beginning to thicken, it is not hard to see Stirner in an unfaithful, ambiguous, Russian version, which suits him much better than the inflated language of Hegel's German heirs. Then one need only open to any page of Dostoyevsky's *Notes from Underground,* where the anonymous voice that speaks (and here too we are dealing with a "collegiate assessor") sounds immediately like Stirner (in Stirner, it is the underground of philosophy that speaks), or follow the destinies of Raskolnikov, Kirillov, or Ivan Karamazov—all characters who in one way or another have been touched by Stirner's demon. It seems only right that the first to perceive the Stirner phenomenon clearly should be a Russian, and one certainly not a devotee of the shining Western Enlightenment but, rather, no less than the most influential theologian of the Slavophiles, Aleksey Khomyakov. In connection with *Der Einzige,* he observed,

> [Here is a work that] has a historical significance not only unnoticed by
> the critics, but which—one must assume—went unobserved by the author
> himself: that of the most total and final protest of spiritual liberty against

every arbitrary shackle imposed from outside. It is a soul's cry for the immoral truth, but immoral only because devoid of all moral support, a soul tirelessly though unconsciously engaged in proclaiming the possibility of submitting to a principle of which it has become conscious and in which it believed, rising up with indignation and hatred against the daily practices of Western "systematizers," who do not believe but insist on faith, arbitrarily create bonds, and expect others to adjust to them humbly. Contemporary history is a living commentary to Max Stirner, an actual revolt of life, in its simplicity, against the bookish lucubrations that planned to delude it with the ghosts of spiritual principles created artificially, where the spiritual principles by which it once really lived now no longer exist.[34]

STIRNER REDISCOVERED

After 1848, Stirner's name appears less and less frequently. He takes his place among those many obscure figures who appeared at a moment—the *Vormärz* of the subversive Young Hegelians, though they were often scared by their own audacity—that Germany, avid and productive, would have liked to put aside. In 1866, however, Stirner was again mentioned in two books on the history of thought that were destined to have considerable influence: *Grundriss der Geschichte der Philosophie,* by Johann Eduard Erdmann (all of paragraph 341,4) and *Geschichte des Materialismus,* by Friedrich Albert Lange. And in 1869, Eduard von Hartmann was to discuss Stirner's ideas in his most ambitious work, calling *Der Einzige* "a book that should be read by anyone interested in practical philosophy."[35] But the decisive words would be Lange's, when he speaks of *Der Einzige* as "by and large the most extreme work we know."[36] Years later, a young Scotsman, John Henry Mackay, found himself in the British Museum with Lange's book in his hands, and hit upon Stirner's words. The curiosity they aroused would soon be transformed into devotion: "After almost half a century, Stirner finds in Mackay his first and most faithful evangelist."[37] Thus we witness the formation of one of the many paradoxes surrounding Stirner: the creation around this most impious figure of a climate of sanctimonious, uncritical, and fatuous veneration. For years, Mackay would swoop down on the traces of Stirner's life, guided by a dubious principle: "Is it possible that a life of such greatness was not also rich in great outer experiences?" Well, yes. Thus, whether because of the biographer's ineptitude or because of a certain mockingly elusive quality that we find in every manifestation of Stirner, the results were rather meager. And the more uncertain the signs were, the more Mackay gave vent to a pompous and emotional glorification, which also aimed to conceal the depressing reality of his hero's life. Mackay's book is, however, the first and only biography of Stirner to date.[38] It is therefore an indispensable reference, not only for the material it contains (fairly scant, but we do not have much more) but as a monument of that cult of Stirner, heedless and hugely ridiculous, that would soon give birth to the figure of the "Stirnerian," a variation of the "anarchic individualist."[39]

BIOGRAPHY

The most singular element that emerges from Mackay's biographical research is the dearth of material: All the manuscripts had been lost, almost all the people who had known Stirner were dead or vanished or unapproachable, and there were no surviving letters and no pictures of him (the only one extant was sketched from memory forty years after Stirner's death by the hand of his enemy Engels). His signature on a document has been unearthed with some difficulty. What little we know about his life speaks of a student from the provinces who arrives in Berlin just in time to hear a few lectures by Hegel and Friedrich Schleiermacher; he passes, not exactly brilliantly, the exams for becoming a teacher in the state gymnasiums (where he will never be appointed); he frequents the group known as *Die Freien* and becomes a teacher in a private school for girls. There are even fewer details of his later years: poverty, furnished rooms, debtors' prison (twice), the humiliation of publishing an appeal in the *Vossische Zeitung* begging for a loan, his obscure death. Stirner's new worshippers were to find very few relics. The ones collected year after year by Mackay and offered in vain to the authorities in Berlin were bought in 1925 for a modest sum by the Marx-Engels Institute (later the Institute for Marxism-Leninism) in Moscow, in whose department of forbidden books they are still—presumably—stored. In this instance, at least, the Soviets were undeniably faithful to Marx and Engels.

STIRNER AND NIETZSCHE

Stirner was rediscovered in the 1890s in the wake of Nietzsche's sudden rise to fame. And a dispute soon developed that would continue for years.

There are those who say that Nietzsche derived many, too many, of his ideas from Stirner without ever acknowledging him. Others deny that Nietzsche ever read Stirner (this was the position taken by his sister, Elisabeth, and accordingly by the Nietzsche Archive). Still others, like Franz Overbeck, were plagued by doubts and uncertainties, but it was he who ended by collecting the decisive proofs: He consulted the list of books borrowed from the library of the University of Basel and discovered that in 1874 *Der Einzige* had been read by Nietzsche's favorite disciple of the moment, Adolf Baumgartner. He then sought confirmation from Baumgartner, who remembered very well having read the book at Nietzsche's insistent suggestion. And he even remembered a few words about *Der Einzige:* "Nothing more daring and consequential has been conceived after Hobbes." Baumgartner's testimony was later augmented by Ida Overbeck, who remembered two conversations in which Nietzsche mentioned Stirner to her with a kind of grim exaltation, saying also that he should not talk about him because one day he would be accused of plagiarism. After reaching a disagreeable level of bitterness (it would be one topic raised by Elisabeth in her various vendettas against the Overbecks), the controversy faded away with time. Since then, the question of the connection between Nietzsche and Stirner has never been put forward in all its implications, though they are immense. Scholars have mostly been content to refer only briefly to this turn-of-the-century controversy. As an introduction to this intricate matter one might read: Robert Schellwien, *Stirner und Nietzsche* (Leipzig, 1892); a silly book, but the first to put the two writers on the same level as "consequential prophets of individualism." Ola Hansson, *Seher und Deuter* (Berlin, 1894), pp. 92–136; (here Stirner is included among the favored seers of the moment, in the elect and composite company of Edgar Allan Poe, Arnold Böcklin, and Paul Bourget; as for Nietzsche, Hansson writes that Stirner was his "John the Baptist." C. A. Bernoulli, *Overbeck und Nietzsche* (Jena, 1908); this is by far the most important source; it reports the statements by Franz and Ida Overbeck and offers an account of the controversy. R. F. Krummel, *Nietzsche und der deutsche Geist* (Berlin, 1974); from this valuable annotated bibliography of writings about Nietzsche up to the year 1900, one can reconstruct the intertwining of Stirner's fortunes with Nietzsche's in the 1890s, leading to the formation of two factions in certain German cultural circles of the time, both bursting with excessive claims: one that sees Stirner as the shadow of Nietzsche; the other, Nietzsche as the shadow of

Stirner. Ernest Seillière, *Apollon oder Dionysos?* (Berlin, 1906); one of the most unusual books on the Nietzsche of those years, it treats in detail the Nietzsche-Stirner connection and is the first to list a series of textual parallels that are most certainly convincing, pp. 191–200. Albert Lévy, *Stirner et Nietzsche* (Paris, 1904); primarily interesting for its reconstruction of Nietzsche's reading in the Basel period, based on the books he borrowed from the university library. C. P. Janz, *Friedrich Nietzsche,* vol. 3 (Munich, 1979), pp. 212–13, 343–45; this is the fullest biography of Nietzsche, but on the Nietzsche-Stirner connection it lacks sufficient documentation and contains errors.

STIRNER STRIKES AGAIN

H. G. Helms's book includes an excellent Stirner bibliography (no one had attempted one before).[40] This work, which purports to be a version of *The German Ideology* updated to the multinational corporations of our day and twice as long as the original (which was already more than long enough), is marked by its shrill and nagging tone and its frantic persistence in tracing all the evils of the world back to Stirner: from Nazism to German television, homosexuality, revisionism, the cult of vacations and the cult of Being, *Kitsch,* imperialism, counterrevolution, nudist colonies, the free market, and anthroposophy. All these wicked phenomena, to pursue the thread of Helms's argument, are the more or less direct consequence of some publication or translation or glorification of *Der Einzige,* a book that can be said to embody (even if those to whom it was actually addressed seem unaware of it) that "middle-class" ideology that is, moreover, the favored instrument for the intrigues of capitalism. So far the thesis is merely an adaptation of *The German Ideology.* But it had never occurred to anyone before Helms to establish certain connections, albeit such obvious ones: for example, the triumph of the counterrevolution in Russia after 1905 coincided with the appearance of no fewer than three translations of *Der Einzige* between 1906 and 1910. Helms is a master at dwelling thoughtfully on things like this, and also at demonstrating that all that is needed to explain something is the wish to explain. Let us watch him in action: "The fact that in the counterrevolutionary period *Der Einzige,* a text that until that moment had been officially undesirable, should be hurled so profusely at Russian minds attested both the need for this ideology and the basic agreement between the ruling counterrevolutionary circles and a considerable portion of those being ruled" (p. 351). So everything is clear. Put any kind of obscure plot into Helms's hands, and he will shortly jolt you with the cry: *"Cherchez Stirner!"* But luckily, not everyone in the world is helpless in the face of deception. There are still "the Marxists," observes Helms, weary but unbowed toward the end of his labors, and "the Marxists seem to have begun to perceive and localize the source of the infection" (p. 495)—which would obviously be Stirner in all his "present danger" (p. 495). The word has finally been spoken.

And speaking of dangers, one is obliged to offer some observations that can also be applied to Nietzsche. It is time to relinquish such official defenses (that they are now universally accepted only testifies to their inadequacy) as "Nietzsche was used by the Nazis only because his wicked sister Elisabeth manipulated and falsified his texts." No; for those who teach "how to philosophize with a hammer" (Stirner was the first to dare to do so, suggested Mauthner—and Marx the second, one might add), these dreadful misadventures are in a sense prepared from the start. Those who practice *experimental philosophy* must expect that abominable people will one day experiment with this same philosophy. And when the veil of aversion dictated by worthy sentiments is lifted—if it ever is—from the image of Nazism and fascism, it will have to be noted that those two phenomena are clear instances of that compulsion to experiment, not only on nature but on ourselves, that is the mark of the century in all its manifestations, whether Soviet, Yankee, Chinese, or finally, Old World. It would only be surprising, very surprising—and special research groups could be organized to explain the phenomenon—if Nietzsche and Stirner had *not* been used by the Nazis.

Helms has thus done a praiseworthy job in collecting the many picturesque instances of degeneration for which Stirner is responsible, somewhat the way a "Marxist" might compile a record of Soviet degeneration. With this difference: whereas in the latter case one hopes to return to a wholesome body of Leninist and Marxian doctrine, in the case of Stirner the degeneration is openly present from the beginning. Stirner *is* degeneration. But here the paths diverge: For a surgeon like Helms, who has unassailable convictions on wholesomeness and all the rest, all that is needed is to operate, with sharp, cruel instruments, to extirpate the infected flesh while there is still time. For those who preserve a residue of curiosity about thought, it will be important instead to investigate the meaning of that majestic degeneration that Stirner placed at the empty heart of his work. What degenerates, in fact, is emptiness itself, operative nothingness, which is also the element in which our everyday life unfolds.

Propelled by hatred, Helms has in any case succeeded in assembling an overflowing wealth of material, which he then ruins, as is his wont, "for the good of the cause." The pathetic testimony of a certain European left, which has always lived (like, one might say, Mme de Cambremer) in the nightmare of never being advanced enough and in perennial expectation of being once and for all debauched, this massive and rancorous work is still undeniably useful, indeed *the* most useful work on Stirner. One should be grateful not only for its bibliographical soundings, especially in the muddy waters of pre-Nazi Germany, but also because here the hasty reader will be able to find a nearly complete collection of the many linguistic and psychical stereotypes ranging from the Third International to the sanctimonious left, here presented—and it is no small feat—in an overwrought focus that makes them a bit more attractive compared to their more plainly ugly manifestations.

ANARCHIC COMMUNISM

Stirnerian currents also appear in the history of the ill-fated Bavarian Soviet, but this time in the form of that "anarchic communism" with which Erich Mühsam countered, with enlightened naïveté, the obtuse naïveté of the individualistic anarchists. Mühsam was an exemplary figure of the period. After preaching the recovery of society's dregs by the revolution (criminals, prostitutes, and tramps seemed to him psychologically more interesting than workmen seated at their benches) and discovering Ascona and Monte Verità (a sacred site for all "alternative and underground culture," which blossomed there in grandiosely esoteric and ridiculous circumstances before becoming known exoterically and worldwide, still ridiculous but no longer grandiose), Mühsam was imprisoned, first by the Social Democrats and then by the Nazis, who tortured him to death.[41] One can immediately recognize in him the very image of the intellectual loathed and despised by the right. Impatient with all discipline, chaotic, and given to wild and exuberant daydreaming, divided between utopia and loose living,[42] he was, however, no less loathed by every law-

and-order leftist. In Munich, he worked side by side with an eminent figure on that political stage, Gustav Landauer, a leader of the Bavarian
Soviet who was brutally killed by soldiers. Landauer, who some years before had helped Mauthner in his research, was also imbued with Stirner's
ideas, though he seldom mentioned him. But some of his youthful writings were even signed "Caspar Schmidt." And Landauer's right-hand
man, at the time of the Bavarian Soviet, was a provincial actor who went
by the name of Ret Marut. Thanks to Rolf Recknagel's meticulous research,[43] today we can recognize this man as B. Traven, author of *The
Death Ship* and *The Treasure of the Sierra Madre.* Between 1917 and 1919
(and then until 1921, under increasingly difficult clandestine conditions)
Marut published *Der Ziegelbrenner,* a magazine edited wholly by himself.
Graphically (and also in certain of his themes, such as an overwhelming
hatred for the press), it took its inspiration from Karl Kraus's *Die Fackel,*
but the breeze that blows through it is pure Stirner. Before vanishing completely into the anonymity of multiple aliases, thus becoming the *only* fully
Stirnerian figure so far, Marut-Traven gave expression to his thoughts and
dreams, all orbiting around Stirner, in the frenzied pages of his magazine.
Meanwhile, he helped Landauer in the stormy government of the Bavarian Soviet, still the single, hapless attempt at power by "anarchic communism." (There is a piercing irony in the fact that his only verified assign-
ment was that of press censor.) With the collapse of the Bavarian Soviet,
lynching and death were also in store for Marut-Traven, but he was able
to escape—how, we do not know, for we know almost nothing about
him. Shortly thereafter, in Mexico, he seems to have begun the elusive life
of a man with many names but whose real name we still do not know.

CLANDESTINE ENCOUNTERS

The greatest affinity with Stirner can be detected in readers who seldom or
never name him. Aside from Nietzsche, who never wrote Stirner's name,
and Marx, who wrote about him *only* in a work he never published, these
affinities can be found in the most incongruous places, and even more
often in the cinema than in books. The "unfathomable" characters of
Orson Welles tell us more about Stirner than whole bookshelves of studies
on the Young Hegelians. And Stirner's anomie is a hidden benchmark to
which one constellation in the Hollywood zodiac unwittingly refers: the

"lawless" character forced to become a "law unto himself" (in accordance with an epistemological paradox that lies at the base of *Der Einzige*). But Stirner also watches over the marvelous ravings of Nagel in Knut Hamsun's *Mysteries*. And in general all of Hamsun, his desperate and criminal variety of uprooted vagabondage, is incomprehensible without Stirner. And who can be the guardian angel behind the stubborn, irrational adventures of the hobo who rides the rails, as told by Jack London in *The Road,* if not Stirner, the metaphysician of tramps? (In this case, great literature unloved by professors, that of London and Traven, does well in the movies, in the more than befitting adaptation of the hobo's adventures that Robert Aldrich—hats off!—has given us with *The Emperor of the North.*)

PHILOSOPHY OF EXISTENCE

It seems obvious that there is a connection between Stirner and various so-called existential philosophies. Karl Löwith had already placed Stirner alongside Søren Kierkegaard in a plainly existential context,[44] and even Martin Buber was to combine Kierkegaard *and* Stirner in a laborious examination of the question of the "individual."[45] Then along came Juliette Gréco, and in the devastated Europe of 1945 people murmured about existentialism and pointed out the new guru, Jean-Paul Sartre. But in the search for ancestors, Herbert Read quickly thought of Max Stirner, whom he called one of the most existentialist of past philosophers, and he observed that whole pages of *Der Einzige* could be read as anticipations of Sartre.[46] And Günther Anders, reflecting on the inevitable existential rebirth from the ruins of war, had already tried to trace early Heidegger back to Stirner.[47] As for Albert Camus, his critique of Stirner, though noble, neglects to mention the vital impulse that many of his own characters received from him.[48]

But many others would also try to go back "to the fount." Among them, Henri Arvon, with his book that claims—true, more in the title than in the text—that Stirner was the ancestor of existentialism.[49] Today the subject is commonplace: One finds it taken up, for example, in the book by R. W. K. Patterson,[50] who seeks to juxtapose Stirner with philosophers (Nietzsche and Kierkegaard, as usual) and writers (the masters of decadence, those who might have said to themselves, *"Le Néant fut ma Béatrice"* [Nothingness was my Beatrice], the anagogic version of the first and last Stirnerian statement: "I have founded my cause on nothing").

PSYCHOLOGY

From the idealistic terminology of *Der Einzige,* derided and then abandoned as wreckage, it is easy to go back for revelation to a cloud of psychological aberration. But psychiatrists and psychoanalysts have rarely
ventured to do so. Ernst Schultze examines a case of Stirnerian paranoia.[51] It involves a young woman who stole, disrobed in public, and
committed other indecent acts because she was convinced that *any*
manifestation of her will was lawful. The psychiatrist shrewdly places
some of her assertions side by side with scattered ones by Stirner in
Der Einzige. But the argument does not go beyond this obvious comparison, thus stopping precisely where it should have begun. The only
renowned psychiatrist to take account of Stirnerian *données* in his research is Ludwig Binswanger.[52] But here, once again, we come back to
that "philosophy of existence" of which Binswanger represents a kind of
psychiatric extension.

Quite different, however, is the *psychological* potential of Stirner's
quest. It was Oskar Panizza, another "damned soul," not a philosopher
but a literary man driven by a physiological affinity, who noted it. In
"Der Illusionismus und die Rettung der Persönlichkeit,"[53] a pamphlet of
1895 dedicated "to the memory of Max Stirner," Panizza carries to its ultimate conclusions—and with the same inexorable and irresponsible
acumen with which, two years earlier, he had demonstrated "the immacu-
late conception of the popes"—the idea of the *spectral* nature of thought
as we find it in *Der Einzige.* After a few initial indulgent jokes on the
positivism of the time, which had lethal psychiatric consequences by
continuing to treat the psyche as a secretion, Panizza launches into his
bristling paradoxes. By swift transitions, he deduces from Stirner's premises an image of the world as perpetual hallucination, proof of a radical il-
lusionism that could easily move in the direction of certain masters of
Buddhist epistemology. But Panizza is a coastal smuggler of philosophy
and prefers to navigate in psychical inlets of the West that will soon be
taken over by psychoanalysis. In any case, his conclusion is perfectly
Stirnerian: "If we do not destroy thought, thought destroys us" (p. 169).
This brief pamphlet, so impudent toward science, can be read as a glorious contribution to that science of "psychical coercion" (p. 176) then
looming on the horizon.

TRANSLATIONS

The first country to translate *Der Einzige* was France. And the text lands right in the most lively literary arena of those years, between symbolism and anarchy. The first extracts appeared in the *Mercure de France* and were translated by Henri Albert, who was also Nietzsche's translator. Then, in 1900, two translations, one by Reclaire, the other by Lasvignes, were published, respectively, by Stock and Éditions de la Revue Blanche, the latter being another center—together with the *Mercure*—where the best literature of those years came together. Stirner thus appears in France in an intermediate place among Marcel Schwob, Félix Fénéon, Alfred Jarry, and Stéphane Mallarmé. Gustave Kahn was one of the first in France to write about Stirner. And André Gide would sigh over the differences between Stirner and Nietzsche, while obviously leaning toward Nietzsche.

The Italian climate was quite different. Again, there were two translations: One in 1902, published by Bocca, was extensively cut and preceded by an introduction by Ettore Zoccoli, who was also the translator. Worried about the favorable reception that Stirner's "criminal individualism" was encountering, Zoccoli outlines the vicissitudes of *Der Einzige* in some detail, and in particular, in accordance with the tendency of the time, he draws a comparison between Stirner's ideas and those of other anarchist leaders. The other Italian edition, whose translator is not named, did not appear until 1911, when it was published by the Libreria Editrice Sociale. Meantime, Zoccoli, who had already published a short book on Stirner and American anarchism,[54] devoted the first chapter of his more ambitious work to him.[55] This book, immediately translated into Russian and German, was one of the principal channels through which Stirner's name was spread in Italy.

SPECULATION IN A PROVINCIAL ITALY

Stirner was received in Italy in much the same way that Nietzsche had once been: with a total inability to grasp the kernel of his thought and with conspicuous effects instead on the attitudes, customs, and language gestures of a provincial mind set that still flourishes today. Benito Mussolini himself was part of it. Though physiologically unsuited for the role, he would have liked to become *"ein echter Deutsch,"* an "authentic Germany," and early on had placed Stirner among the "Dolomites of thought," next to

"Nietzsche, Goethe, Schiller, Montaigne, Cervantes, and so on."[56] And every so often, he would remember to toss out the name of Stirner, as in a 1914 article in *Avanti!,* in which he responds to "Comrade Bordiga" on the subject of neutrality and allows himself a rapid aside after criticizing the vision of "a socialism totally extraneous and refractory to the play of environmental influences." Here, Stirner fleetingly reappears in an obvious reference: "A marvelous but absurd construction. Even the absurd can be marvelous. We are thinking of Stirner's 'ego.'"[57] On one occasion, Mussolini would be driven to proclaim, "Leave the field free to the elementary forces of individuals, because no other human reality exists outside the individual! Why not bring back Stirner?"[58] But this was in an article of 1919, in the *Popolo d'Italia,* skillfully tuned to the mood of the moment.

An official philosopher of fascism like Paolo Orano will speak quite differently in the glow of the Empire (and from the start he had condemned Marx and Stirner as "the apostles of the philosophic left," representing in his view "the crowd and the den" [of terrorists]). The paragraph devoted to Stirner in his *summa* is entitled "Political Poison."[59] It singles out as a terrible danger the kind of thinking that "has found its glacial formulation in Max Stirner's *Der Einzige und sein Eigenthum*" (p. 255), the driving edge of a "narcissism of ideas" that fortunately "has nothing in common with the raw, concise, resolute realism of the Blackshirts" (p. 269). He still felt, however, an obligation to warn young people not to lose their way on such dubious paths. "The youthful soul must not poison itself with the formula: 'I have made the world,' 'I create it at this moment'" (p. 270). But a fascist like Orano, for whom history had to culminate "in a Roman and Catholic way" (p. 17), was unable to go beyond a certain condescension, albeit paternal, toward "the youthful soul." Instead, it took a genuine member of the *Herrenklub* of Berlin, a ferocious Germanophile like Julius Evola (he was never enrolled in the Fascist Party, which he despised for its "feminine" softness), to arrive at the real conclusion, which could be only one: Stirner was a Jew. Thus, without any foundation (but what do factual proofs matter in such a grandiose design?), we find Stirner, as the "father of total anarchism," included by Evola among the agitators who have carried out the "destructive work" of Hebraism "precisely in the cultural field, protected by the taboos of Science, Art, and Thought." These agitators are, in the order in which they are listed, Sigmund Freud, Albert Einstein, Cesare Lombroso, Stirner, Claude Debussy (conceded to be only a "half-Jew"), Arnold Schoenberg, Igor Stravinsky, Tristan Tzara,

Salomon Reinach, Max Nordau, Lucien Lévy-Bruhl, Henri Bergson, Emil Ludwig, Jakob Wassermann, and Alfred Döblin.[60]

In early-twentieth-century Italian culture, Eugenio Garin discerns a Stirner-Corradini-Valli line to be placed beside the "Nietzsche-D'Annunzio-Orestano triad."[61] By following these two lines, one will doubtless find certain juicy conspiracies still lurking in the shadows. But one finds nothing of importance in relation to Stirner himself and his ideas. Much can be gleaned, however, from the covers of books: The funereal Art Nouveau of the Bocca brothers (who published Zoccoli's translation) shows a candelabrum with multiple flames coming together in a single cloud of fire and smoke. The Libreria Editrice Sociale has an eagle standing out against a metaphysically empty sky, with the tips of some of its feathers protruding beyond the frame. Again, for Zoccoli's *L'anarchia,* the Bocca brothers offer a solemn, big-breasted, and muscular caryatid, tired of her job, who finally raises her arms to break the columns and architraves that she has been holding up for too long.

YOUNG HEGELIANS, ANARCHY, AND THE YOUNG MARX

Anyone concerned with the above three topics will generally not deny Stirner a chapter or a page or two or at least a few notes. On the vicissitudes of Hegel's followers, there is nothing yet to take the place of Löwith's classic work *From Hegel to Nietzsche,* which is still valuable in examining the historical scene around Stirner, treated here, moreover, with a certain conciseness. The literature on the young Marx, in all its ramifications, customarily conceals or omits the deeply troubled and violent connection between Marx and Stirner, who usually gets inserted in innocuous lists of Young Hegelians (thereby raising comical problems: Stirner is an extremist par excellence and by tradition belongs to the left-wing Hegelians; therefore, he should be to the left of Marx, but no one can be to the left of Marx, who is *the* Left, and therefore . . .). Paradoxically, certain studies of the group around the young Marx written *before* the publication of *The German Ideology* seem much more balanced in evaluating the figure of Stirner.[62] One would almost say that the Marx-Engels text has had the effect not of giving Stirner greater importance, albeit as adversary, but of squeezing him forever in a vise of scorn. Even in 1936, Sidney Hook, in his best-known book, could legitimately remark that it was not generally known that Marx had written a book about Stirner.[63] According to the prevailing opinion of experts on the subject, Stirner should be considered primarily as an eccentric writer whose luck it was to trigger Marx's polemical verve. And in their holy zeal, many such experts are astonished that Marx and Engels should have taken such pains to refute so obviously unpresentable a work. For a recent example of woeful legerdemain, take a look at the first volume of *Storia del marxismo,* edited by Eric J. Hobsbawm and other scholars (Turin, 1978): In this project, which claims to represent *the* Marxisms, a meager flowering in plurality, Stirner gets mentioned four times—and always in insipid contexts. Even such elementary information as any school textbook ought to contain is not given. It would be all the more pointless to expect these works of corpselike synthesis to recognize that Stirner can be useful not only in reading *The German Ideology,* a book of which whole sections are incomprehensible unless one has *Der Einzige* open beside it, but also, for example, in reading the *Grundrisse,* where only the presence of Stirner, this too intimate enemy, as much an enemy as Richard Wagner was for Nietzsche, can help in understanding certain obscure passages. Another illuminating example is provided by Cesare Luporini's long, cautious preface to the Italian translation of *The German Ideology.*[64] Here, after a beginning that professes, albeit in an undertone, good intentions of every kind (on the classic Khrushchev model: Just have a little patience and by the end of the century we'll rehabilitate you all!), where Stirner is promoted to the honor of being called *"lo Stirner,"*[65] where audacity goes so far as to recognize that we will need "to rethink the role of Stirner himself, now that we have got beyond that dispute with anarchism that was later associated with him,"[66] Luporini then proceeds—perhaps with his hand on the brake after having dared too much—to mention Stirner cursorily five more times in the seventy-nine dense pages devoted to introducing the reader to a work where Stirner's name recurs obsessively for more than three hundred pages.

Since the beginning of the century, Stirner has been habitually assigned to the family of "anarchist individualists." But let us not forget that in *Der Einzige* he hardly mentioned the word "anarchy," and unlike the other founding heroes (Bakunin, Pierre Proudhon, Pyotr Kropotkin), he never took part himself in any political activity (so far as we know). Stirner's position in the span of anarchism was already obvious anyway, even before Mackay's biography, in Max Nettlau's book, where Stirner is the most important entry in the chapter on German anarchism between 1840 and 1880.[67] And the claim is made for Stirner's basic importance to anarchism in Georgy Plekhanov's little book, which was to have an enormous circulation.[68] Finally, Paul Eltzbacher was to include Stirner's among the seven basic varieties of anarchism (alongside Bakunin, Kropotkin, Proudhon, Leo Tolstoy, William Godwin, and Benjamin Tucker) in his treatise, which resembles a kind of botanical handbook of anarchism.[69]

MAUTHNER

Common to all studies on the Young Hegelians is their obvious concern to "situate" Stirner in their midst. And the obligatory frame of reference is Feuerbach rather than Hegel. But Stirner was not so much an extremist disciple of Feuerbach as he was someone who unmercifully mocked him. The criticism aimed by Marx and Engels at Feuerbach was much milder and more incidental by comparison. Basically, what they demanded was that ideas should be "put into practice," that alluring praxis that bewitched the century (and imbued the everyday atmosphere, as even Dronke observed: "The 'praxis' of the century lays hands on material means, when mere conviction, mere theory, no longer help").[70] But actually Marx and Engels had little to find fault with in the "religion of humanity" that the modest philosopher had proposed as a liberating solution. On the contrary, they had been profoundly nourished by it. Stirner, on the other hand, saw in Feuerbach's good-natured "free thought" something hugely sanctimonious, an encouragement to the abysmal *sottise* that would later draw Flaubert and Baudelaire to its epos, to culminate in Homais, Léon Bloy's shopkeepers, and the Soviet "new man." But the historians of philosophy were ill suited to recognize these passages: They noted that Stirner made use of a language largely derived from Feuerbach and argued that *therefore* he must be offering a continuation of it, albeit an aberrant one. To catch the element of radical derision that links Stirner to his alleged comrades, it took an eccentric of philosophy, a mystic of skepticism like Fritz Mauthner, who gave a masterly description of it in a few pages.[71] The calm lucidity of his prose helps us finally to forget the farrago of comments on Stirner—often mere paraphrases—that had been accumulating for thirty years, and we begin to understand what ought to be the premise for any reading of Stirner: to reduce *Der Einzige* to a series of "positions"

(anarchism or Hegelianism or existentialism or whatever) is the surest
way to neutralize its *unique* monstrousness. Likewise, the digressions on
the insolence of the "I" who speaks in *Der Einzige* make no sense unless
one grasps the way such insolence is vitally interwoven with a singular experiment in knowledge: Stirner puts into operation (or into praxis, if we
wish to respect the habits of the time) an absolute nominalism, unprecedented in its consequentiality, and at the same time, he severs the complicity of thought with language, with its implication, at least in all post-
Cartesian philosophy, that thought is the same as discursive thought. For
how otherwise would one arrive at that *certainty* that is philosophy's goal,
without the intersubjective help of linguistic signs? And at this point it is
clear why Mauthner has been the only one to grasp this process in a perfectly natural way: His words come from that "Vienna of language" wherein dwelt Wittgenstein, Kraus, Freud, and Adolf Loos. His eye singles out
immediately, and almost by instinct, the savage epistemological machine
operated by Stirner, something that none of his most solemn readers had
been able to perceive. Stirner's criticism leads not to a "position" but to
aphasia, and only by starting from silence can one get through.

EDITIONS

After the first edition of 1844, Wigand reissued *Der Einzige* in 1882, an edition that seems to have passed unnoticed. The book, however, became
mandatory reading with the 1893 edition in Reclam's Universal-Bibliothek
series, costing eighty pfennigs, which had an introduction by Paul Lauter-
bach. Since then, *Der Einzige* has been constantly in print. The current
edition in Germany today is still in the same Reclam series. Since 1972 it
has included an essay and notes by Ahlrich Mayer.

WISDOM OF THE CELL

Locked "in the desolate expanse of a narrow cell" because of his political
past, Carl Schmitt recalls a few words sung by Wagner's Siegfried ("I
alone inherited my body / by living I consume it") and notes, "The music
is by Wagner. But the words go back to Max Stirner"—an allusion to
Stirner as an obscure connection in the quarrel between Nietzsche and
Wagner. And thereupon a memory of Stirner comes back to Schmitt that

applies not only to him. But many others who encountered Stirner in the same years remained marked by him and at the same time embarrassed and offended—and they may not have talked about it:

> I first read Max Stirner in high school. To this I owe the fact that I found myself prepared for many things I still encounter today and which otherwise might have caught me by surprise. Anyone familiar with the depths of European thought between 1830 and 1840 is ready for the greater part of what finds a voice throughout the world today. The field of rubble left by the self-decay of German theology and idealist philosophy was transformed in 1848 into a field of forces traversed by theogonic and cosmogonic signs. What is exploding today was prepared before 1848. The fire that burns today was lighted then. In the history of the spirit there are a few uranium mines. Among them I would put the pre-Socratics, some of the Church Fathers, and certain writings from the period before 1848. Poor Max fits in there perfectly.
>
> Considering him on the whole, he is repellent, coarse, a braggart, a show-off, a degenerate student, a boor, an egomaniac, and clearly a serious psychopath. He screeches in a high-pitched, unpleasant voice: I am I, nothing matters to me except myself. His verbal sophisms are unbearable. His bohemianism, enveloped in cigar smoke, is nauseating. And yet Max knows something very important. He knows that the "I" is not an object of thought. Thus he found the best and in any case most German title in all of German literature: *Der Einzige und sein Eigentum.* At this moment Max is all that comes to visit me in my cell. This, on the part of a rabid egoist, moves me deeply.[72]

Schmitt's ambivalence toward Stirner is that which all modern culture of any interest has had for him. The other part of that culture, which is very vast, has blotted out Stirner without even realizing it. No one will visit it in its cell.

LUKÁCS

It is hard to see why Stirner should not have a place beside the other criminals of thought discussed in *The Destruction of Reason.* Could it be because it would have been too easy to revile him? Or because he is not even granted the dignity of a corrupting philosopher? Or for some other more recondite reason? Perhaps Georg Lukács wanted only "respectable" delinquents. But was it not Nietzsche who extolled Prado, the "decent criminal"?

HEIDEGGER

Heidegger has nothing to say about Stirner. Yet Heidegger is nihilism's greatest theorist. And Stirner is a pure lump of nihilism. Heidegger's silence quotes another silence on Stirner: Nietzsche's.

PARODY

When Ueberweg-Heinze names Stirner for the first time in his authoritative history of philosophy, it is to say that he wrote an "ironical caricature of Feuerbach's criticism of religion." Years later, Mauthner was to correct that judgment slightly by amplifying it: "Stirner's book can be seen as a grandiose critical parody of Feuerbach."[73] But one might go a small step further and say that Stirner wrote a grandiose parody of philosophy itself.

ENVOI

"Today there are still certain dedicated men who because of his book take the anarchist Stirner for a madman and for Satan in person; and today there are still certain men, dedicated in other ways, who make a new epoch of humanity start with him, precisely because he was an anarchist. But he was not a devil, and he was not crazy; on the contrary, he was a silent and noble man, whom no power and no word could be said to corrupt, a man so unique that he found no place in the world, and consequently more or less went hungry; he was only an inner rebel, not a political leader, since he was not even bound to men by a common tongue."[74]

12 Prelude to the Twentieth Century

When I think of The Book of our century, I don't turn to *À la recherche* or *Ulysses* or *The Man without Qualities,* those majestic constructions, exemplary not only for their genius but for their precision and obsessiveness as well, to which public opinion now grants due respect, as to those cathedrals made of toothpicks that some provincial hermit has spent the best years of his life silently building. I think, instead, of a book in which one seems to breathe the more exclusive air of the last century. That was the time when it was written, and it remained unfinished at its author's death. I am thinking of *Bouvard et Pécuchet* by Gustave Flaubert. This book is the inevitable pavement on which all our footsteps move: in Kamchatka and in Patagonia, *par les champs et par les grèves,* between suburbs and ruins, wherever the ground has been leveled by those two Titans who met one hot Sunday afternoon in summer on a bench on the Boulevard Bourdon and immediately recognized that each had a hat in which he had written his name: Bouvard, Pécuchet. "Look, we've both had the same idea, to write our names in our hats." "Good Lord, yes, somebody might take mine at the office!"

Sub specie aeternitatis, the meeting between these two obscure copyists is probably no less significant than the one between Napoleon and Goethe. And its two actors deserve the title of Founding Heroes of our world. Just as the twelve labors of Hercules correspond to an equal number of constellations in the zodiac, so the sorry adventures of the two clerks eager to draw on Knowledge run from one end to the other of our Psychical Earth and enfold it on every side. The convolutions of their brains are a labyrinth in which one day, with ecumenical faith, all the things of which we had long been proud were received: the Arts and

Sciences, in a mutual embrace. They speak to us of a world that for the first time had been completely written down: in newspapers and recipes, in bons mots and condolences, bold paradoxes and fearful warnings, cold technical manuals and spiritual guides. And every element in this Scripture adhered to every other, thanks to a wonderful *universal glue:* Stupidity.

That was the background of everything, behind which opened only the silence of sidereal spaces. Bouvard and Pécuchet, these two geniuses who are still misunderstood today (they had at least one indispensable quality of genius: They took everything literally) and who are even accused of being imbeciles, were the first to have a horrific vision of the solidarity of the Whole. They saw the Universal Equivalence produced by Stupidity the same way that visionaries once saw oneness in a speck of dust and the flaming stars. And they understood that in the face of that Ineffability, no word need be added. All that was left was a single act of devotion: to *copy,* because repetition, here as in any ritual, is commemoration of the Unrepeatable.

"What are we going about it?—Don't think! Let's copy. The page has to be filled, the 'monument' completed. Everything equal, good and evil, the beautiful and the ugly, the insignificant and the typical. Nothing is real except phenomena." Having come to the end of their adventures, they have a double copyist's desk built for themselves. And they start copying *everything,* buying piles of wastepaper by weight. The unfinished second volume of *Bouvard et Pécuchet* was to be a vast, still pond of quotations.

In his last years, Flaubert was "a ravaged old heart." From the windows in his house at Croisset, he watched the boats drift by on the Seine and talked to his dog. He even avoided taking walks because they ended by plunging him into depression, forcing him to endure his own company. Then the past attacked him to the marrow of his bones, and he remembered that he was not only a fanatic of "Art" (always with that pathetic capital letter) but "the last of the little seamstresses," a soul that had always had to barricade itself against a sharp and painful sensibility, unable to sustain the conflict of life. Perhaps his doctor did not realize how right he was when he called him "an overgrown hysterical girl."

"Life only seems bearable to me when one succeeds in avoiding it," Flaubert once wrote to his friend George Sand. And behind those words one glimpses the "complete presentiment" of life that he had had as a very young man: It had presented itself to him as "a disgusting odor of cooking issuing from a ventilation duct." And yet he would go on craving it in the hallucinatory state of writing. In these last years, with his mother dead and his income reduced, Flaubert all of a sudden found himself in an "endless solitude," exhausted by his stubborn march toward an unknown destination. And he was aware of being simultaneously "the desert, the traveler, and the camel."

Once again he was in the throes of a book, a manuscript that grew with maddening slowness: *Bouvard et Pécuchet,* an "abominable book," an "impossible book," "a crushing and *frightful* undertaking," which sometimes seemed to him demented and not far removed from the craziness of his two protagonists. In order to recount the stages of their epos without pedantry, he read and annotated more than fifteen hundred volumes, most of them inane, pretentious, empty, dull. Even "great authors" got mixed up in this ludicrous caravan. Everywhere he found material for his "monument," which he hoped would prove worthy of that jealous and implacable deity, the "infinite" being to whom he was dedicating it: Stupidity.

What was the burning fury that drove him? At first it was the desire for revenge. *Bouvard et Pécuchet* was to be an opportunity to "spit bile," to "vent anger." The plan of the book seemed to be summed up in one sentence: "I will vomit on my contemporaries the disgust they inspire in me." O naïveté! Just as his two characters had been naive when they gave up their jobs and, drawing on a small inheritance, retired to the country to explore knowledge, so their author—the devotee of "Art"—had deluded himself into thinking he was *using* these two characters to demonstrate something, hurling them against an invisible enemy. Instead, these two characters devoured their author. *"Madame Bovary c'est moi"*—this too famous remark shines in its esoteric significance only if we understand it as the corollary to a theorem that Flaubert did not utter but discovered: "We are all Bouvard and Pécuchet" (and obviously Flaubert to begin with).

This is the flash of intuition that illuminated his last years. As the two heroes gradually begin studying landscape gardening (unwittingly inventing and liquidating the avant-garde) and Celticism, geology and mnemonics, tragedy and pedagogy, politics and magnetism—and while their author went on tracking them, reading through thousands of intolerable pages—Flaubert approached the mocking truth: "Bouvard and Pécuchet fill me to such a point that I have become them! Their stupidity is mine, and this kills me."

If the "Art" that Flaubert always mentioned, even in letters to his niece, was of a certain unprecedented kind compared to the art of which Horace and Alexander Pope wrote, then Stupidity, which is the subject of *Bouvard et Pécuchet,* was also an unprecedented and grandiose phenomenon. It too required a capital letter. But why, just at this time, did that primordial characteristic of man advance so many claims? Here we must make a historical digression. Around the beginning of the nineteenth century, one sees the twin emergence of Stupidity and *kitsch.* Both are perennial powers whose signs can be recognized everywhere and in every period, but at a precise point in history they unveil their Medusa faces. Henceforth, everything in the world is born accompanied by its degraded Double; not only every knickknack but every idea.

Just as there is romantic kitsch and classical kitsch, as well as the Renaissance, Gothic, and "modern" varieties, so now Stupidity reformulates Platonism and paleontology, emotions and rationality, rebellion and subjugation, disbelief and devotion. The two *bonshommes* Bouvard and Pécuchet (and Flaubert inside them) then discover that Stupidity is no longer a characteristic of *certain* ideas. On the contrary, with the even-handed impassiveness of a god, it distributes itself in all directions: among believers and atheists, countryfolk and city dwellers, poets and mathematicians. Stupidity is the bloodthirsty paper realm of public opinion.

Thus, *Bouvard et Pécuchet* is not the story of two poor idiots who try to lay their hands on knowledge and founder every time in quicksand. Rather, it is the one inevitable modern *Odyssey,* the debilitating itinerary that every "new man" is forced to undertake, in Flaubert's time as in our own. Knowledge triumphs as soon as all wisdom has foundered along with taste, which was its last, discreet, and volatile heir. Unless there is initiation, anyone can find himself, when faced with knowledge, in the position of Bouvard and Pécuchet. And like them, the "new men" are perfectly formless beings, blank slates (this is what philosophers claim so that they can write on them themselves), elastic and empty bodies, devoid of roots, and yet all the more goaded by infernal goodwill to create for themselves what cannot be created but can only be had beforehand: roots. They clutch at knowledge, at every single branch of the great tree of knowledge, in order to hide in its foliage and from there draw nourishment from the soil. But every bough breaks. Their nothingness is always too heavy.

Flaubert recognized that he too (like the rest of us) was a "new man."

He knew that he was recounting an *Odyssey* with no Ithaca at which to land. But he recounted it also in order to put to the severest test the only antidote he recognized as effective: "Art." Perhaps he thought that "Art" might force Stupidity into a further and still more mysterious metamorphosis, the one to which he had once alluded in a letter: "Masterpieces are stupid; they have a tranquil air, like the actual productions of nature, like large animals and mountains." And it is like a large, unfathomable animal that *Bouvard et Pécuchet* gazes at us today.

Public Secrets

13 Hiding Places

Walter Benjamin was incapable of approaching a form without radically changing it. But this was certainly not out of that defiant experimentalism that gives such a hopelessly decrepit tone to so many monuments of modernism a few years after their appearance. Indeed, his gesture may even seem to be the opposite: There was always something antiquated about it, something outdated, ceremonious, and subtly obsessive. Certain radiant colors could only sparkle for him in the midst of a quantity of faded and dusty trash, a little like the lilac stockings that betrayed Proust's Monsieur de Charlus. Such trash was for Benjamin the preparadisiacal form of culture. Before being redeemed by the eschatological hour, the existence of things attained its unique felicity in total abandon, in the condition of debris, at the edges of a vortex that for Benjamin was the very course of history. Amid his wide-ranging and unpredictable reading, Benjamin moved like a junk dealer conducting a silent friend through the passageways of his vast storeroom. This is his city: The testimonies of madmen pile up on one corner, while under arcades of marzipan, one discovers stacks of children's books, crumpled, tattered, and scribbled all over. Farther on stand treatises on the endless subterranean, peripheral, and celestial stories that accompany, incognito, the monotonous, exhausting pace of history. One then emerges on the grand boulevard of the romantics, a broad square, paved with letters and memoirs.

For someone like Benjamin whose mind lived in such a place, without ever being able to get out of it, writing reviews could not be that banal profession, that promise of humiliation, that it is for so many. He needed to have his reviews, even if only twenty lines long, arrive in the newspaper as coded messages from the Junkman's Storeroom, signaling the displacement of objects, new arrivals, unexpected disappearances. Once in a while these articles sounded like dry, inexorable orders of expulsion: One need only read his reviews of Max Brod's *Kafka* and Theodor Haecker's *Virgil* to see once and for all how to demolish a book. But obviously such messages would not have come only from current topics: It was necessary to rummage among travel diaries and ghostly classics; among the papers of anthropologists, politicians, theologians, and linguists; among pamphlets, children's books, photograph albums, and treatises on handwriting analysis and other disreputable sciences. The list of books reviewed by Benjamin between 1923 and the outbreak of the war is already an illuminating fragment of autobiography. These hundreds of articles plotted a meticulous map, open on the void, of a "physiognomical" culture that simultaneously avoided "nobility of spirit" (the whole "feudal school of German feuilletonism" and those who could still talk about man without shuddering), the dwindling avant-garde, and the impending dullness of the Soviets while successfully plundering valuable elements from these three opposing fortresses.

But no one paid much attention. Although Benjamin, with almost childish satisfaction, wrote that as a reviewer he had achieved a "position" in Germany, even that of "leading critic of German literature," his voice has the sound of a depressed monologue: amiable, mannered, and sociable, like certain madmen who talk to their wardrobes. Except for Gershom Scholem and Theodor Adorno, no one seems to have heard his voice in those years, somewhat as *The Origin of German Tragedy* found only two readers at first: Hugo von Hofmannsthal and the formidable Carl Schmitt. (That Bertolt Brecht ever understood Benjamin has always struck me as highly doubtful.) Nevertheless, these assignments, at once public and private, coincided with one of Benjamin's profound desires. For what could be more esoteric than writing for the newspapers? To reveal one's own secrets, appropriately disguised, on a page that circulates everywhere, but only for a few hours, and to know that by the next day they will have happily disappeared while continuing to exist in that secularized version of the realm of Platonic ideas known as the archives. This produces an ambiguous elation, one that Proust recounted in two memorable pages of *Contre Sainte-Beuve.* But for Benjamin, an eminent formal strategist, it also hinted at a further secret, one very close to the heart of his work: the dazzling connection among maximum availability to the public (to which

Baudelaire had already given a more precise and noble name: prostitution), the ephemeral, and esotericism.

As a result of all this, the most private and idiosyncratic Benjamin can be found not only in his letters and important essays but also in his reviews. A few lines about a bad book can become a repository of confessions. Where in Benjamin would one look for a striking theory of repetition, combining the Nietzsche of *Thus Spoke Zarathustra* and the Freud of *Beyond the Pleasure Principle*? In a review of a history of toys—*and nowhere else*:

> Every great and profound experience would like to be insatiable, would like repetition and return to last until the end of all things, the restoration of an original situation from which it emerged. . . . Play is not only a way for mastering terrible original experiences by softening, mischievously evoking, and parodying them, but also for savoring triumphs and victories with the greatest intensity, and always again. . . . The transformation of the most upsetting experience into habit: This is the essence of play.

Or listen to him on eros: "Indeed, the child and the collector, or rather the child and the fetishist, rest on the same terrain; they both arrange themselves, albeit on different sides, around the steep, excavated massif of sexual experience."

14 On Public Opinion

The most obscure history is the history of the obvious. There is nothing more obvious than public opinion, a term that public opinion holds to be innocuous and that has come to comprise in itself huge areas of what can be said: The vast pastures of public opinion are the pride of civilization. And yet public opinion is a fearful thing, which has undergone tortuous, ridiculous vicissitudes until its triumph in the present. There was a time when philosophers used to start with facts, which have now fled among the unicorns. Public opinion remains: mistress of all regimes, shapeless, everywhere, and nowhere, its oversized presence is such as to allow only a negative theology. With the fall of divine rule and the debasement of the vicariate of metaphysics, public opinion has been left in the open as the last foundation stone to cover swarms of worms, some iguanas, and a few ancient serpents. How does one recognize it? Or rather, how does one recognize what is *not* public opinion? There is no map of opinions, and even if there were it would not be of any use. For public opinion is first of all a formal power, a virtuosity that grows endlessly and attacks any material. Its hoax is to accept any meaning, thereby preventing it from being recognized for whatever ideas it has to offer. Indiscriminate, *perinde ac cadaver,* public opinion swallows up thought and reproduces it in similar terms, only with a few slight modifications.

Karl Kraus is the "proposition builder" who spent his life pointing out these modifications. For thirty-seven years in Vienna, 1899 to 1936, he published *Die Fackel,* the frontline bulletin of his war. It was not so much a magazine as a newspaper about newspapers, a parasite on parasites, and people read it in trams and coffeehouses. Here is what Kraus had discovered: Public opinion can talk about everything but cannot say everything. For public opinion has a style, and only by studying its slightest peculiarities of diction will one be able to gain access to its inordinate crimes, to its familiar poisons, to its smirk over one's death, in short—just as public opinion says—to everyday reality. We still follow the rhetoric of public opinion and continue to use one of its main features: the stock phrase.

What is the *organ* of public opinion? The press—and today, the whole, immense communications network. Thus, Kraus devoted his newspaper and a great part of his existence to the press, as an appointed site of public opinion, where one can have the leisure to contemplate the fluid surface on which we move at every moment finally congealed in letters. And he certainly did not want what insensitive interpreters chiefly praised him for: to improve the press. By 1904, Kraus had left no doubts on this matter, which lies at the core of his argument with Maximilian Harden: "I once wrote: 'Harden, who measures journalism with the yardstick of relative ethics, wants to improve the press.' *I want to make it worse,* I want to make it harder for it to carry out its vile intentions under the cover of spiritual pretensions, and I consider a stylistically better press more dangerous."[1] In concentrating on the press, Kraus had grand visions, such as did not often visit even great poets, who concentrated on the pure word. Consider the words I have used as an epigraph: The world, its substance, is, from an industrial standpoint, a by-product; from a neo-Platonic standpoint, it is an emanation of the press. Facts issue from opinions by superfetation. "Is the press a messenger? No: the event. Words? No: life. It not only claims that its news about events are the real events, but it also produces this sinister identity by which appearance always says that facts become news before being facts."[2]

Let us imagine a great theological civilization: Anyone born in it inherits a total thought, preceding fact, which then is articulated and manifested in a language, narrower than its origin, the reminder of something previous and stable. For someone born in the theological civilization of post-history, thought is a depository from which one can draw everything except the experience from which each single thought is born, while the availability of the past as a depository is itself the disturbing experience common to all forms of the new age. If the Enlightenment had realized its utopia, the subject would really have been a tabula rasa, able to endure that total abrasion of meaning produced by all-consuming nominalism and by the method that endlessly dissolves substance. And it would also have had unprecedented agility. But that is not so, and therefore it is not utopia that belongs to post-history but rather its inversion and parody. Once the substance is exhausted, the method spins artificial substances from its own slime: Buildings by now have no foundations but are still more solid, as though they grew from the earth. And we certainly find neither the fake tabula rasa in the subject nor the acknowledgment of a previous thought; rather, we find the continuity of opinions, a homeostatic whirl of utterances swarming from past and present, a Cartesian forest of mental railroad tracks, the permanent explanation of history prefigured in the endless speculative fairground, or *Académie des Jeux,* described by Leibniz.[3] But the subject knows nothing about it. *One opinion is as good as another:* The abyss yawns in this commonplace as in every other. These few words enclose the paralyzing formula of post-historical algebra.

The continuity of opinions is the material chosen by Karl Kraus for his prose work, thousands of pages, the 922 issues of *Die Fackel.* It is an essential characteristic of Kraus's prose that it carries within it a specter: It may be a passage explicitly quoted from a writer or newspaper, the composition of a word, a stock phrase that gets reworked, a punctuation mark. In any case, until the spectral element has been identified, Kraus's proposition cannot be read correctly. This procedure is required once one recognizes that the world has become a newspaper. The result of this procedure, to which Kraus stubbornly clung, is that the author must renounce any thought of his own that can be expressed, as is customary, in a series of propositions. The *primum* is now the continuity of opinions, a totality of language in constant proliferation. The writer pretends to be concerned only with opinions in order to make his way through their jumble and capture thought. His Ariadne will be language. Indeed, Kraus's relations with language might only be told as an erotic epos:

I do not rule language, but language rules me completely. For me, she is
not the handmaiden of my thoughts. I live with her in a relationship that
lets me conceive thoughts, and she can do with me what she likes. For the
fresh thought leaps out at me from words, and the language that created it
is formed retroactively. Such pregnancy of thoughts has a grace that obliges
one to kneel down and requires all kinds of trembling attentions. Language
. is sovereign to thoughts, and if a man succeeds in reversing the relationship, she will make herself useful to him around the house but bar him
from her womb.[4]

(In this passage the spectral element is woman, with the phraseology that
traditionally pertains to her. The equivalence of woman and language, recurring in all of Kraus, is implied and made all the more obvious by the
fact that the word *Sprache*—language—is feminine. In consideration of
this, the various pronouns have been translated as though they applied to
a relationship between persons.)

The work of the "proposition builder" is to abandon himself to language, which is supposed to contain a force of its own, a latent thought,
the only one capable of breaking the spell of public opinion. "Thoughts
come to me because I take them at their word."[5] But once it is removed
from the immediate exercise, from being captured by the work of language, thought departs. It is indissolubly bound to the word that called it
forth. When Kraus writes, "Progress makes coin purses out of human skin"
(p. 279), we see him establishing, with no waste of words, the "dialectics of
the Enlightenment." But Kraus would never have wished to *describe* that
dialectic. And if we have reason to be grateful to Theodor Adorno for having done so, we recognize at the same time that the implications of Kraus's
metaphors continue to multiply beyond the point where Adorno's involved
explication begins to rest on its oars.

Thus, Kraus's thought can only be recounted by someone who does
not understand it: "Many who have fallen behind me in my development
can state what my thoughts are in a more comprehensible way."[6] On the
other hand, Kraus himself, who does not like to "get mixed up in [his own]
private affairs" (p. 293), would surely not be equally clear and certain.
Kraus believes one cannot know where thoughts come from, and therefore he supposes that they are formed beforehand and go wandering
about; only those who have formed their language can receive them. A
writer would be someone who "believes in the metaphysical path of

thought, which is a miasma, while opinion is contagious and therefore has need of the immediate infection to be received and spread."[7]

But why not even consider all of Kraus's aphorisms as a series of opinions? There would seem to be nothing to keep one from doing so. As such, they make a bizarre and contradictory collection, insolent and incongruous, in which the author often seems to support with one hand what he destroys with the other. In the end, one notes that these are the opinions of a man who cares nothing about being "consistent with his own opinions." But one will also note this: The things Kraus says become unrecognizable as soon as they are restated in other words, because "if a thought can live in two forms, it will not feel as much at ease as two thoughts living in a single form."[8] If at this point in its history, thought is no longer the sovereign organizer of language but must necessarily pass each time through the hell of opinion, it is precisely language that will tip the scales: "the difference between a way of writing in which thought has become language and language thought, and one in which language represents simply the shell of an opinion."[9] Opinion has the appearance of a formally homogeneous continuum and tends to abrogate the mimetic power of language; Kraus, on the contrary, heightens the difference and makes language into theater, to the extent of calling his work "written recitation,"[10] while always stressing the lightest and most elusive element: the tone. "If I must make a liberal demand, I do it in such a way that reactionaries obey and progressives repudiate me. What matters is the accent of the opinion and the detachment with which it is stated."[11]

Where the man in the street is prompt to offer his *de gustibus non est disputandum,* Kraus talks like a mathematician or an underworld judge. But what is his Euclid or his law code? We will never find out, but we do find, equally vehement, the imperative to rectify language. This undertaking was called "rectification of names" in ancient China; but whereas Confucius could appeal to a powerful all-inclusive custom to reestablish order in words and thus in China, Kraus, in the Byzantine but enervated Kakania, had at his disposal only a musical metaphor: to speak as though appealing to a *perfect pitch* for language. And the language that reaches his ear has only words in common with what public opinion means by language. In the information culture, the pages of *Die Fackel* constitute an enclave in which language is presented with characteristics that cannot be reduced to those that newspapers have imprinted on the world: Instead of the deadening clarity of words as an instrument of communication, what we find there is the illuminating complexity of language as a "means for coming to terms with creation."[12] Kraus looks back to an origin that refuses to define itself: "The origin is the goal"[13]—such is his first axiom. The great Judaic heritage resounds in these words, the memory of Adam giving names. And this origin is mirrored in a messianic end, when—according to a legend that also influenced Walter Benjamin and Adorno—the Kingdom would be established by leaving everything as it is, *except for a few slight modifications.* Holy Writ and its counterfeit copy, the newspaper, can pass into each other,[14] in both directions, precisely by means of slight modifications: If it is true that the *"supreme stylistic task* [of satire] *is its graphic arrangement,"*[15] then this is the basis for Kraus's theory of quotation, the height of his satire. This slight modification might be merely the addition of quotation marks to a text and its reproduction, without comment, in the pages of *Die Fackel.* Because these pages are a trial by ordeal, the quotation will emerge dead or alive, in any case transformed; it will have spoken another language. At the outset of World War I, Kraus wrote, "It is my duty to put my epoch between quotation marks, for I know that that alone can express its unspeakable infamy." Thus, at times, the simple typographical combination of two newspaper quotations on the eloquent blankness of a particular page is enough for the language of infamy to pass judgment on itself.

By adding Judaic esotericism and the obsession of modern formalism, whereby language becomes equivalent to musical material, Kraus achieved a frenzy of words that in the short run should have led him to the Cabala or to absolute literature. It led him instead, like his demon, to apply both of them on a wild and difficult terrain: the press—words coded, then as now, to say something overwhelming and too close for comfort, the world transformed into *universel reportage,* as Stéphane Mallarmé put it. No other great writer of the century has dared to weave the magic of words and the black magic of society into so dense a web. Kraus's political polemics are the most exacerbated *art pour l'art,*[16] and his *art pour l'art* gives his polemics a force unknown to political speech.

Public opinion appears for the first time, as δόξα, in five lines by Parmenides (fr. 1, 28–32),[17] on which all manner of exegesis has been and will be tried. The goddess Δικη speaks as follows:

It is necessary that you learn everything
both the untrembling heart of well-rounded Truth
as well as the opinions of mortals, in which there is no true certainty.
But likewise this too you shall study, how appearances
must gloriously be affirmed by passing whole through everything.

The enigma of these words lies perhaps in their impressive clarity, in the forgotten gesture of expressing together the two separate realms of Ἀλήθεια and δόξα, the joint relation of being and appearing, the heaviest burden, one of which subsequent thought has never ceased trying to throw off. The δόξα of Parmenides is still, simultaneously and in the fullest sense, opinion-appearance; the ordeal between word and thing has not yet been broken. In four lines, three words (δόξας—δοκοῦντα—δοκίμως) indicate variations in appearing and oddly correspond to fr. 28 in Heraclitus, where a similar variation (δοκέοντα—δοκιμώτατος) comes in two lines. The path of names and opposing forces—indeed, all cosmology belongs to it—δόξα lets us foresee the interruption of the discourse, which takes shape against the background of the undivided heart of Ἀλήθεια. (The reluctance on the part of philologists to recognize in Parmenides a twofold affirmation of δόξα and Ἀλήθεια, and not their incurable opposition, can only be explained if one compiles a case history on the whole course of Western thought, of which philologists have been, without realizing it, the perpetrators.) Δόξα is at the same time the image and discourse of appearance; in it, the whole expresses itself in the flashing of names and forms. In Ἀλήθεια the whole is recognized "by many signs" (fr. 8, 2–3) for that which it indestructibly is, in the fullness of the continuum. They are the two φύσεις that the whole admits (see Plutarch, *Adversus Coloten,* 1114 D): superimposed spheres, both enclosed, but the one in the intact *entirety* (οὖλον), without divisions, of Ἀλήθεια; the other in the enumerative *completeness* (τά πάντα), perpetually reshuffled, of δόξα (see fr. 9, 38). A transparently initiatory doctrine that can be traced back—as a variation that already prefigures the nullifying future of philosophy—to the primordial gap between the manifestation and its principle: terms that certainly do not correspond to "intelligible" and "sensible," as the whole Greek tradition from Aristotle on would like, applying to Parmenides a pair of opposites that do not pertain to him. What holds Ἀλήθεια and δόξα together and keeps one from crossing over into the other is their common obedience to the same goddess, Δίκη-Ἀνάγκη—

as stated, respectively, in frs. 10, 6 and 8, 30. The bond of necessity cannot be dissolved, since appearance "will never sever being from being" (fr. 4, 2).

Gorgias is the great figure who marks the severance of the connection between opinion and appearance, the devious and ruinous corollary to the weakness that prevents appearance and Ἀλήθεια from remaining joined. With Gorgias, the terrible sobriety of the West speaks out: "Being, [because] unmanifested, does not have appearance (δοκεῖν) in store; appearance [because] powerless, does not have being in store" (fr. 26). This rift cannot be crossed, and the lack of contact abrogates the *criterion,* which is a reference to Ἀλήθεια: Now, opinion, the discourse of appearance, becomes discourse *about* appearance and its manipulation. We enter the combinatorial realm of the modern in the released forces of the discourse, the algebra of power. But the whole history of nihilism, that is, our history, shows us a timid nihilism that does not dare to go all the way: The criterion of truth having collapsed, truth itself has not collapsed, as thought would have required. This timidity is actually the most astute and overwhelming act of reason, which has seen the prime instrument of social control in maintaining the notion of truth. Plato, in the *Theaetetus,* described this process with admirable bluntness, once and for all: "But in the things I am talking about, namely, questions of right and wrong and holy and impious, they want it firmly stated that these things have neither a nature nor a reality of their own, but that society's opinion becomes their truth, when such opinion exists and for as long as it exists" (172 b). Here, by now, opinion has emancipated itself, becoming an autonomous force adjusted to nothing external except to society as a tangle of opinions, while one of the meanings of an ancient judgment attributed to Simonides of Keos is revealed: "Appearance (τὸ δοκεῖν) does violence to truth (τάν ἀλάθειαν)" (*Republic,* 365 b–c).

The bond of necessity stated by Parmenides is replaced in Plato by that of proportionality between categorically divided regions, according to a process of assimilation—the relation between model and copy—whose pattern one finds in the *Republic* (509 b–e). And given Plato's inexhaustible ambiguity, one will not be surprised by the passage in *Parmenides* (130 b) where he abruptly mentions that such proportionality has neither the force nor the audacity to extend itself to everything. The correspondence stops before the ridiculous and dirty debris of appearance:

"And of things, O Socrates, that would seem to be ridiculous, such as hair, mud, dirt, or any others that may seem low and contemptible, do you wonder if it is necessary to say that a separate form exists of each, distinct from the one we touch with our hands?" Socrates does not dare, and perhaps his hesitancy is not the last of his ironies; but the degradation of appearance also involves the ruin of whatever, beyond appearance, did not want to join with it, even metaphorically. From now on, the great nihilistic analysis, the one that runs through the whole history of Western philosophy and culminates in the Nietzsche of the years 1884–88, will reveal each successive essence to be a disguised appearance. At history's high noon, announced by Zarathustra, unprecedented words ring out: *"With the true world we have also abolished the apparent one."*[18] This final passage of nihilism, which would turn the wheel of Western thought back to the point preceding its first movement, is precisely what history, by emerging from itself, has not granted. The whole network of oppositions that until today have formed the grammar and syntax of thought, in the end, risking being deprived of authority, has been deposited in facts, and there it gloriously lives on, without foundation and as though in play. Its immense power has become perhaps even greater: Even if no one believes in the theorems anymore, everyone practices their theater. The structure has reached its maximum strength once it is not stated but simply staged. Now crowned opinions occupy the hyper-Uranian τόπος: they are the gods of operetta, parodic and earthly stand-ins flung into the realm of being, to inhabit the place ironically prepared for them by the dispersed ideas.

Opinion, from the moment it is no longer a momentary mental disposition but has become the unmentionables of appearance, surreptitiously usurps an authority that had belonged to thought and removes itself from the actual play of appearance. And people of opinion are adults and no longer have any need to project the source of authority onto the faraway Plain of Ἀλήθεια, "where the reasons and forms and models of what has happened and what will happen lie motionless" (Plutarch, *De defectu oraculorum,* 422 b–c). Opinion finds confirmation in itself, it flows by itself, and servitude has become spontaneous. The totality of opinion then constitutes a body, the Great Beast described in a memorable passage in Plato, the prime source for Simone Weil's theory of society:

All these private individuals who ask to be paid, whom the politicians call Sophists and consider to be their rivals, teach nothing else but these beliefs of the crowd, which it expresses when it assembles, and this they call wisdom; as if one were to learn to know the impulses and desires of some Great Beast, grown strong, how to approach and touch it, and when it is more intractable and when more docile, and what are the sounds it is likely to emit, and what sounds emitted by another make it tame or fierce; and after learning all this and living with the creature, with the passage of time should call it wisdom, and having organized it as an art, should turn to teaching it, without knowing anything about the truth of these beliefs and desires in relation to the beautiful and the ugly, the good and the bad, the just and the unjust, but should only apply all these names to the opinions of the Great Beast, calling the things it likes good, and those it dislikes bad, and without knowing any other reason for these things, should call what is necessary fine and just, never having seen or been in a position to show how the nature of the necessary differs from that of the good. (*Republic*, 493 a–c).

Today we no longer need Sophists to incite the Great Beast, since the Sophist is the immediate self-regulation of society, an organism nourished by the tensions it itself incessantly generates, an order that is preserved only so long as it expands. The last, anonymous subject of society is the destiny of science as a total experiment on the world, an experiment in which humanity is the chosen material. The Soul of the World no longer has a human face, nor does it appear on horseback in the streets of a city. Likewise, deceit no longer needs to be personified in a subject. The decline of Mephistopheles as a dramatic character is actually his triumph.

There is no way to distinguish opinion from thought except by analyzing its language. Ever since the trial by ordeal between word and thing was broken, this curse has accompanied discursive thought. Though the Sophists were the first to reveal it, Socrates was the first to see its consequences and to attempt to rescue thought from the fatal trap. Faced with the parasitism of opinion on thought, he chose to become a parasite on parasites, to disguise his own language in theirs, and in short, to extract thought from the discourse of others. In the *Republic* (340 d), he is accused of "arguing like a sycophant." In Socrates, thought, under the pressure of sophistry, abandons the seat of authority and substitutes irony at a distance: The stink of the rabble that Nietzsche sniffed in him is the price, heroic and degrading, of this first contact with opinion. To cover oneself with opinion in order to wear it out is a mortal risk: Opinion is thought's shirt of Nessus. Socrates' behavior carries out the renunciation of original words; henceforth, thought agrees to move on the plane of social violence, which is the violence of opinion; was it not to be public opinion that killed Socrates? This is the first attempt to extract thought from language that speaks without consciousness. Language that speaks in us beyond our consciousness is also that of the robber and guest to whom, by applying Occam's razor, the name of unconscious has been given. But opinion neither robs us nor claims the ambiguous status of guest; on the contrary, like a paternal benefactor, it reassures us and fortifies the bastions of our ego, which are festooned with opinions. What does the emancipated man have to boast of except his opinions? They are one way to display the fingerprints of his ego. The black magic of opinion is so incomparably effective because opinion is a reasonable language, and reasonableness does not involve consciousness. Originally the mobile physiognomy of appearance and the process of forms in language itself, opinion seems increasingly to congeal in the course of its history. In the end, it is paralyzed in its "majesty."[19] Now opinions can be defined as statements uttered violently and spontaneously, apart from all consciousness, and this leads to the cautious hypothesis that the petrification of opinion is the last phenotypical mutation stamped by culture on man. On this prospect of motionless horror, the future has also opened.

The altar of opinion is the commonplace. Every time a commonplace is uttered—to guarantee ceremonial orthodoxy, the officiants will have at their disposal no more than a certain number of tones and modes of expression—the original abyss yawns once again, and the elements are divided. Léon Bloy suggests that a commonplace be defined as the parodic inversion of a *theologoúmenon,* a way of speaking about God: "Without their knowing it, the most vacuous bourgeois are tremendous prophets; they can't open their mouths without convulsing the stars, and the abysses of light are immediately invoked by the chasms of their Stupidity."[20] And his words find a sequel in Kraus: "to learn to see abysses where there are commonplaces."[21] Flaubert in *Bouvard et Pécuchet,* Bloy and Kraus, they all tackled this enormous phenomenon, but only Kraus lived to witness its final, dreadful metamorphosis.

Commonplaces, stock phrases—these are stones of language "that take us back to that little known epoch immediately preceding the catastrophe. 'At that time,' says Genesis, 'the earth had only one language.'"[22] The supreme goal of writing has always been, to quote Mallarmé once more, to get away from languages that are *"imparfaites en cela que plusieurs"* [imperfect in that they are many] and, at the same time, to discover in things a language written and spoken in silence, as attested by centuries of speculation on hieroglyphs. But if, at a certain point in time, everything turns into parody, even this doctrine, which no tradition has developed as has the Hebrew, will have to encounter the current presence of its counterfeit. Nazism will bring this about. Its operation implies "the annihilation of metaphor":[23] The image, retranslated into a language of facts, now gives off the sounds of torture. This is the event that silenced Kraus when Hitler took power. Brecht noted what had happened:

> When the Third Reich was founded
> only a tiny message came from the eloquent one.
> In a poem of ten lines
> he raised his voice, only to complain
> that it wasn't enough for him.[24]

But Kraus did not simply fall silent, as he had announced in his last poem, the one to which Brecht refers. The "eloquent one" denounced in the harshest terms the loss of words that resulted from the advent of Nazism: He wrote *Die dritte Walpurgisnacht* (The Third Night of Walpurga), a mighty oak growing over the common grave of the century, a forbidding massif, an ironclad work of which only the incipit is generally known—one might say almost justly, since, in accordance with the rule of the "proposition builder," the first proposition in the book corresponds to the whole: "Apropos of Hitler, nothing comes to mind." And the text goes on:

> I am well aware that, with this result of prolonged thought and many attempts to grasp what has happened and the force behind it, I fall considerably short of expectations, which perhaps were stretched as never before toward the polemicist from whom a popular misunderstanding demands what is called taking a stand, by doing precisely, every time an evil has in some way touched a sore spot in him, what is also called facing up to it. But there are evils where this ceases to be a metaphor, while behind the face the brain, which also participates in some way in these actions, would no longer think itself capable of having any thoughts at all. I feel as

though I've been hit on the head, and if, before actually being so, I never-theless would not like to consider myself satisfied to appear to be silenced as I in fact am, it is in obedience to something that obliges me to take ac-count even of a failure and to explain the situation in which such an abso-lute collapse in the sphere of the German language has placed me, and my personal sense of weakness on the occasion of the reawakening of a nation and the establishment of a dictatorship that today commands everything except language.[25]

If writing has always aspired to lead metaphors back to their origin, which is then once again found to be something improper, the Nazis immedi-ately did something all too similar, with their "eruption of the stock phrase into action" (p. 123). This is the event that imposed silence on Kraus and then made him write the grandiose commentary on his silence. When "rubbing salt on open wounds" is a present fact and not the remote and forgotten origin of a metaphor, when dead metaphors reawaken to be ap-plied directly to the bodies of the victims, the metaphor itself decays, and its end is the hellish mirror of the origin: "Since the thing has happened, the word is no longer usable" (p. 123). Finally, "blood spurts from the scab of stock phrases," and the word is silent. "This is—in the new faith, which isn't even aware of it—the miracle of transubstantiation" (p. 121).

"Incognito like Haroun al Raschid, he passes by night among the sen-tence constructions of the journals, and, from behind the petrified façades of phrases, he peers into the interior, discovers in the orgies of 'black magic' the violation, the martyrdom of words"[26]—this is Walter Ben-jamin's marvelous image of Kraus. In almost forty years of these nightly forays, Kraus had already discovered what was to happen until our own day, but he did not care to be a witness of Nazism in the same manner. He had never disdained any kind of enemy, enveloping them all, from the least significant to the most infamous, in the miasma of *Die Fackel,* but now for the first time an immense adversary looms and he does not treat it as such. In *Die dritte Walpurgisnacht,* one can see that many things cross Kraus's mind concerning the lackeys or hierarchs or inadequate oppo-nents or propagandists of Nazism, but the figure of Hitler is the only one to remain indistinct. And this is the last and most difficult revelation left by Kraus: He was the first to recognize that he stood on the threshold of an age that drains the conceptual and dramatic notion of adversary by ex-tending it to everything, dispersing it in fog, easily turning anyone into his own enemy. Afterward, nothing is left but to listen attentively to the sounds of the world, the great slide from one archon to another, and to spell out the signs that allow one to tread cautiously in the amorphous.

Here there is no need to take up the tragedy of Kraus's last years. That is a secret door over which he himself wrote, "On the occasion of the end of the world I want to retire to private life,"[27] while he was dying of public life. But his last works have a special significance: After writing and not publishing *Die dritte Walpurgisnacht,* Kraus published instead a very long issue of *Die Fackel* with the title "Warum Die Fackel nicht erscheint"— which contains large extracts from the unpublished work—to explain his own silence and to mock those who were still counting on his "taking a stand" in the face of Nazism. Before his death, he published a few more issues of *Die Fackel,* devoted primarily to Johann Nestroy, Jacques Offenbach, and Shakespeare and only marginally to politics. "When the roof is burning, it's no use praying or washing the floor. Praying, however, is more practical,"[28] as Kraus had written many years before. It is to this activity, supremely defenseless and yet practical, that his last work returns: the preparation of *Die Sprache,* a volume of writings on language containing, among other things, memorable essays on the comma, the apostrophe, subject and predicate, rhyme, and typographical errors; the book would be published only after his death. The political significance of these pages is condensed in a few words: "If humanity did not have stock phrases, it would not need weapons."[29]

Meanwhile, right on that threshold where Kraus recognized the insufficiency of his and all other words, the perfect appropriateness of his previous words was retrospectively confirmed by events. Apart from the unprecedented, Nazism added nothing new. On the third night of Walpurga, the Nazis are ignes fatui that become a funeral pyre, but the theatrical machine that operates the phantasmagoria is the same one that Kraus had been observing for years, a machine in whose gears the world is still caught. In the end, Kraus was able to address these words of farewell to the press, his first target and the mouthpiece of opinion for all other evils, shorthand for society as degradation: "For National Socialism has not destroyed the press; it is the press that has made National Socialism. As reaction, only in appearance; in truth as fulfillment."[30]

Kraus died in 1936. Then came the war, followed by years of peace wrinkled with horrors in the new society. Now the divine being is society itself. The new society is an agnostic theocracy based on nihilism.

15 A Chinese Wall

THE RED NOTEBOOK

In a province known as the last empire, which neither knew nor cared to know whether it was one or the other but was convinced it could always reach an agreeable compromise among all the incompatibles, "one day everything—wherever you looked—turned red. . . . Whispers, murmurs, shivers! On the street, in trams, in the park, everyone was reading a red notebook."[1] It was April 1899, and "there, in Kakania, that state since vanished, in many ways an exemplary state, though unappreciated,"[2] Vienna welcomed with greedy curiosity the first issue of *Die Fackel*, written entirely by a twenty-five-year-old newspaper contributor named Karl Kraus, who was clearly up to no good ("we're not asking ourselves in a high-sounding way what to do, but honestly what to do away with")[3] and promptly unveiled his secret aim, the ruthless ambition to be impossible in the city of "pleasant relations,"[4] where actually, "one can't become impossible."[5] No one can take offense, since a mandatory doubt does away with all good and evil: Everyone is too acquainted with everyone else, having seen each other since they were children; everything has something else behind it, revenge for a benefit not gained, flattery for a benefit in the offing. From that year, "already stiffening at such a change"[6] (the turn of the century), for the next thirty-seven years, *Die Fackel* disseminated without letup "betrayal, earthquakes, poison, and fire from the *mundus intelligibilis*."[7]

CAFÉ GRIENSTEIDL

Many writers were then ripening precipitously in the hothouses of the cafés, and to found a magazine was the most normal of gestures. What was unusual, however, was the proposal to criticize everything within range. And the intention to make a frontal attack on the *Neue Freie Presse,* Vienna's so respectable, so elegant, big daily newspaper, was rash indeed. Kraus had arrived at these decisions after swift and tortuous years of apprenticeship, whose symbolic beginning can be placed on a day in the spring of 1892 when he and Hugo von Hofmannsthal celebrated their liberation from final exams by meeting in the gardens of the Beethovenplatz.[8]

Hofmannsthal was then the archangel Loris: His first writings— published in *An der schönen blauen Donau,*[9] in the style of the Viennese "gay apocalypse"—were the meteor that had had the delicacy to stop in the middle of the sky in the city where "everything stands still and waits" ("Best wishes for a good end of the world, Your Grace!").[10] And even before he was out of short pants, he had been welcomed to the Hall of the Muses, where he had been assigned a velvet niche. December 1891 had witnessed his meeting with Stefan George, the beginning of an astonishing ballet of torments and misunderstandings, broken off, like his schoolboy crushes, by the intervention of Hofmannsthal's concerned and understanding father. The friendship is documented by a month-long exchange of frantic notes between the two poets; by Hofmannsthal's acknowledgment that "You reminded me of things / That lie hidden in myself";[11] and finally, according to an oral tradition traceable to Hofmannsthal, by the image of George, the twenty-three-year-old "prophet," hysterical over the breakup, kicking a dog and muttering *"sale voyou"* [dirty hooligan].[12] By now Hofmannsthal was already taking walks "amid acacia and jasmine"[13] with Hermann Bahr, the tireless and long-winded majordomo of the New, who so often changed his livery and would later become a constant target for Kraus's vituperation.

The ultimate essences of Viennese decadence gathered in the Café Griensteidl, the Jung-Wien [Young Vienna] group, only mildly toxic as compared to those being cooked up in the same decade by the *Mercure de France.* In addition to young Hofmannsthal, those seated there included Arthur Schnitzler, Felix Salten, Richard Beer-Hofmann, a few forgotten figures, and finally Bahr, who had momentarily drawn the battle lines of modernism on those little tabletops and proclaimed the "overcoming of naturalism"[14] to an inattentive civilization that had so far succeeded in ignoring it.[15] On the sidelines of the group sat Karl Kraus, who in 1892 had embarked on a sporadic career of literary journalism contaminated by life. "Friends?" Beer-Hofmann said of him, "We're not exactly friends; we just don't get on each other's nerves."[16] But Kraus soon developed a lack of tolerance, first for Hermann Bahr, then for the whole group. The reasons for this rejection were to pile up, layer upon layer, for the rest of his life. In January 1897, the Café Griensteidl was closed so that the Palais Herberstein, in which it was located, could be renovated and divided into apartments. This is alluded to in Kraus's first developed piece of writing, *Die demolirte Literatur,* an all too biting squib, a *jeu de massacre* carried out on the Jung-Wien group. "Life will break the crutches of affectation:"[17] As far as he was concerned, this so-called Young Vienna had now turned out to be the final avatar of the decrepit Vienna of decoration.

> ANATOL: Something else now occurs to me.
> MAX: What's that?
> ANATOL: The unconscious!
> MAX: The unconscious?
> ANATOL: I mean, I think that unconscious states
>   exist.
> MAX: Well . . .
>
> *—Arthur Schnitzler*

VIENNA, CAPITAL OF DECORATION

Around the end of the century, "Vienna was not so much the city of art as the city par excellence of decoration,"[18] its wings evenly protected by a fine aesthetic dust. Schnitzler's "sweet little girls," spices in the city's eros; the rare aristocrats whom the "difficult" Hofmannsthal is supposed to have taken as models of language and behavior; the functionaries who still succeeded in experiencing the bureaucracy as ceremony; the fast set, faithless and silly but above all gallant; the feuilletonists who powdered every trifle; the Gustl lieutenants,[19] victims of incongruous frenzies of honor—all this, and

> Smooth words, variegated pictures,
> Divided, secret feelings,
> Agonies, episodes

and "the many things that fall like frost and rust on overly refined souls,"[20] amid screens, family albums, wax figures, *cabinets particuliers* [private din-ing rooms], uniforms, chronic misunderstandings, are fastened around a center, which was—as the Viennese Hermann Broch saw from the distance of exile[21]—the empty box reserved for the emperor in every Kakanian theater, a dark cavity, resigned to a necessary absence. Vienna was also said to be the city of corruption par excellence, and it certainly was, but with a kind of pathetic cynicism, as we can see in hindsight. Having been overtaken by industry, which had its fire elsewhere, it was almost forced to specialize in the enamel with which to cover itself. It was the first city to produce aesthetics as raw material; it was a colony in the center of Europe, too absorbed in the complicated relations, Byzantine and prehistoric at the same time, among its various peoples and races, to be able to conceive the existence of Asia. Professional charm was thus sketched on a dark background, and the same thing happened to the sparkling city as to Schnitzler with his "cheerful ideas," which became gloomy in his hands as soon as he stopped for a moment to think about them: like a story "that I told my friends one day, and as I told it, the thing kept getting more serious, until at the end, to my surprise, the hero got stabbed and died an awful death."[22] Years later, Bertolt Brecht would say of Kraus, "When the age laid hands upon itself, he was the hands."[23] But at that time, around the end of the century, the tale, full of arabesques, digressions, and anxious pauses, went on being spun "in the best of demimondes."[24]

THE MORGUE OF SYMBOLS

Throughout history, from Plato's *Republic* to our own time, a curse of the improper (metaphor—ornament—decoration) as a sign threatening to escape the *logos* is periodically confirmed in classical and neoclassical poetics, where, behind the appeal to Aristotle, one glimpses the terror of the erratic sign. With the first radical romantics, the final escape of metaphor is announced; henceforth, it hides in a forest that has become the site of literature. But this event, which society finds regrettable, is followed by a devious readjustment, and the great romantics themselves, in all their ambiguity, were the vehicle for it. The order of rhetoric was increasingly losing its binding power, and it was replaced, with lethal tolerance, by a dyarchy of Ornament and Instrument in which the two opposites, pretending as always to be enemies, re-create the lapsed equilibrium along very different lines. Ornament is now found to be highly useful as a shell, a tireless chaperon without which Instrument would never agree to appear in society. The aura of these two undivided powers is ambiguity. They are festively welcomed in an immense salon where there are only two kinds of guests, "those who use an urn for a chamber pot and those who use a chamber pot for an urn."[25] On the sidelines, "speaking in the void," two implacable individuals keep insisting that there is a difference between the two objects: Adolf Loos and Karl Kraus. In 1908 and 1910, respectively, they will each publish a scandalous manifesto-essay: "Ornament and Crime" and "Heine and the Consequences." The titles themselves reveal that they were driven by a judgmental fury that forced them to involve the whole culture in their aesthetic intolerance. With one of his abrupt gestures as a fictitious "good American,"[26] Loos immediately notes an important fact: namely, that in the present, "ornament has no organic connection with our civilization"[27] and is therefore degenerative. Like an immense tattooed criminal body, the city spreads out before the frightened eye. Aberrant sirens project from respectable facades. "Houses have tumors, the bow window. It will take surrealism to paint it: Houses exude a fleshy excrescence."[28] In an operation that takes up all of history, insistent nominalism dissolved the body of images and symbols; the city became their morgue. In his outburst, Loos already portrays an enlightened humanity that will prefer smooth objects, free of necrotic images, and will forget the ornamentation it destroyed. This did not happen: Though there was no apparent liturgical justification, a body of images, guided by the infernal Beatrice of kitsch, emerged and regained possession of the world. But, our age being secretly docetist, that body is phantasmal, a pure envelope. Kraus wanted to retrace the history of form as envelope and exemplify it in a name. He hit on Heine as poison and wound, a poet who was self-assured in his torment, conscious of his degradation, and too gifted not to try to disguise it: "But form, this form that is the envelope of the content, and not content itself, clothing for the body, not flesh for the spirit, this form would still once have had to be discovered, before being established forever. Heinrich Heine took on the job."[29] The precision of the attack (which seized on the peculiar weakness of romanticism, incapable of producing middle values, and for which "every slip from the level of genius meant a slide head over heels from the cosmos into kitsch")[30] has often kept people from seeing that what Kraus was attempting in this essay was less an "evaluation of Heine's poetry than the criticism of a form of life"[31]—the same form of life that triumphs today in a more cunning version. Ornament and Instrument still govern the state of things, at the intersection of two tendencies: "For one, art is an instrument; for the other, life is an ornament."[32] This mutual homage, which corrupts art and life, produces a compact euphony; what is lost is only a memory: "Art disrupts life. The poets of humanity re-establish chaos every time. The poets of society sing and lament, bless and curse, within the order of the world."[33]

VIENNA, CAPITAL OF LANGUAGE

Latent, incompatible with the decoration by which it had been nourished to the point of disgust, another Vienna began to be formed in those years, in the place where unnoticed crystallizations of thought occur: behind history. Just as Paris, the arsenical city, "where bodies soon consume,"[34] was the privileged soil for the release of the Double in the early part of the century, so Vienna, city of sweetness and merciless analysis, everywhere frizzled, a suicide with impeccable manners, rotated around the pivot of language in the same years, and from there the final disease was transmitted to the rest of the world.

This was the Vienna to which Kraus belonged, a city not to be found in documents or commemorations because it exists only behind barred gates in the works of a few great solitaries who were guided by the same obsession, which they exercised on different materials. Freud, Kraus, Wittgenstein, Schoenberg, and Loos are the principal stars in this constellation.[35] To all of them, language appeared to be a vital, initial, all-inclusive question, with an urgency that the times were able to counter only with the zeal of semiology congresses. In an extensive network, still largely to be explored, analyses of female undergarments connect with unconscious cryptographies; the search for "what can be said in general," with the "unconscious logic" of what musical language says; unsparing *Witz* [wit] about psychoanalysis, with the psychoanalytical investigation of *Witz;* the *Es* that Freud borrowed from Nietzsche and Georg Groddeck, with the grammatical *es* [it] to whose use in language Kraus devoted a memorable essay. *Es*: This neglected little word presides over the obsession with language, and thanks to that obsession rediscovers its powerful archaic features, as glimpsed by another Viennese, Leo Spitzer, who devoted all his inventiveness to language: "The great neuter of nature is the most correct definition of the *es*; in other words, the *es* derives from the mythopoietic imagination of men: *es regnet* [it is raining] is as mythical as *Iuppiter tonat*" [Jupiter thunders].[36] And Spitzer here refers explicitly to Kraus's essay, which says: "*Es*: chaos, the sphere, the whole, what is largest, most felt, which is already present before what is born first. Light, day, evening are not subjects (as grammarians erroneously suppose) but predicates; they cannot be subjects, because it is the *es* that must first bring them to the light, to the day, to the evening, while developing itself in them."[37]

Why this convergence on language? All history was fostering it: With the reign of rules ended, the adventurous study of them was beginning. "Man is no longer, only his symptoms are left"[38]—such was the implication, and the great Viennese haruspices took note of it. They had in common the severity of militant monks: With the abrogation of morality, "which wore shackles like jewels,"[39] a much more exacting etiquette came to establish clear distinctions in the practice of language. Kraus's words could stand in epigraphs to the works of each of these highly different individuals: "That someone may be a murderer proves nothing about his style, but the style may prove him to be a murderer."[40] Meanwhile, murderers all over were trying to ennoble themselves by style: "Every gesture is an arabesque, every breath is orchestrated, every beard is a statement. All this is necessary because otherwise horror would abide in the desolate cavities of windows. But I'm not fooled by the facade! I know how much art has had to leak out of life, and how much life out of art, to make this children's game between art and life possible."[41] All the Viennese theorists grew up "roofless behind artistic facades"[42]; they turned their backs on those facades and, in a no-man's land strewn with historical rubble, sought language, with different procedures, equally convinced that the secret was waiting for them, until language again revealed itself as a neutral, total, overhanging power of which we are the object before being the subject. It was an upsetting discovery, which destroyed the wings of the surrounding stage. Thus, the capital of decoration vanished in the dust of crumbling stuccoes shortly before life finally abandoned it to its ghosts.

THE LONGEST BREATH

Kraus's aphorisms are easy to get into but much harder to get out of. Flashes of intemperance, dizzying antitheses, and systematic paradoxes at first seem perfunctorily to delineate a trenchant, domineering character. If, however, one explores his other works, the clarity disperses. Anyone who has read through the more than 30,000 pages of *Die Fackel*; the 209 scenes and epilogue of *The Last Days of Mankind,* where the world and the theater finally agree on what cannot be represented; the long essays addressed to the events of the day and to the punctuation in an edition of Goethe; the implacable "operettas in prose" on trials for moral turpitude; the nine collections of *Worte in Versen,* where so many obsolete rules of versification are respected and so many unprecedented themes are imposed on poetry; the endless quotations; the couplets added to Jacques Offenbach; the two indispensable critical introductions to Heine and Johann Nestroy; the quarrel with the rascally newspaper publisher Imre Békessy and with the infamous Johan Schober, the Viennese police chief; the new translations of Shakespeare into the language that had already provided the best Shakespearean translations; the polyp-like periods of *Die Dritte Walpurgisnacht,* in which the difference in language designates by antiphrasis the brutality of its object, Nazism—anyone who has navigated among these omnivorous words and then revisits the aphorisms will find the clarity of the image that emerges from them confirmed, but ironically, for this clarity now appears to be the result of a monstrous compression. The aphorisms epitomize the whole work, but only after having been through the whole work does one realize that inexhaustible catacombs open beneath them.

For Kraus, the unit of measurement is the proposition: As in certain Shang bronzes, a ram's chest is also the face of an owl and the horns are also salamanders, so every one of his propositions is complete in itself but at the same time the expression of an unbounded organism, which is not even so much the individual work to which it belongs as the totality of Kraus's writings. In its turn, this totality, from the homogeneity that comes from its exuberant execution, appears—at a distance—to be a single block, a sort of single aphorism, a single breath held for an unbearably long time, almost as though the meaning of Kraus's words had become literal: "The longest breath is of the aphorism."[43] The aphorism is thus the laboratory for the "builder of propositions"; it is also the end of the process, its first and last step, the easiest and most difficult. The same goes for the reader: He will recognize the aphorisms as the most immediately accessible texts, which later turn out to be the most reluctant to yield their multiple allusions. The masters to whom Kraus is related are Georg Lichtenberg and Nietzsche, both of whom also found in the aphorism a deceptively discursive form, the greatest condensation on the surface as it emerged from language, a form that has "something dark, concentrated, obscurely violent . . . —entirely opposed to the maxim, which is an adage at the service of fashionable society, and worn smooth to the point of becoming lapidary, while the aphorism is as unsociable as a stone . . . (but a stone of mysterious origin, a heavy meteor that would seek to be vaporized as soon as it falls)."[44] Compared to his great predecessors, Kraus will again exacerbate that *lex minimi* that for Jean Paul was the token of *Witz*,[45] because he was drawn even more than they were to a form where the distinction between theme and development was annulled, where every element was at the same time material and structure. The accusation, first formulated by Kraus's early critics and many times repeated, that his essays were "mosaics of aphorisms" is thus all too exact, but this is a sign not of weakness but, rather, of their originality of form. Indeed, many of his aphorisms, which Kraus collected in three volumes, appear for the first time in the text of his essays, and they are equally in the right place whether isolated or interwoven. Their perspective changes, however, even when Kraus lifts them from the text without making any of his customary alterations. Now, preceded and followed by silence, stripped of presuppositions and consequences, the words of this writer who weighed every detail on the scales of absolute justice explicitly take on that *excess* of truth ("an aphorism never coincides with the truth; it is either a half truth or a truth and a half")[46] that redeems all of Kraus's work from the coercion of the law and its weapon: proof. For "it is not a question of 'proving' a thought to a reader, since a proof is not a thought."[47] Many times the aphorism succeeds, as Kraus demands, in "getting ahead of the truth." Superbly: "It should jump over it in a single bound."[48] This is a severe requirement, and the reader will necessarily be slow to discover which aphorisms actually correspond to it. He may even be surprised to find them almost hidden in the middle of idiosyncratic outbursts, nervous flutters that do not try to be anything more. But this too corresponds to a principle that Kraus always followed: to seek the most ephemeral pretexts, to occupy the most degraded materials, the most corrupted forms, so that often his finest aphorisms are and should be hard to distinguish from generalizing platitudes about life.

> I could not have built the Great Wall without
> cutting the veins of the earth.[49]
>
> —*Meng Tien*

THE GUARDIAN OF THE GREAT WALL

Here is how Kraus's work looks from the outside:

> Pages are strung evenly on pages. They may have turned out better or
> worse—but in a peculiar concatenation, which is purely outward, they
> keep on going with no necessary end in sight. . . . An overall structural
> principle is never present.
>
> For the structure, lacking as a whole, is present in every sentence and is
> instantly conspicuous.[50]

And here is how it looked to Kraus:

> When I begin a work, at the moment I take my pen in hand, I have no idea
> of the structure or the particulars of the work. And yet after having writ-
> ten the first proposition, I already feel, from its grammatical tension, how
> long the work will be, and this has never deceived me. (One could com-
> pare this feeling with that of an engineer, who recognizes the complete
> arch of a bridge from its junction.) The writing then proceeds without in-
> terruption until I am completely exhausted.[51]

Except this is not a bridge. Kraus's work connects only with the soil on
which it grows. It belongs to another grammar of space, of which there is
no closer example than the Great Wall of China, which also provided the
title for one of Kraus's astonishing essays. It stretches out, compact and
endless; many have seen its fortifications, uniformly squared, but few have
made the complete circuit, which takes years, and no one would be able
to tell you the form of the whole. Elias Canetti, in Vienna around 1930,
made a stubborn tour around that wall and left a description of it that is a
perfect gloss on Kafka's story:

> Sentence joins sentence, piece joins piece into a Great Wall of China. It is
> joined equally well everywhere; but no one knows what it actually enclos-
> es. There is no empire beyond this wall, the wall itself is the empire; all the
> juices of the empire that may have existed went into this wall, into its con-
> struction. No one can tell what was inside or what was outside; the empire
> lay on both sides, the wall stands towards both the inside and the outside.

The wall is everything, a cyclopean end in itself, wandering through the world, uphill, downhill, through dales and plains and very many deserts. Since the wall is alive, it may think that everything else is destroyed. Of its armies, which populated it, which had to guard it, only a single, lonesome sentry is left. This lonesome sentry is also its lonesome expander. Wherever he looks into the countryside, he feels the need to erect a further section. The most diverse materials offer themselves; he is able to form them all into new ashlars. One can promenade on this wall for years, and it will never come to an end.[52]

Certainly, this builder's activity is a very strange one, and he himself insisted on distinguishing it clearly from other writing possibilities:

While, for example, I deem myself nothing but an ordinary *proposition builder,* innocent of any effect on life and of any ethical enhancement that language can produce, nevertheless within this modest activity I think I have more reasons to be megalomaniac than everything that today calls itself *writer,* though I always direct all the intensity of work and sensibility only to the single proposition and never, for example, to a novel (and just the same for each proposition, so that there can be no difference in value among my propositions, and each construction appears equally finished and well done).[53]

Convinced that "civilization ends when the barbarians flee from it,"[54] Kraus could bear to live only on the frontiers, on a wall that was both a sign of protection and of the impossibility of escape and that he sometimes called *the wall of language:* "I am often close to the wall of language, and now I catch only its echo. Often I bash my head against the wall of language."[55] When, in his last years, he was accused of becoming incomprehensible and inaccessible, it was because the sentry, squeezed between a civilization abandoned by the barbarians and a barbarism brought up on civilization, felt "buried alive"[56] in the wall and now turned only to the underground streams of water that had long been flowing there.

> Every art is erotic.
> —*Adolf Loos*

EROTIC OVERTURE

Disguised as a cynical flaneur whose wisecracks impart a knowledge of life by definition suspect, Kraus the aphorist appears with issue 198 of *Die*

Fackel (March 1906) in a cluster of remarks collected under the heading *"Abfälle"* (rubbish). And what will such a dubious character talk about as he sits unceremoniously in one of the city's coffeehouses if not *about women*? Of these first aphorisms, many deal with women, and the worldly priority of this topic over others will be maintained in the three collections of aphorisms that follow over the years: The first section of *Sprüche und Widersprüche* (1909) bears the title "Woman, Fantasy"; the first of *Pro domo et mundo* (1912), "About woman, about Morality"; the first of *Nachts* (1918) is devoted to "Eros." Such regularity must surely have much significance for a captious formal spirit like Kraus: As in Mozart's *Don Giovanni,* the light and grim overture to his work comes, to every degree, under the sign of woman. Here the network of antitheses and conflicts begins to get knotted, and the tourney of contradictions opens that will run through every one of his pages. And to cover up somewhat the subtle grafting operation, Kraus here plays at hiding himself in a fairly disreputable social guise, that of the entertainer, and the fierce, divine face of Eros flashes forth in Viennese drawing-room chatter. But even in the other registers of the work, successively revealed in the first ten years of *Die Fackel,* woman maintains her initiating function. First of all, in the satire on topics of everyday life: After a rapid, devastating, but not indispensable digression through the scandals of Kakania, there follow in quick succession the stock exchange, the trade unions, industry, the university, the menu with which the Krupps placate journalists at a reception (the same Krupps who dock the wages of their workers for the day of the Kaiser's visit to the factory, an honor that dispenses with food). The first pretext that finally and forever separates Kraus from the deadly addiction to pretexts is that peculiar scandal that "begins when the police put an end to it":[57] government intervention on the side of sexual morality. With issue 115 of *Die Fackel* (September 1902), which is taken up almost entirely by a piece entitled "Sittlichkeit und Kriminalität," the form of Kraus's essays emerges complete: Ample quotations from Shakespeare, wickedly attuned to the present, introduce the excitement of the tritest court proceedings—a trial for adultery!—on a cosmic scale. The female sex, guilty in its origin, stands always at the center of these instances of male justice: Cocottes, procuresses, adulteresses, and prostitutes appear in sordid courtrooms to be subjected to the vexations of a juridical system that makes it possible easily to control the misery of the civilization inflicting it. Finally, that range of intentionally literary essays, which will later include, among others, the two memorable ones on Nestroy and Heine, starts in June 1905 with a discussion of Frank Wedekind's *Pandora's Box*; in those pages, myth makes its entrance in the narrow arena of a circus cage.

One must, however, take the aphorisms as a guide if one is to find, behind the flurry of witticisms, those morganatic associations that for Kraus will always remain adamantine bonds. First of all, the woman/language combination: With radical archaism, Kraus sees in woman and speech the two fragments of nature that society constantly exchanges and subsumes in its own pure element, money, without ever succeeding, however, in eliminating their still extraneous features, the gaze they direct at orders other than the civil one. "In the art of language 'what is improperly used' is called metaphor. Therefore metaphors are perversions of language and perversions are the metaphors of love."[58] To remove the subjects of the exchange from their function is a perverse practice par excellence, the unforgivable impropriety in social custom. And in the background of the dark paths of metaphor and perversion, the *coniunctio* in pleasure of womankind and language is celebrated. The erotic relation with the word and observation of the syntactical abuses perpetrated by woman on society are the shining aspects of a search, whose sordid reverse side is the de-eroticizing of thought in the suppliers of public opinion and the persecution of the woman who acts for pleasure or even—horrors!—for pleasure and money at the same time.

On the level of immediate satire, there is a swarm of vicissitudes gleaned from the judicial annals of Vienna: Transposed into Kraus's version, they produce moments when we might think we are witnessing the "birth of operetta from the spirit of prose":[59] The Riehl case (Regine Riehl, brothel keeper), the Hervay case (Leontine von Hervay, accused of bigamy and evil practices), and many others are monuments to the ludicrous nature of justice, the majestic heights of a civilization ignorant of life. Here, then, at the center are the hammered and indelible sentences ("A trial for crimes against decency is the necessary development from individual immorality to a general one, against whose grim background the assured guilt of the defendant luminously stands out"),[60] while all around it revolves an inexhaustible and gilded *ronde,* the social romance of Vienna, dreadful but always—it is a point of honor—light.

Indignation, by itself, generally makes for bad poetry, but the perfection of these prose pieces—and even more of those on similar themes in *Die chinesische Mauer,* four years later—is the result of a sensual alliance between feudal homage and vengeful raptus. Walter Benjamin correctly saw there the shadow of Baudelaire, who was the first to establish the "solidarity of the man of letters with the whore."[61] Kraus, as heir of the great dandy, whistled "biting minuets . . . to the *chassé-croisé* of Justitia and Venus."[62] And never had anyone shown so plainly that what is frightful about Justitia is not so much her punitive aspect, which any sort of humanitarianism is quick to mitigate, as her ignorance and clumsy incompetence before the facts of life; and that Venus, who everywhere weaves her immoral plots, in the slums and in the most austere offices, is always a benevolent adviser to one's intelligence, an adviser who has, among her prime tasks, the indispensable one of mocking society.

> *La haine du bourgeois est un phénomène romantique, excessif, comme tous les phénomènes romantiques, mais très sain.* [Hatred of the bourgeois is a romantic phenomenon, excessive like all romantic phenomena, but very sound.]
> —*Élie Faure*

MIZZI VEITH

For [Mizzi Veith] did indeed lead a certain kind of life. And not by herself, according to what they say. A brutal stepfather prevented her from becoming a telephone operator. Nor did he allow her to work in a match factory or to learn the tobacco trade. On the contrary, from her early youth, she was obliged to take life on its lighter terms and cultivate an impulse that is the worst blot on woman: that of pleasing men. Her stepfather demanded that she be pretty and not even try to hide it. And therefore he disgraced her into profiting from a physical defect that human society deems worthy of only a penny of alms and its own contempt. Had she been born without hands, to live this way would have been decent, albeit punishable for vagabondage. But since her hands were beautiful, she was a fake cripple, therefore dishonest, and threatened by the law against vagabondage all the same. The father, who had not forced those hands to ruin themselves working at a factory bench, behaved with her like a criminal. She sank so low that her figure ended by being emphasized by her toilette instead of being hidden behind an apron. Such exhibitions are a form of prostitution, and those who abandon themselves to them are all the more despised since by doing so, they arouse an aesthetic enjoyment in the indignant spectator, while the defects shown by other cripples arouse only moral sensations. And the excuse that a woman can't help it if she's beautiful will never be accepted by society, since the latter has countless veils at its disposal to conceal the evil. A father who fosters or tolerates such exhibitions becomes guilty of a crime. Mizzi Veith was brought up to earn pleasure for herself and with it the scorn of bourgeois society.[63]

CHINATOWN

In that remote epoch, some people—who did not share the tendency, which today has become a sign of maturity, of not acknowledging "the bipartition of humankind" ("it has not yet been recognized by science"!)[64]—used to construct, demolish, and construct all over again tables of vices and obligatory virtues for man and woman. Nietzsche had recalled the whip and Ariadne; August Strindberg, in his *Plaidoyer d'un fou,* testified to the exuberant comedy of the war between the sexes, and there was an undoubted pang to it; Wedekind hunted down the last specimen of woman as Wild Beast in the sawdust and papier-mâché of the circus; Peter Altenberg lovingly described his erotic little girls; Otto Weininger, in a scientific frenzy, tabulated female defects and affirmed the original bisexuality that Freud, during his shadowy friendship with Wilhelm Fliess, was convinced he had discovered. It seldom occurred to anyone that mythology and Plato's *Symposium* might have much to suggest along these lines; the age of anthropological common sense was only about to begin, and in the tribe of Europe the *numerus clausus* was still in force. At this surprising point came the ubiquitous infiltration of sex: Nietzsche aphorized, "The degree and kind of a man's sexuality reaches up into the topmost summit of his spirit."[65] And what for our earliest ancestors had been a cosmic implication now had to be discovered and experienced as social destiny, that is, natural catastrophe, on the occasion of its fearful reawakening:

> We have built our huts on a crater that we thought was spent, we have spoken with nature in human language, and since we did not understand its language, we thought it would no longer move. . . . We have dared to warm our feet at the sacred fire that once aroused the male spirit to action. And

now that fire has ignited the house. The social structures that should have guarded the fire and protected us are valued as fuel.[66]

Kraus, smiling ominously, contemplates the sanctimony of that "continuous amazement that nature has failed to allot the same measure of insufficiency to both sexes; that it has created woman, for whom pleasure is only a foretaste of pleasure, and man, who is left exhausted by it."[67] He observes, and without expressing an opinion, he begins to channel a flood of associations. Meanwhile, he suggests that what he has noted about woman also applies to nature itself; likewise, the ridiculous and authoritarian part of man is also that of society and the spirit. All the themes on which German philosophy, from Kant onward, had discoursed, with its tendency toward solemn moralizing about the behavior of man, are here surreptitiously derided, because the poisonous thread of sexuality has been introduced into the fabric of the discussion. Any prolegomenon to future metaphysics now leads directly to libertine witticisms. Thus, on the basis of certain neglected sexual observations, Kraus elegantly, firmly, and quietly dismantles the platform of dignity. And against the light, he already sees all of Western civilization taking refuge in the back rooms of Chinatown laundries, where are preserved excited letters from ladies beyond suspicion to a Chinese waiter, the gentle, impeccable satisfier of white women who becomes, on occasion, their murderer. Of course, the ladies who hastened toward the "great bath of pleasure"[68] in the dens of Chinatown did not know they were being moved by the same impulse to salvation that Western civilization clumsily tries to suppress: "the yellow hope"![69] But though clarity was never great in society in this movement and was great, if limited, in its ladies, in Kraus, on the other hand, clarity was so prominent that he diligently listed the reasons for this impulse. He invented a utopian model, which corresponds in many respects with the historical reality of China, in the manner of the eighteenth-century theorists but with different intentions:

> A Chinese does not commit a sin when he commits it. He does not need scruples of conscience to find pleasure in pleasure. He is backward because he has not yet finished liquidating the treasures of thought that have accumulated for him over thousands of years. . . . He is a juggler who commands life and love with a finger, while the panting athlete engages his whole person. . . . He keeps morality and pleasure separate and thus prevents them from being a nuisance. . . . He is not sentimental and does not

have that lack of economy in the soul that we call morality. He does not know the duty to love his neighbor, where it requires that two be hanged with one noose. His life is quite removed from a sick ethics that weakens the strong man, since it enjoins him to protect the weak. . . . He lives fully and feels no need for the humanitarian spirit. . . . Convinced that he is replaceable, he gives exceptional proof of a social sense that in Western ethics is disguised egoism. He is able to make room; his love for his neighbor operates not in a spatial dimension but a temporal one. He does not live in the delusion of individuality, which tries to assert itself in the world of facts. He submerges himself in the teeming mass of the crowd and is thus indistinguishable to himself as to the eyes of others. Since all are equal, they can do without the benefits of democracy.[70]

ANTITHESIS AND ORIGIN

Kraus's insolent asides—on incessant female sensuality and male sexual ineptitude, on the pleasure of the woman who provokes the spirit of man, on such disastrous anthropological impoverishments as the woman who *also* has a brain and the man who *also* has an insistent sexuality—must all be traced back to the peculiar function exercised by *antithesis* in his work. First of all, if Kraus is not a thinker but a language that thinks, then it will come as no surprise that his ideas should present themselves in pairs of opposites, as is especially required by the structure of language, which, from its bilateral phonological oppositions to the fatal bifurcations of the abstract lexicon, is built on opposition. But it would be naive to consider Kraus's curt statements, the abrupt caesuras that recur in his pages, as binding: One must always keep in mind that what is at stake here is the extreme truth of the aphorism. And as a surplus over truth, these aphorisms constitute a device that is of no use in describing the world of opposites, now translated into a language of opposites. It is useful only in making it revolve toward its origin, which does not acknowledge them: "The antithesis is not included in creation. For in the latter all is incomparable and devoid of contradictions. Only separation of the world from the creator makes room for the longing that for every opposite finds its lost image."[71] Here that private cosmogonic abyss over which all of Kraus's work hangs suspended suddenly opens. In this writer who demanded the absolute in fine print but did not refer to any explicit certainty, the word "origin" crops up in crucial passages. "You remained at the origin. The origin is the goal"[72]—Kraus's secret is hinted at in this line. And it is precisely the word "origin" that has attracted the interest of critics, from certain well-intentioned apologists, who have seen in it an appeal to "authenticity," a word that on some lips is a stab in the back, to various thoughtful castigators who have recognized in it a vicious superstition, so that Kraus seems reactionary to more advanced minds. (Sometimes they add: what a pity, since he was antimilitarist.) And it is hard to say which is more gross: the enlightened, progressive intelligence, which sniffs the stench of elitism in anyone who thinks for the pure vice of thinking or even simply pays attention to words, or the parvenu of the spirit, for whom nothing is sufficiently free from contact with modern life; remote from the vulgarity of the times, of which he himself is a striking example, he is the last descendant of all those who followed the precepts succinctly stated in Gilbert and Sullivan's *Patience:*

> Be eloquent in praise of the very dull old days which have long
>   since passed away,
> And convince 'em, if you can, that the reign of good Queen Anne
>   was Culture's palmiest day.
> Of course you will pooh-pooh whatever's fresh and new, and
>   declare it's crude and mean,
> For Art stopped short in the cultivated court of the Empress
>   Josephine.
> . . . .
> Then a sentimental passion of a vegetable fashion must excite your
>   languid spleen,
> An attachment *à la* Plato for a bashful young potato, or a not-too-
>   French French bean![73]

But the question remains: "What's the use of yearning for Elysian Fields when you know you can't get 'em, and would only let 'em out on building leases if you had 'em?"[74]

According to two prevailing strands of Western thought, the origin can be invoked as a reference either to nature or to a *primum* that is both chronological and metaphysical. Rousseau and Plato stand as leading spokesmen for these two paths. In Kraus, on the other hand, the origin does not have a clear ancestry, although one can recognize the Hebraic phylogeny in it: This origin, which is only "the gleam"[75] in which the word dissolves its guilt, is not only extraneous but hostile to conceptualization, unable to transform itself into an instrument. It does not serve to pay homage to historical or prehistorical models. Kraus, this theologian of language, offers no verbal exits. If anything, he offers only an orientation of one's gaze: The word, with all the heavy armor of its antitheses, cannot do more than turn toward the fluidity of the origin and reecho—not state—the Adamic intermingling of sound and thing. There would be nothing marvelous in the word without the look it sends far back, the farthest from itself and everything, when it is contemplated in its clandestine encounters with the writer: "The closer one observes a word, the farther back it sends one's gaze."[76] And all this serves as presentiment, with nothing imperative about it; here it is not Hamann speaking, or a latter-day cabalist, but "only one of the epigones / who live in the old house of language."[77]

And yet, unlike many who glorify the origin, Kraus does not see in the epigone a spent force; indeed, for him, it is only for those who live in the end that the origin is freed from the misleading ambiguity of the *primum*. This was clearly understood by Benjamin:

> Now if language . . . is a woman, how far is the author removed, by an unerring instinct, from those who hasten to be the first with her, how multifariously he forms his thought, which incites her with intuition, rather than slake her with knowledge, how he lets hatred, contempt, malice ensnare one another, how he slows his step and seeks the detour of epigonism in order finally to give her the pleasure that is the sum of all the previous ones plus the last thrust that Jack [the Ripper] holds in readiness for Lulu.[78]

VOICES

There is another important corollary to the theorem about woman and language. As early as 1903, Kraus wrote that in the origin of the sexes, "woman's free sensuality is the full value by which nature compensated her when it gave imagination to man."[79] This mythical division of elements gives rise to a complex game of exchanges and balances by which art is nourished. Thus, the society that has domesticated eros simultaneously undergoes an atrophy of the imagination; in the end, the two events coincide. And society keeps going precisely because it is incapable of imagining the separation from life in which it continues to live. Kraus thus observed a world that continued to produce machines that it could not conceive: The great social theories are in certain ways also to be classified among such machines, huge experimental apparatuses that, under laboratory conditions, were to operate on all humanity. For the age is experimental—and in art less than elsewhere; indeed, the greatest experiment takes place where the capacity to imagine it is lacking. In this sense, World War I is the unsurpassed experimental event of the century. And that is how Kraus saw it. For himself, he chose the opposite path. What the age did without perceiving it *had* to be experienced and expressed by Kraus, by a hidden accord of counterbalances indissolubly linking the two parts. Like his master Nestroy, Kraus knew that art is "the quickest connection between a gutter and the Milky Way,"[80] and in exercising it he found himself continually invaded by the swarm of implicit hallucinations that were not consumed by everyday banality. These are images projected on the "wall of fire"[81] in front of his desk, *at night,* and they are also voices, bomb fragments of sentences that loom during the day and grow gigantic in the darkness: The page of the newspaper, for example, is immediately translated into an oral jumble. As in a fable, Kraus knows he is doomed to hear these voices forever. All the inflections, accents, cadences—they envelop him acoustically, challenging, jeering, piercing. This spiritualism with the living was forced on Kraus by the precision of his ear. For him, the quotation is first of all a magical means. Whatever he quotes has been felt as a threatening, hallucinatory presence, but in the end it has been overcome by the fury of the writer who, lying in wait like a marauder,[82] has wrenched the ghoulish words from their context to enclose them forever, as though in amber, in their stiff and ultimately revealing gesture in the pages of *Die Fackel.* They retain few signs of the treatment—at most some typographical spacing—and the perfect example is the one in which there is no visible trace of the shamanic operation.

THE DEMON

"It is deeply rooted in Kraus's nature, and it is the stigma of every debate concerning him, that all apologetic arguments miss their mark. The great work of Leopold Liegler springs from an apologetic posture. To certify Kraus as an 'ethical personality' is his first objective. That cannot be done. The dark background from which his image detaches itself is not formed by his contemporaries, but is the primeval world or the world of the demon."[83] Every magical encounter presupposes a profound mingling of opposing forces: This is why the apologetic defense of Kraus is so inadequate in trying to make him into a kind of champion of good causes, a "defender of the rights of the individual" and whatever nobler things an inert imagination is able to come up with. He was all this too, of course. But Kraus's relations with the world seem much darker, more ambiguous, infernal: He was compelled, driven by his demon in the midst of demons. In many issues of *Die Fackel* a feeling of oppression was produced by the endless flow of print, page after page without a single heading, where, once involved, one gets the feeling of being caught in a thickening tangle, a sense of urgency that takes one's breath away, the omnipresence of an avenging judgment. All these allude to the scenes of torture that take place in the cellars of the Great Wall, scenes in which Kraus does not only play the part of victim. What goes on there, what exchange of torments and pleasures, can only be perceived at intervals. But a bargain-priced nobility is insufficient today. And besides, it is vulgar.

Not by chance, it was Elias Canetti, one of the great experts on present-day demonry, who wrote the only eyewitness account on this aspect of Kraus. There are few pages so illuminating—about Kraus or their author. Canetti describes a state that many experienced but, paralyzed either by adoration or a deserter's hatred, were unable to talk about: their obsession with Kraus, who transformed many of his admirers into purely emotional zombies. Himself ruled by voices, Kraus ruled through his voice. For Canetti, the experience of Kraus's readings[84] is the moment when his captivating power was symbolically discharged:

> In spring 1924—I had only just returned to Vienna a few weeks earlier—friends took me to my first lecture by Karl Kraus.
>
> The huge concert-house auditorium was jammed. I sat far in back, able to see very little at that distance: a small, rather frail man, slightly hunched, with a face that came to a point below, of an incredible agility, the movements of whom I did not understand, they had something of an unknown creature to them, a newly discovered animal, I could not have said which. His voice was sharp and agitated and easily dominated the auditorium in sudden and frequent intensifications.[85]

Canetti saw in those readings the splendor of a law that scorched and destroyed in its fervor.[86] He was violently engulfed by Kraus's power, and it took him years to free himself. He condenses in a few lines the demonic tension of that period of his life:

> For at that time I truly experienced what it means to live in a dictatorship. I was its voluntary, its devoted, its passionate and enthusiastic follower. Any foe of Karl Kraus's was a corrupt, an immoral creature. And even though it never reached the point, as was customary in subsequent dictatorships, of exterminating the alleged vermin, I nevertheless had what I must confess, to my shame, I had what I cannot term any differently, I had my "Jews"—people whom I snubbed when passing them in restaurants or on the street, whom I did not deign to look at, whose lives did not concern me, who were outlawed and banished for me, whose touch would have sullied me, whom I quite earnestly did not count as part of humanity: the victims and enemies of Karl Kraus.[87]

THE REJECTION OF DEATH

"Nothing more distressing than his followers, nothing more lost than his adversaries."[88] Solitary amid these ruins, Kraus had a relationship with his enemy object that has nothing to do with the good conscience of an accuser. To approach it, one is obliged to set foot in a secret zone, where Kraus's connection with the world will appear to be of a different order—at worst, reversed. Having passed the barrier of burning light, one now enters a place of lasting twilight, and there once again one finds the countless voices and specters that had besieged Kraus's desk for so many years. But this time they are there with the tacit consent of the writer, who never came to terms with them. They are waiting for something: They are postponing death, because in Kraus's heart was the mad Jewish rejection of death, the struggle with the jealous Lord to hold onto life. The figures in every scandal are collected to expunge the primordial scandal, which is death itself. Unlike Stefan George, who tried by ceremonies to separate himself from the rabble that honored him (a "flight from time toward eternity" that was rather the "flight of a contemporary toward the hieratic"),[89] Kraus does not mind mingling with the foulest everyday rubbish in order to involve it in words. For he is certain that if the word is not interrupted, death is forestalled. With the violence of biblical characters when they turn to the Lord, Kraus revealed in two of his most important poems—"Todesfurcht" and "Bange Stunde"—the root of his obsession:

to write endlessly is the ultimate exorcism granted him by time to stave off death. He lives with death, because the word directed to the origin is endless, and thus the hellish forms that evoke it proliferate as always. And this word *is incorporated*[90] in those figures:

> they hang in a bloodstained chain
> from my form the many forms
> that you have granted me to keep
> and in a blessed bond of pain
> endless voices from my mouth.[91]

It is now clearer how the pages of *Die Fackel* functioned as a magical barrier, as is the reason for the tendency to fill them entirely with type, eliminating heads: Death can infiltrate every interstice in the Great Wall. Faced with extinction, Kraus recognizes that he is entangled in an enormous chain with his own specters: All of them, bound to him forever, will have to join him in constraining death; unlimited existence must be imposed on the most mortal forms in the world. In this blasphemous refusal lies Kraus's true prophetic gesture. Damning or saving himself but always dragging behind him, as in a medieval Triumph, all that he himself has condemned: This move of pure frenzy alone cancels whatever blinding effect his satire may have. Beyond the imaginary theater of voices and hallucinations, it re-creates a faint curtain of light, which this time, however, does not destroy but conceals, allowing everything to go on spinning its crazy wheel. "He used to say he would like to live forever, that he didn't believe he would have to die . . . That the spirit ought to have the power to prevent death. . . . He said verbatim: 'Only in a state of madness can I fall into the hands of death. It's not true that Goethe died peacefully. He howled for three days and three nights because of his fear of dying.'"[92]

GUILT AND ORIGIN

In Kraus, the origin is so strong it lifts the chain of guilt; in Benjamin and then in Adorno, the opposite will occur: The chain of guilt will forever blight the origin. Roberto Bazlen used to say that Kraus, Benjamin, and Adorno represented three successive and increasingly vulnerable ways of emerging from the ghetto: Actually, considering them in order, one notes a progressive decrease in the capacity to sustain reality (but it should be added that, as in every great decadence, each step liberates not only new weaknesses but also certain qualities that were scarcely apparent in the previous phases). The stylistic lineage is obvious: the extreme syntactical mobility, the quivering play of antitheses that devour each other only to be promptly regenerated, words unexpectedly brandished like escutcheons, contempt for gradualness, aphoristic tension in every sentence—all this comes from Kraus, as does the construction of a stage on which to place society and culture. Benjamin will add his mournful, exalted sense of allegory; Adorno, an incipient yet already rigid formalization of thought but especially an inexorable and unequaled eye for industry, as revealed in his most admirable book *Minima Moralia.* And in music he will no longer read the cosmos but the astral light of the psyche, of forms, and of society.

Nature, ambivalent stand-in for the religious element, is in Kraus not only an object of thought but also a model of thinking, the site of the manifold play of appearance. Kraus has not just one thought, but many. He ignores philosophy; if he reads Nietzsche or Schopenhauer or Kant, it is primarily because they are great writers. His maniacal insistence on precision in language is combined with a surprising indifference to the discipline of speculation. He stands up in the midst of the tribe and speaks; a prior certainty accompanies his gestures. This is no longer so in Benjamin: A gnostic condemnation of reality as such is instilled in him from the beginning, along with repugnance at recognizing its dark ancestry. So Benjamin became a Marxist: All of nature appeared to be ensnared—by magic—in guilt. But in nature lies the only possible liberation: There the messianic light appears that will later be called revolution. For those who turn to doomed nature, destiny, having now become only a baleful power, has destruction in store. This is explained in Benjamin's admirable essay on Goethe's *Elective Affinities:* "If they, not caring about the human, fall prey to the power of nature, then the natural life, which does not preserve its innocence in man unless it is linked to a higher life, drags the latter down with it as well."[93] This is a grim mythology but it has noble precedents, and it reappears here in all its splendor. It was on this basis that Benjamin judged Kraus, thereby deriving the arguments to distance himself from him:

> That the sociological area never becomes transparent to him—no more in his attack on the press than in his defense of prostitution—is connected to this attachment to nature. That to him the fit state of man appears not as

the destiny and fulfillment of nature liberated through revolutionary change, but as an element of nature per se, of an archaic nature without history, in its pristine, primeval state, throws uncertain, disquieting reflections even on his idea of freedom and of humanity. It is not removed from the realm of guilt that he has traversed from pole to pole: from mind to sexuality.[94]

But actually Kraus does not *want* to remove himself from guilt; he is not seeking a paradise of origins nor one of postrevolution, and his inflexible immobility has a strength that criticism leaves intact: "Spellbound I stay on this spot, / and I can't go back and don't want to go away."[95] Benjamin's mythology, on the other hand, will not resist the temptation to transform itself into historical doctrine, thereby distorting itself and history: The fundamental fragment "On the Mimetic Faculty" simultaneously presents these two faces. Here a flow is already outlined from mimetic power (and hence: speaking nature, chain of guilt, magic as coercion) to the semiotic power of language, understood as a depleting liberation. And to grasp the slavery of prehistory, as his myth requires, Benjamin must suppose a utilitarian origin, one of terrified self-preservation: "[Man's] gift of seeing resemblances is nothing other than a rudiment of the powerful compulsion in former times to become and behave like something else."[96] What here is concisely alluded to will later be made clear, far too clear in Theodor Adorno and Max Horkheimer's *Dialectic of Enlightenment:* splendid pages if we include them in a series of glosses on Odysseus and the Sirens; awkward and fumbling when taken as an interpretation of the past. And this time it is truly a rudiment of the Enlightenment that keeps one from looking back at the origin without superstitious terror.

MIRROR DECEPTION

"In this great big time, which I knew when it was so little, and which will be little again if any time remains to it; and which, a metamorphosis of this kind being impossible in the sphere of organic development, we should have to call rather a fat time and in truth heavy as well; in this time, in which what could not have been imagined is just what is happening, and in which what can no longer be imagined will have to happen, and which, if it could be imagined, would not happen"[97]—"in this great big time" in which Kraus is fated to live, the intermingling of word and thing is not only a dream of the origin but tends more and more to be diabolically fulfilled in everyday reality. To have recognized this constitutes the uniqueness of Kraus's vision of language; he is thus not only one of the last archaic human beings who stabilize with words a rapport prior to any sort of nominalism but also one of the few new human beings to perceive how, at the outset of nominalism, the polluted waters of the word impiously combine again with the thing. This is the moment when "pens are dipped in blood and swords in ink."[98] As long as the shells of opinions floated on the waters and hid them, a breath of unknown origin still blew over the word, but it was the word of the end. If in 1908 Kraus could already declare that, in his view, "the pressure gauge stood at ninety-nine,"[99] it was to demonstrate not a thoughtful expectation of disaster (which it was not all that hard to foresee) but the sober certainty that the word was already by this time word of the end—namely, a word standing precisely as a mirror reflection of the origin. He knew very well that "the last days of mankind" were a whole epoch. To turn the word of the end back toward the origin, to live in the *mirror deception* of a world that destroys not itself but the discriminating spirit in order to produce a deadly equilibrium, a parody of Eden—this requires a paradoxical strategy that accounts for many of Kraus's methods, including the decision to move in the *continuum* of public opinion, to draw from it all his materials. For public opinion, that Platonic idea that goes about the city in civilian clothes, by now happily released from any antiquated participation in earthly matters, is the place par excellence for mirror images.

Here one can grasp the ultimate reason for Kraus's opposition to Hofmannsthal. Kraus rejects the quest for noble, uncontaminated materials, which for him is a knee-jerk reaction to the "transformation of our tradition into a corporation."[100] (Later years have merely extended this process to Tradition in its exoteric sense.) Indeed, all aestheticism can be seen as the interference of industrious *"sténographes acérés des nuances"* [sharp stenographers of nuances][101] who begin to amass and catalogue prestigious signs in "mythological trunks, theological hatboxes, and baskets of quotations":[102] from sensation to taste to vice and to rarity, the great collection that today the multitudes have exclusive access to begins to build up. In the first issue of *Die Fackel,* one already finds Hofmannsthal described as a "collector of gems from all literatures."[103] A few years later he is actually compared to Maximilian Harden, the virtuoso of flowery journalism: "Common to both is the fact that when they drink wine, they go into raptures over the vessel, with this sole difference, that Hofmannsthal afterward describes to us the precious stones that are mounted on it, while Harden after each sip goes to consult his card file under the letter G, and copies whatever he finds written there about goblets."[104] And later Kraus was to heighten the metaphor still more, writing that Hofmannsthal "has gone on living, by now sober for some time, from the intoxication of drinking from gold goblets in which there's no wine."[105]

What Kraus revealed and established for the first time is the moment in which form enters as an essential part of the production process. Style becomes available: It is a commodity administered by civilization like oil reserves and the past. The claim that *one* style is the objective spirit of a particular moment thereby also disappears. The last attempt to aim so high was Art Nouveau, which lived and died in this contradiction, expressed in the wishful thinking that made the industrial product regress to a form of nature. The rise of the category of dress, or rather of presentation—what was designated at the time as "ornament"—marks the entry of all of history into the closet. Today all this envelops the world, and the blunting of perception is so advanced that in the end, Harden's convoluted prose and certain articles by Stéphane Mallarmé—though only born from the same death—may be judged interchangeable: Both of them are examples of exquisite fin de siècle journalism. The moment of aestheticism as a final intrusion of the spirit on the market, seen with the hindsight of slaves, may also seem quite similar to the moment when literature *took leave* of itself, which was indeed heralded in Mallarmé and then continued to be manifested off and on, often clinging to a pious obedience to form, silhouetted against a background of absolute negation. Hegel had already noted this in the romantics while rejecting them. Thus, if in both cases it is a question of form, the ambiguity of the game was fated to worsen with time, and today we are living in its perpetual death throes: the late mimesis of *rupture,* combined with the reawakening of the masses, converges primarily on a picnic of French theorists; it is nothing but the homage of bigots to the heroes of *transgression.* In a gnostic world inhabited by agnostics, there is no gesture guaranteed to transgress, and there is nothing sadder than a community of enlightened minds still regretting the final, familiar sin.

NEW FORMS

> We have broken
> the ages in half.
> What to do with forms,
> the New, the Enormous!
> Not for one, not for all
> were we constructed.[106]

So sing the café bacchantes in the "magical operetta" *Literatur,* still one of the sharpest satirical skewerings of the avant-garde. And in other works as well, Kraus had withering words to say about the advanced art of the "parasites of the end of the world":[107] The expressionist and dada crew, and sometimes even great writers like Gottfried Benn, were caught in his net. But Kraus's criticism of new forms has no connection with the foolishness of those critics of the decline of the arts who shudder with horror at the principles of fragmentation, montage, and hybridization. On the contrary, Kraus knew perfectly well what reckless claims, rigor in darkness, were implicit in those principles, and he was unsparing in his attack on those who once again proclaimed them without being able to imagine their meaning. Only in specific differences in these forms can one grasp their poverty, see how far short of their axioms they fall, while to reject the axioms themselves is sheer bigotry. Kraus was able to criticize the feuilleton article, which was devouring literature from within and ended by offering its prey as an encouragement to good living. But he applied the principles of random digression, the fleeting impression, and the transposition of *flânerie* into an art form, which is a feuilleton discovery, in such perfect prose as "Lob der verkehrten Lebensweise." And the perception of the surreality of the city, which runs from Baudelaire to Benjamin in *Einbahnstrasse,* André Breton in *Nadja,* and Louis Aragon in *Paysan de Paris,* is already contained in the aphorisms about certain petrified rebus-landscapes of Vienna or Berlin. The same goes for the theater: All the audacities of expressionist theater look timid in the presence of the inexorable excess of any setting, any reduction to images, in *The Last Days of Mankind,* where countless forms inherited from literature, from the Goethean strophe to the *disputatio,* the Chinese quotation, Nestroyan farce, the diatribe, the plot for a puppet theater, the curtain-raiser, the essay, come together in mutual slaughter. And the many who have thought it clever to remark that the famous first sentence of *Die Dritte*

Walpurgisnacht ("Apropos of Hitler, nothing comes to mind") would correspond to a total lack of ideas in the whole book are unaware of the terrible formal unity of that text, in which quotations from the Nazi press are enclosed by a counterpoint that has no precedents in German prose, and the simple typographical arrangement provides an illuminating shock that one would expect in vain from the pedagogy of *The Resistible Rise of Arturo Ui.* For years now, the monopoly on writings against the evil powers has been assigned to Brecht, but a few words by Adorno are enough to demonstrate the inconsistency of some of his efforts in that direction:

> To present processes within large-scale industry as transactions between crooked vegetable dealers suffices for a momentary shock-effect, but not for dialectical theatre. The illustration of late capitalism by images from the agrarian or criminal registers does not permit the monstrosity of modern society to emerge in full clarity from the complex phenomena masking it. . . . It harmlessly interprets the seizure of power on the highest level as the machination of rackets outside society, not as the coming-to-itself of society as such.[108]

Kraus expressed that coming-to-itself. In every ramification of his work he introduced new forms, without ever theorizing about them, and he was always looking back to a fictitious place of perfection inhabited by a few classics, at whose center was Goethe's *Pandora.* In this, he surely showed that "interplay between reactionary theory and revolutionary practice"[109] that Benjamin attributed to him.

> The enemy is the new power with old emblems
> at its disposal.
>
> —*Karl Kraus*

CHINA AND QUOTATION

In March 1931, the young critic Erich Heller delivered a lecture in Prague in which, in connection with Karl Kraus, he referred to a famous passage from Confucius: "If concepts are not correct, works are not finished; if works are not finished, art and morality do not flourish; if morality and art do not flourish, justice is not exact; if justice is not exact, the country does not know where to lean. Therefore one must not tolerate words not being in order. That is what matters."[110] Karl Kraus reproduced this "magnificent quotation" in *Die Fackel,* thus accidentally meeting the source from which all his work derives: a Chinese sorites. He had discovered its principles through undisciplined practice, without the help of a cultural bond: All he knew about China was what he read in the newspapers. Yet Benjamin's allegorical fancy was once again precise when he likened Kraus to a "Chinese idol with a furious sneer, whirling two naked swords in a war dance before the crypt of the German language."[111] China is, in fact, a sort of secret horizon for Kraus: In relation to the world, as an acceptable image of civilization, it is the only one not to exhaust itself in the "civil war of customs against nature";[112] in relation to writing, because it is in the description of certain features of Chinese that we find the most precise definition, transposed, of Kraus's linguistic utopia, which one could say is represented particularly by that language, one that is not made to spare mental exertion, while combining the maximum clarity of detail and the maximum complexity of resonance. And if all of Kraus can only be understood as "written recitation,"[113] if he was able to deduce the punctuation of a Goethe manuscript on the basis of an incorrect canonical edition,[114] it would certainly have comforted him to know that in Chinese, "'to read the classics' is said with the same expression as 'to recite a prayer'; Chinese texts generally have no punctuation; it is by *reciting* them that one learns to place the period: To understand means to feel the rhythm."[115] Like the thinkers of ancient China, Kraus considered the world *through emblems,* and like them he seems to have understood that "the changes that can be noted in the course of things are identical with the substitutions of symbols that are produced by thought."[116] Thus, for example, the present reality *is* the ocean of public opinion, the changing mass of linguistic stereotypes that follow one another in the public psyche and of which the newspaper offers a convenient abbreviation. And in this ocean we recognize precisely the mirror image of that surface of *stock phrases* on which the Chinese classics draw, "literature based on centones." Perhaps the most outstanding work of sinology in this century, Marcel Granet's *Danses et légendes de la Chine ancienne,* concludes that, strictly speaking, the whole of archaic Chinese literature is a single disguised quotation and that to seek in it "the prime fact or the original text . . . would mean exposing oneself to a dangerous error."[117] Relying on a quotation from the same text, Chinese authors lead the reader by different paths to thoughts that are even opposed. Relying on original opinions, contemporaries live in necessary agreement. With a twofold gaze in a twofold space, Kraus contrasted an origin that implies a scripture comprising the whole with an end where what speaks is a multiform and nameless voice, which has a word for every fact and ahead of that word, every fact. The use of the quotation was therefore indispensable to him, since the quotation is precisely the form that denotes extreme proximity either to the origin or to the end. Kraus, a Chinese of the end, finds himself obliged to quote continually, but in accordance with Western rules, his quotations constantly proclaim the order of the day, and the day is precisely the Day of Judgment.[118] And like his great Chinese predecessors, Kraus *does not indicate the source.* After "the fundamental note of our time, the echo of my bloody delusion," has sounded, where "the most striking inventions are quotations," the destroying whirlpool that surrounds the "cosmic point" from which "even what happens at the corner of the Sirk-Strasse is regulated"[119] creates a sufficient void for the inscription, in solitude, of the epitaph:

> What emptiness here
> in my place.
> Every anxiety consumed.
> Nothing remains of me
> except the source,
> which it did not indicate.[120]

The desert around the Great Wall is now identical with the blankness surrounding the locus of Kraus's text.

"THE ROOT IS ON THE SURFACE"

Before so complex a vision of universal interdependence, the accusation that is still repeated against Kraus—that he saw only symptoms, not causes—appears vacuous. In this, surly messenger boys claiming to be Marxists are in agreement with such "spiritual" authors as Max Brod. It seems ironical to level such an accusation at the writer who soberly illustrated the economic function of World War I: "to transform commercial areas into battlefields, so that these in their turn become commercial areas."[121] If we examine the reasons for this accusation more closely, we immediately encounter the petty notion of cause that we still drag around and that is one of the most distressing symptoms of a general incapacity to perceive what is going on. If the Bad Guys in power were really sufficient reason for any disaster, the world would certainly be more understandable, much less wicked, and also of scant interest. With obtuse gravity, Max Brod scolds Kraus for having devoted a little of his attention, at the outbreak of World War I, to a "silly advertising poster."[122] But Kraus continued to look at advertising posters during the war also because, before the war, he had seen in advertising posters the war that others, who now were looking only at the war, had persisted in not recognizing. Many academic chairs in sociology have been established since, and many people are now convinced that looking at advertising posters is not an idle pastime. It should be added, however, that Kraus is not a tireless decoder of social messages; he perceives emblems and manifests himself through emblems, where others see hoaxes and explain deceptions— always a bit too obvious, oddly enough, since the whole remains obscure. Whoever thinks he can quietly trap an image in a semantic grill is a little like the legitimate lords and masters of those ladies who happily took refuge in Chinatown. And it is primarily for this that Kraus attacks psychoanalysis: He had recognized it as the first great social model for reducing the totality of meaning to a one-way street. For Kraus, here once again Chinese, totality requires continuous circulation: Causes can become symptoms, and symptoms turn out to be causes. His argument tends to proceed like a Confucian demonstration, which at first sight looks like a chain of causes and effects and instead is a circular order, an endless movement, in which we are caught up as soon as we set foot in his work. From the outset it is hastily suggested to us that "diagnosis is one of the most widespread diseases."[123]

("The root is on the surface":[124] The symptom is not reabsorbed into the cause, and what eludes the cause can become the most difficult riddle, of which the cause will be the outer aspect. In this fixation on the sign as such, Kraus is in agreement with a movement of thought that has had a disquieting effect on all of modernity, and we would be misled were we to limit it to the area of literature. "The beginning is the sign":[125] These are not the words of a symbolist poet but of the mathematician David Hilbert.)

OLYMPIA AND PERICHOLE

Many were surprised to observe the constancy and energy with which Kraus devoted himself to Offenbach in his last awful years, when actually he might have seemed to be governed by the archetype of Timon of

Athens, squandering his assets among false friends and knowing them to be such, while the Nazi program had already been largely revealed. Yet there is nothing more consistent: The mirroring of origin and end, which Kraus had always lived in his work, now found a form in his life as well.

When Kraus was three years old, his family moved from Jičín, the Bohemian town where he was born, to Vienna:

> His first contact with the big city had left him with a feeling of shock. He was frightened by Vienna, and his earliest memory was of being lost. He looked back on himself as a little savage, wholly confused by the uproar, the difficult winding streets, the enigmatic dangers lying in wait at every turn. To take a walk was an adventure on which he would embark with his heart in tumult, anxious, thinking he would never find his way home. His elder brother Richard, who was a practical sort, would take along a whole loaf of bread. Maybe he had a healthy appetite, but Karl saw in this fact a measure of caution dictated by circumstances, a little like the rations of hardtack with which sailors are supplied for every eventuality. As far as he was concerned, he was not interested in material life; but since he was afraid of never coming back, he carried in his arms the thing that was most precious to him, his puppet theater, and under no circumstances could he be persuaded to part with it.[126]

The map of the city as a childish realm of fable and anxiety was to develop along similar lines in Benjamin's *Berliner Kindheit*. But what distinguishes Kraus is his dogged, mad decision never to be separated from his "sacred ark" in his travels through the world—and above all, the fact that it was a puppet theater. Later it would be replaced by language, and what better way than operetta to bring the two things together and merge them?

Presumably, a few years after his walks in the park with his puppet theater, Kraus

> got from Offenbach's operas, which he happened to hear in a summer theater, much more decisive impressions than from the classics, which his teachers had urged him to accept without understanding them. Perhaps through the caricature of the gods, the real Olympus was disclosed to him. Perhaps his imagination was spurred to the task of forming, on the basis of *La Belle Hélène,* that image of the heroes not yet granted him by the *Iliad.*

And from rustic farce, which leads to the magical world of *Bluebeard,* he had drawn more lyrical meaning, from the buffoonish murder of women more genuine horror and romance, than what those poets who had aimed at it intentionally could offer him.[127]

Offenbach, "sorcerer of parody and parodist of myths,"[128] was to be for Kraus the occult psychopomp who would introduce him to the *Terra Specularis,* interwoven with rapture and torment, where the parody of the end makes it possible to grasp the glare of the origin. For in his eyes, operetta is the only world that still follows the laws of chaos, where causality is suspended, and every event thus floats uprooted from its leaden pedestal. Nonsense bursts forth undisturbed to soothe those who had always noted its presence behind the disguises of reality. At this point, the equivocal becomes the rule, and only the flimsiest membrane separates the two worlds, Paradise and Hell. It is "the inimitable forked tongue of this music, its way of saying everything with a positive and negative sign at the same time, its betrayal of the idyll through parody, the joke through the lyrical,"[129] that operates in this double realm. This is the eschatological hybridization that Kraus recognizes in contemporary post-history through the lens of operetta: dreadful, when one thinks of the endless "last days" in which "characters from operetta recited the tragedy of humanity";[130] paralyzing, when one thinks that "Offenbach triumphs in the demonical wit by which, during the last military parade before Hitler, at the moment when the cavalry passed in front of him, the orchestra felt moved to play, not, for example, the march from *Tannhäuser,* but the infernal can-can, the one from the realm of the dead";[131] dazzling, if in the figures in the operetta one also recognizes, as does Kraus, the promise "of transforming, not gods and heroes, but playing-card kings and fairy-tale princes into men, and men themselves into puppets."[132] The unblemished life of marionettes can reemerge only in operetta, and this is what Benjamin meant when he wrote, in his review of a public recital from Offenbach given by Kraus, that "the souls of the marionettes have ended up in his hands."[133] Protected by Olympia, the automated doll in *The Tales of Hoffmann,* "who smelled of that perfume / with which Eros blessed my dream,"[134] Kraus begins moving his puppets to the tune of Offenbach, thus obeying the supremely ambiguous imperative of music in general: "to loosen the cramp of life."[135] The rigid marionette in the dissolving flux of sound is precisely the emblem of that music that simultaneously promises death and a different life, freed of all defensive constriction, where every gesture would have the necessity and perfection of Kleist's fencing bear. And like the unforgettable Kleist, Kraus recognizes in the marionette a form of higher life, which the automatism of the machine offers to the world and which the world has not accepted, making it instead its ruin. In "Frauenlob," that difficult poem of his last period, Kraus alludes to his vain flight, in a dream that takes place within chaos, toward a puppet who is the supreme image of Eros: an Offenbach Marie Antoinette "throttled by bourgeois evildoers."[136] It is thus at a paradoxical dream presence, Olympia and Perichole, woman-machine-word to the strains of an Offenbach operetta, that Kraus directs his gaze, the only solution, almost alchemical, that one is permitted to predict in the *Terra Specularis,* the obscure but distinct voice in a dream. We hear it resound at rare intervals in an enormous work: That the solution is obscure will appear reasonable to anyone already aware that "artists are merely those who are able to make a riddle out of the solution."[137] For the others, one can only repeat: "Never mind, you seekers! The mystery will be illuminated by its own light."[138]

16 The Practice of Profane Illumination

Around Walter Benjamin, theorist of aura, an increasingly shining and legendary aura has gathered since the publisher Suhrkamp, in 1955, issued the two volumes of his writings, edited by T. W. Adorno; 240 copies were initially sold. In 1968, many young Germans spent their days reciting crude slogans of Third International vintage, but at night they dreamed of Benjamin, his Empires of Quotations, his enigmatic and decisive judgments, his capacity to connect the tiny and the immense. Meanwhile, posthumous publication of his writings has gone on multiplying, each year offering the thrill of some new text: the book on hashish, reviews, essays, fragments.

Among them, the one that immediately comes to mind as a majestic block of shorthand symbols (Benjamin's handwriting, which is an essential part of his work, was virtually microscopic), a mountain crisscrossed by gorges and eroded by caves, canals, and ravines, was the edition of the *Letters,* published in 1966 in two volumes totaling 862 pages. The book, precious in itself, is also useful in refuting anyone who claims to possess a clear and distinct image of Benjamin. Of all such images, three are the most common, and in recent years, venomous quarrels have been waged over their respective truths. They correspond somewhat to different faces of himself that Benjamin presented to three of his illustrious correspondents: Gershom Scholem, Bertolt Brecht, and Theodor Adorno.

To begin with Adorno: A close friend of Benjamin's since 1923 (but they never addressed each other by the informal *du,* though Benjamin addressed Adorno's wife so), he quickly perceived the immense authority of his person: "It is hard for me to find the right words without falling into the kitsch of enthusiastic expressions whenever I try to convey what an intense impression he made." When Benjamin was an exile in Paris, and by then without resources, Adorno got him assignments from the Institut für Sozialforschung, directed by Max Horkheimer. About their later relations much has been said that miserably poisoned Adorno's last years; and I have no wish here to go over painful, often violent recriminations. I will only observe that those relations seem to have been secretly governed by a singular paradox: The affinity between the two was as strong as a fundamental divergence. In the long, flowing letter in which Adorno explains to Benjamin the reasons why the institute is rejecting his splendid essay on Baudelaire for publication in its journal, there is a constant wavering between remarks that display a grasp of Benjamin's methods almost in their inaccessible crux, and others in which one can see a strange wish on Adorno's part to give the recalcitrant Benjamin a few philosophical raps on the knuckles, accusing him of not knowing how to use the Hegelian category of mediation. And yet Adorno himself, many years later, would perfectly clearly formulate the reason why such criticisms left Benjamin untouched: "In contrast to other philosophers, even Bloch, his thought, paradoxical as it may sound, did not develop in the sphere of concepts."

The protective mantle wrapped around Benjamin for many years by the institute has caused him to be taken too often for a general "cultural critic" and exponent of the Frankfurt School. Both are equivocal definitions (even if justified). But one might more justifiably see Benjamin as Ernst Bloch's wife saw him for the first time: Deep in thought, he was walking by himself along the Kurfürstendamm, and Karola Bloch dared to ask him what he was thinking about. Benjamin replied: "My dear madam, have you ever noticed how sickly the little marzipan figures look?" In these words speaks the Berlin child who goes on spinning cobwebs of melancholy fantasy about objects and who, even after donning the adult clothes of the flaneur, moves amid the shifting scenery of the city as once in the encoded world of the nursery. Unless one hears this voice in all of Benjamin's work, I fear its aroma is irreparably lost.

The second common image of Benjamin, to which the German students were loyal in '68, is the Marxist one, and this time the connection is with Brecht. But ambiguities abound here as well. The fact is that Benjamin, an omnivorous reader, had always avoided studying Marx (by 1933 he had read only *The Class Struggle in France*). And his conversion to Marxism was for completely abnormal reasons, which Benjamin himself explains with great acuteness in an important letter to Max Rychner:

"I've never been able to study and think except in the theological sense, if I may put it that way, that is, in accordance with the Talmudic doctrine of the forty-nine steps of meaning in every passage of the Torah. Now, my experience tells me that the most worn out Marxist *platitude* holds more hierarchies of meaning than everyday bourgeois profundity, which always has only one meaning, namely, apology." Memorable words—but one might add that when Benjamin got his hands on Nikolay Bukharin's *ABC of Communism,* not only was he not transported into an ecstatic ascent of the forty-nine steps, but he confessed that the book had been a "disastrous experience" for him. And his attempts to swallow "dialectical materialism" were to be embarrassing to the end. This man, who was almost physiologically incapable of being banal, seemed driven by a malign wish to inflict wounds on himself. Only this can explain why he was actually sometimes attracted by the most dismal Soviet version of Marxism.

The last image is the one drawn by Scholem, Benjamin's oldest and closest friend. This great scholar of the Cabala communicated with Benjamin from the start in terms of the "metaphysics of language." And their correspondence is one of the most fascinating of the century. It was with increasing sorrow that Scholem watched Benjamin pass under the mantle of Brecht. He feared his friend was succumbing to a fatal self-deception and continued to invite him to Palestine. Benjamin kept postponing his departure. But I doubt if he would ever have been able to follow the path laid out for him by Scholem: The peculiarity of Benjamin's cabalism was that he had to exercise it chiefly on *non*-Hebraic subjects. And all places were better suited to this eminent scriptural commentator than the real places of Holy Writ. Also Benjamin, like Paul Klee's *Angelus Novus,* in which his "secret name" was hidden, was dragged along by a storm that blew from Paradise and kept him from keeping his feet planted on any land at all, much less a Promised Land.

Reading Benjamin's correspondence, we find these three quite different images exposed to the three correspondents even on the same days. How did they manage to coexist? No differently from the way such a wildly esoteric fragment as "Theory of the Similar" and the essay "The Author as Producer," which provided many watchwords for the German students, coexist in Benjamin's work a few months apart. And if, as Adorno suggested, Benjamin's thought did not develop "in the sphere of concepts," what then is its true sphere? It may perhaps be a place that can be recognized only when one enters it, like a landscape of ruins or a garden surrounded by high walls.

To cross that threshold does not require any special mental discipline. Rather, what is indispensable is to have sought, and found, an experience that has the paradoxical singularity of being at the same time fully esoteric and fully secular, of the kind Benjamin alluded to with disconcerting clarity in his essay on surrealism:

> [W]e penetrate the mystery only to the degree that we recognize it in the everyday world, by virtue of a dialectical optic that perceives the everyday as impenetrable, the impenetrable as everyday. The most passionate investigation of telepathic phenomena, for example, will not teach us half as much about reading (which is an eminently telepathic process), as the profane illumination of reading about telepathic phenomena. And the most passionate investigation of the hashish trance will not teach us half as much about thinking (which is eminently narcotic), as the profane illumination of thinking about the hashish trance. The reader, the thinker, the loiterer, the *flâneur,* are types of illuminati just as much as the opium eater, the dreamer, the ecstatic. And more profane. Not to mention that most terrible drug—ourselves—which we take in solitude.[1]

17 Brecht the Censor

"Bert Brecht is a difficult character," Walter Benjamin once noted. As indeed he was, but he has become all the more difficult by dint of being easy. Let me say it at once: I, for one, prefer to flee into the night rather than have to watch the actors once again join hands at the curtain call and speak harsh truths to an audience of ladies and gentlemen who are already putting on their fur coats while casting benevolent looks at those talented boys and girls on the stage. Like Federico García Lorca, like Georg Lukács, like Jean-Paul Sartre and Cesare Pavese, Brecht has been triumphantly received for some time now as one of the heroes of a vast middlebrow culture with good and progressive intentions. And so, to read him today, one must first rid his writings of that thick crust of solemn social kitsch that has gradually settled on them. A boring job but not an overly arduous one: All one needs do is forget for the moment the plays and didactic perorations and turn instead to the poems and the *Stories of Herr Keuner* to refurbish the image of an enigmatic, coarse, almost disagreeable, and very, very insolent writer. And one sighs with relief: This "character" is most certainly difficult, but he is a great writer and no longer grist for well-meaning souls.

It is part of Brecht the "difficult character" that his most private and secret book—the *Work Journal* (1938–55)—should be subtly self-censored. In drafting these notes, for almost twenty years, in Denmark, Sweden, Finland, the United States, and Berlin, Brecht was forever thinking of the possibility that an enemy eye might see and use them. And one day he noted that he actually found his own diary "much distorted due to possible undesirable readers."

One could say that all the vicissitudes of Brecht's life are marked by this fear of falling into the enemy's hands. For him, the first enemy to escape from—and this is to his everlasting credit—was culture itself, understood as a manifestation of the "nobility of the spirit," in the words of the hated Thomas Mann. Whenever he heard the majestic wing feathers of the *Geist* fluttering around him, that tireless spirit that, especially in German lands, never stops chewing its cud, Brecht spat on the ground—then, with his characteristic mocking gesture, put out his hand and "begged for tobacco." By this twofold movement, Brecht repudiated the realm of essences (and therefore of Great Authors, Great Works, and the Expression of Free Culture) and at the same time declined to renounce the superfluous: "The theater, indeed, must absolutely be allowed to remain a superfluous thing, which means, of course, that it is for the superfluous that one lives." As long as he remains enclosed in this eloquent irony, Brecht's behavior is perfect and makes one think of certain invincible Chinese sages, "with fine and limpid hearts," who moreover were among his secret models.

But the story of Brecht is much more twisted and murky. One of his regular vices was to lock up his many enemies in the same prison, forcing them to serve the same sentence: "slaughterers who emerge from libraries"; harmless seducers, guilty only of pleasing women (perhaps even the women who pleased Brecht); and in general all those authors whose work he considered lacking in an "Enlightenment nature." We thus find in the *Work Journal* an overflowing stock of accusations, insinuations, and sarcasms striking out in all directions, at Lukács and Thomas Mann, Johannes Becher and W. H. Auden, Christopher Isherwood and Alfred Döblin. His judgments are almost always acute and almost always too acid. The same goes for certain great events: At the outset of the war, Brecht, from his solitary observation post, looked contemptuously at England and tried to equate it with Hitler's Germany. Imperialism against imperialism, he said.

Years later, in Hollywood, he scanned the American cinema with surly incomprehension, scolding it in a manner typical of the European intellectual he abhorred so much: He accused it of being hostile to the Author, the Great Work, and Culture. Moving in the sad circle of German refugee writers in America—one must remember they were officially designated "enemy aliens"—who were often pushed aside as annoying petitioners, Brecht looked with obvious rancor on the group from the Frankfurt School, headed by Theodor Adorno and Max Horkheimer, almost as though they were a bunch of hysterical college professors primarily in search of funding, servants of capitalism. And yet, in those very years, Adorno and Horkheimer were able to discern, for the first time and with unsurpassed lucidity, the outlines of the culture industry in the reality of America; by comparison, Brecht's analyses seem rudimentary and, above all, marked by a tiresome certainty of being on the right side.

Even his relations with Walter Benjamin, by far the greatest and most devoted reader Brecht ever had, reveal some fairly odious aspects, as can be gleaned from Benjamin's notes on his stay in Svendborg. When Benjamin showed him his admirable essay on Franz Kafka, Brecht commented that it "carries water to the mill of Jewish fascism" (once again, the obsession with enemy readers). When he saw that Benjamin was reading *Crime and Punishment,* he promptly burst out in one of his provocatory judgments: "Brecht attributes to Chopin and Dostoyevsky an especially detrimental influence on health."[1] Finally, when in America he received the news of Benjamin's terrible death, Brecht noted the fact in his diary without a word of farewell to his friend and immediately went on to nitpick the manuscript of "On the Concept of History," the last Benjamin submitted to the Institute of Sociology, concluding, "In short, this brief essay is clear and clarifying (despite its metaphors and its Judaism)."

"Despite its metaphors": Largely untrained in speculation but with a good nose for smelling out where and why thinking becomes dangerous, Brecht tried for years and years to create an airtight artistic theory and practice that would withstand the assaults of what, with a certain clumsiness but sure intuition, he called "metaphysics." He did not succeed, for which we can be grateful. It is still, however, of extreme interest to reconstruct how this need to defeat the invisible enemy was created in Brecht. Certainly the enemy was not, as he would have us believe, the "Aristotelian theater"; rather, it was the specter of art itself, insofar as it remains intrinsically ambiguous, elusive, and loath to lend itself to any worthy social action. "Art is on the side of destiny": This sentence, tucked away in the dialogues in *The Purchase of Brass,* may perhaps hold the key to Brecht's attitude. The side of destiny is the ungovernable side, overwhelming and divorced from will; it is the cloud of unknowing from which all writing emerges. One cannot understand Brecht's stubborn insistence on making his theater instrumental, governable, stripped of all magic, unless one recognizes the formidable presence of his antagonist in the shadows. Brecht's "epic theater" sought to extirpate the magic of the theater. But magic is not

something that was superimposed on the theater under particular historical circumstances and that can therefore be eradicated by other techniques. Magic abides in the theater; indeed, it abides in every word, in that it names an absence. A few decades of Brechtian performances have given us experimental proof of this: Brecht has become a style of staging, a new magic—sometimes powerful, sometimes trite. Who today can honestly maintain that in attending a Brecht play, one is not subjected to that magic "torpor" that Brecht so feared in the theater?

There is still much to be discovered, however, about the peculiarity of Brecht's magic. And I would look less at the much-abused category of the "alienation effect" than at the technique of quotation, which is in a way the esoteric face of his art. A monument of that technique, much richer than any theatrical text by Brecht, is Karl Kraus's 770-page-long *The Last Days of Mankind*. Brecht derived a powerful impulse from it, one that he never openly acknowledged. But it is also true that in him the category of quotation took on new aspects, which we find throughout his work, even in the *Work Journal*, a paradoxical and abnormal creation, all interwoven in counterpoint between Brecht's personal notes and the photos and newspaper clippings he glued to his pages.

By concentrating on quotation and working on preexisting materials, Brecht was accepting a fact more fundamental today than ever: the rejection of *direct expression*. Whoever no longer recognizes himself in a society—and this is the situation of all new art—does not even recognize the fictive ego that society grants him by inviting him, with false magnanimity, to express himself. The writer accordingly becomes an imaginary subject who no longer has available a *language in common* with society and who therefore is obliged to waver between a personal encoded tongue and the whole repertoire of languages and forms handed down to him by the past. By mounting these scattered fragments, making these languages and forms collide, the writer will tell the unprecedented story in which he has been allowed to participate. This explains, for example, why certain poems by Brecht, in appearance so direct, seem to have been extracted from the works of some ancient Chinese poet. And it is just this unbridgeable distance that gives these few words of "basic German" an immense resonance.

Nothing in Brecht is more valuable than his conspicuous contradictions. The man who wrote, "What times are these, when a dialogue about trees is almost a crime!" committed that crime more than once, devoting to trees some of his best poems, which remain more deeply engraved on the memory than *Arturo Ui* or his *Galileo*. The man who always harped on the need to *utilize* writing confesses, through his alter ego Keuner, that when leaving his house he loves to look at trees because in a society where people are "objects of use," trees still maintain "something autonomous and therefore comforting," for one can hope that even carpenters recognize in them "something that cannot be utilized." And this same man, who had mocked all sublime qualities in literature, devoted to an elder tree one of the few poems of the century that can, without exaggeration, be called sublime.

Its title is "Difficult Times":

> Standing at my desk
> Through the window I see the elder tree in the garden
> And recognise something red in it, something black
> And all at once recall the elder
> Of my childhood in Augsburg.
> For several minutes I debate
> Quite seriously whether to go to the table
> And pick up my spectacles, in order to see
> Those black berries again on their tiny red stalks.[2]

No explicit denunciation of the world's evils has the intensity of these few indirect and reticent lines.

18 The Ancient Egyptian Character of Art

The great era of modern aesthetics is quite short: It begins with Kant's *Critique of Judgment* and ends with Hegel's *Aesthetics*. After that, one must instead seek artistic enlightenment in glimpses and by indirect paths: a few lines from Baudelaire or Nietzsche, a letter by Mallarmé, aphorisms by Kraus, malicious remarks by Valéry, gibes by Benn. The chief purpose of aesthetics today seems to be to provide work for academic institutes. Adorno is one of the last links in that succession of writers who were able to speak of art after it had been proclaimed dead, as can be seen in many pages in his best works: *Minima Moralia, Philosophy of Modern Music, Mahler,* and some of the essays in *Noten zur Literatur.* A master of the art of obliqueness, Adorno dealt with aesthetic problems in an offhand way. Thus his last work, published under the title *Aesthetische Theorie* as a posthumous fragment of 533 pages with few paragraph breaks, seems all the more disconcerting.

One opens the book only to find oneself perpetually on the edge of quicksand—for Adorno this may be dialectics. One is drawn into a kind of transposed raving à la Samuel Beckett (and indeed, the work was to be dedicated to Beckett). Horror of the origin governs all of Adorno's thought and also forces him not to allow his inordinate discourse to have a beginning: "It is simply a matter of this: from my theorem, according to which there is no philosophical *primum,* it also follows that one cannot build a structure of argument according to the usual gradual progression; on the contrary, one must put together the whole by a series of partial units, more or less of the same weight and arranged concentrically on the same level; for it is the constellation, not the sequence, that conveys the idea." This is a perfect description of the archetypal form of *Aesthetische Theorie,* which is only partially, yet splendidly, manifested in the book.

But the book can also be described in the opposite way: as a system of aesthetics, vast in structure, immense in ambition, and constantly ashamed of itself. Massive main walls are continually being hidden by tangles of vegetation, wild underbrush, and carnivorous plants. One rediscovers the great Adorno by losing oneself in this ungovernable luxuriance, but whoever penetrates as far as the bare construction will be surprised to recognize there not a renovated Hegelian Escorial, heavy and majestic, but at most a timid Petit Trianon. (But think of the abyss that separates any Petit Trianon from the oppressive ministerial edifice evoked by so much recent aesthetics.) It is clear, therefore, that this is by no means a work to be recommended to anyone wishing to maintain the illusion of Adorno the rigorous philosopher: Here, as never before, it is easy to see that his dialectics is first of all a disguised rhetoric. But this is not to say that an orthodox dialectician is closer to the truth than a prodigious rhetorician. It is certain, however, that Adorno does not share the grim heaviness of the new dialecticians. His prose—formed in the school of Kraus and Benjamin and then emancipating itself—is a siren: Those who find it awkward generally find Wagner empty and Proust long-winded. Such people are consistent but a bit deaf to form. If anything, one would have to call it a contagious prose: Many who have heard it have then been afflicted by a stylistic rictus that also blocks their ability to think.

So let us overlook the theoretical premises of *Aesthetische Theorie,* which are its weakest part, and look at it instead as a work that, despite a certain academic allure, is desperately autobiographical. Miserably vexed by young people who in their eagerness for praxis spell out the *Dialectic of Enlightenment,* Adorno turned back at the end to the secret center of his thought, unknown to his official followers, a center that is certainly not in Marx, nor even in Hegel, but close to the animal muteness of art. This was where Adorno had started, and here he closed his circle. Adorno conceived art, from the beginning, in the mirror of utopia. In his references to utopia, a recurrent fata morgana, one can often find signs of an appalling Enlightenment naïveté, even and especially in this last book. For example, he conveys the idea that the possibility of paradise on earth should correspond to an advanced stage of the forces of production. But "utopia" for Adorno is rather a zone of fantastic light, where the Hebrew tradition of the Kingdom, clandestine and all the stronger in its defenselessness, lives stripped of any doctrinal support. Many of Adorno's marvelous passages filter into the dialectic thanks to a safe-conduct from utopia, as though making an arduous ascent among gnostic archons: the image of music as the gesture of bursting into tears; the sleep of Albertine watched over by Marcel and by Adorno, his philosophical double; the convergence of the realms of nature and grace in the last scene of *Faust II;* even the dazzling definition of art as "magic liberated from the lie of being truth"; or finally, in *Aesthetische Theorie,* the impassioned vindication of the "beauty of nature." Adorno's truth lies in the interstices of his philosophizing, fissures, tiny at times, opening on a no-man's land between forms and thought. One could actually harvest from *Aesthetische Theorie* a rich anthology of these flights, which turn out to be so many blind alleys in the argument. The silent *non confundar* of the image, the pure extraneousness of the object that "opens its eyes," motionless presence, hypnotic opacity—these are characteristics of art that find in Adorno an advocate whose words are disturbing: For him, the origin and goal of his thought lies in the chimerical sound of a "language of things"; in a radical, albeit concealed, revolt against his master Hegel, who had described and approved the domesticating aspect of art as a seal that serves to "remove from the external world its reluctant strangeness."

For Adorno, instead, the central category of art is precisely the enigma. And this already serves to belittle aesthetics as "science": "All works of art, and art in general, are enigmas; this has dogged the theory of art since ancient times. The fact that works of art say something, while at the same time concealing it, points to their enigmatic character in terms of language." There exists for Adorno a secret alliance between nature and art to remove themselves furtively from the tyranny of the spirit, but on the other hand—and this makes all the knots inextricable and the twists and turns of thought that tries to unravel them fascinating—Adorno, like Benjamin, is completely immersed in the Enlightenment nightmare according to which the original face of nature is that of a "chain of guilt," or rather, myth as blinding destiny. (I am speaking, of course, of the utopian-Judaic wing of the Enlightenment, not the Rousseauian wing.) To free itself, nature has to be dead: "It is owing only to their mortal element that works of art participate in reconciliation. But in this they remain slaves of myth. This is their ancient Egyptian character." Splendid words, which only a slave of the Enlightenment could have written.

19 The Siren Adorno

America, 1944: a place of easy hallucinations, especially for German-speaking refugee intellectuals, who were reduced to the role of "petitioners in mutual competition." At the same time, they were exposed to their first, brutal contact with *pure* industrial society, often shuddering and retreating in the face of the "mechanization of the spirit." There were several suicides in those years, and there was desolate solitude in small apartments in New York and Los Angeles. Many did not give up but became pathetic ghosts of the old Europe, relics of a culture that no one now had any use for. From this humiliating condition, Theodor W. Adorno was able to draw valuable material for his greatest book: *Minima Moralia.* And his moment of maximum creative strength coincided with his situation of maximum helplessness: An unknown intellectual, desperately melancholy but at the same time highly curious about everything, with bulging eyes and the little hands of a delicate child forced to grow up too soon, he assumed the guise of an empirical sociologist in an effort to be of use and offer some concrete research to the American Jewish Committee.

But the true concreteness lay precisely in his troubled and shifting gaze as it rested on the looming objects in the New World, on scraps of sentences from newspapers, on the professional smiles of his colleagues, on the fortified cottages of horrible, happy families. Adorno revived an aphoristic form that had been Nietzsche's, then Max Horkheimer's, Ernst Bloch's, and Walter Benjamin's, and now put it to a different use, allowing him to plunge decisively into the private life of the society around him: a life of trivia that emerged already televised and that no philosopher had hitherto thought worthy of consideration.

Adorno allowed his gaze to wander at length over these trivial things, until he saw shining through them the whole past of our culture, a landscape of catastrophes now contracted in hellish harmony and fragmented as in a psychoanalytical case history. Observing glossy advertising images or listening to the words of a popular song that carried the distorted echo of a Brahms lied, Adorno knew it was a question not of protecting "culture" from these horrors but, on the contrary, of recognizing in them the mocking origin of culture itself, finally unveiled in reverse at its end: "In their counterfeit light shines the publicity character of culture."

For those able to grasp, through the meshes of a prodigiously dense and tense prose, the mechanism of what Adorno called "criticism of culture," *Minima Moralia* is a contagious book. I do not think anyone can say he has read it properly unless he has experienced it for some time as an obsession, feeling obliged to look, as though for the first time and often with paralyzing fright, at many everyday situations he had hitherto taken for granted. So eventually it becomes healthier to dismiss this obsession and its widespread intrusiveness, and perhaps even return to a more shortsighted and distracted gaze. But it is an obsession for which one remains ever grateful, and when one reopens this book, certain sentences reemerge like talismans that once helped to cross the enchanted forest. For anyone who has had the good fortune to meet them, they remain silent and charitable witnesses whose power is still intact. I should like here to record only one of these sentences, perhaps the most precise definition of art I know: "Art is magic liberated from the lie of being truth."

I said that *Minima Moralia* is a contagious book, a siren book. Of course, to hear that song one must have receptive ears. Otherwise one may end up judging it as did the eminent historian Delio Cantimori: When the publisher Giulio Einaudi requested his editorial opinion of the book, Cantimori pronounced, "It is the belated product of that literature of socio-psycho-philosophical maxims and considerations that were much in vogue during the Weimar period." Case dismissed: two lines of historical framework, as always required, and an implied contempt for a hybrid literary genre with ancestors as untrustworthy as Georg Lichtenberg, Schopenhauer, and Nietzsche.

Speaking of Nietzsche, Cantimori was to have occasion a few years later to spell out his attitude as a responsible educator in a memorable letter published in *Conversando di storia*. It is a text that ought to be quoted in full, an unsurpassed catechism still inscribed in letters of bronze behind many wrinkled brows. I will confine myself here to one of its utterances: "The good educator, in this case the publisher, should not publish Nietzsche, because Nietzsche leads readers astray." But—said Cantimori, now arguing against Cesare Vasoli, who had deemed it urgent to rescind forever Nietzsche's Italian visa—this does not mean that Nietzsche should not be allowed to circulate at all, at least among "people now adult, or in the process of becoming so, or at least intellectually and morally 'mature.'" To avoid a still-dangerous familiarity, however, the cautious Cantimori advised against keeping Nietzsche's books handy in one's own library: "Naturally, I won't keep Nietzsche on the same shelf as the Einaudi edition of Gramsci or the Einaudi and Feltrinelli editions of Salvemini, and not even with the Laterza edition of Nitti, or with Marx or Plato; I'll put him with the poets and tragic dramatists and novelists; I'll put him on the shelf for monstrosities or the one for astrologers, or should I keep him with the philosophers and theologians?"

A truly serious dilemma, and we have no idea how Cantimori resolved it. Many who are much less subtle, complex, and informed than this acclaimed educator and who turn to him as to a secular Madonna of Loreto have instead drawn one simple and rude conclusion from his delicate embarrassment: Whatever he is, astrologer or poet, let's throw the Plague Bearer out! Well, in both his pedagogic thoughts on Nietzsche and in that now distant editorial opinion on *Minima Moralia,* I think Cantimori represented a loftier and more troubled version of something quite sordid that we continue to encounter every day: a certain tendency (obviously masked as educational zeal) to police culture on the part of its more enlightened Italian representatives.

Still, the accusations of censorship leveled at the Einaudi edition of *Minima Moralia* seem to me a bit misguided. It was published in abridged form, leaving out a substantial portion of the original, and the accusations were provoked by the publication by Erba Voglio of the little volume entitled *Minima (im)moralia,* which offers the very pages so far never translated. (And they are excellent pages, but no better or more radical than those we already had; editor Gianni Carchia's idea that Einaudi's criterion for its edition may have been a systematic pruning of Adorno's "excesses" itself appears rather excessive.)

To publish *Minima Moralia* in 1954 (that is, only three years after the German edition) and to publish it this way, in translation and with an introduction of such quality, both owing to the enthusiasm and intelligence of Renato Solmi, was in any case a farsighted act, one almost happily foolhardy, given the bleakness of Italian intellectual life in those years. Indeed, this great book at first passed unnoticed, and only after several years did the force of history require that it be recognized for what it is— and to think that it took French, British, and American publishers, so often generally praised, more than twenty years to offer anything comparable.[1] So this episode consoles me once again in thinking that the most daring and inventive part of culture in Italy is represented by the publishing industry, while the most refractory part, hostile to the "labor of the concept" *[die Arbeit des Begriffs]*, may actually be the bloc of big and little academics.

20 An Apocryphal Grave

A desolate cloud hangs over the last months of Walter Benjamin's life. On the night of 23 August 1939, German radio interrupted a musical program to broadcast the announcement of the Hitler-Stalin pact. A few days later, as the Nazis were invading Poland, German refugees in Paris were made to assemble in the Colombes stadium. There were about six thousand of them, and among them was Walter Benjamin, with a suitcase and a blanket. For ten days they waited in an oppressive heat, while excrement accumulated in large buckets. On the tenth day, Benjamin was sent along with many others to an internment camp at Nevers. It was a completely empty château, with no light and no beds. Benjamin slept at the foot of a spiral staircase, in a cubicle that he had to crawl into on his hands and knees.

A survival market soon developed. Benjamin would offer lessons in philosophy to "advanced" pupils in exchange for three Gauloises or a button. But later he was to have more ambitious ideas: He wanted to found a magazine for the camp, "naturally at the highest level." The editors got together one day for a meeting, entering the philosopher's den on all fours. "Gentlemen, it has to do with getting an armband," said Benjamin with some solemnity. The armband meant permission to leave the camp for a few hours in the morning. They never got it. Two months later, Benjamin was freed, thanks to the intervention of Adrienne Monnier. The idea of creating a magazine in order to get an armband seems to me to correspond to the only conception of praxis suited to Benjamin: an act that opens the possibility of emerging from an internment camp, which is then History itself. This gnostic conception is incompatible with the much more widespread one fostered by those for whom praxis primarily means transforming the world into an internment camp, thereby carrying History to its triumph.

Between his release from the Nevers camp (November 1939) and his flight to southern France (June 1940) months pass, of which we know very little. From this period comes a piece of writing, in part jotted down on newspaper wrappers. Events and the form of the writing oblige us to consider it Benjamin's final testament: the eighteen "Theses on the Concept *[Begriff]* of History"—nine pages, dense and glittering, carved on a lump of lava. It is on them, more than any of his other writings, that the fury of interpreters has been unleashed as they continue their efforts to drag Benjamin in opposite directions.

It looks from the start as though Benjamin has here returned to being what he always was: a prodigious allegorist. With the pretext of presenting a series of speculations, the theses hold out a garland of images. The first is right out of Edgar Allan Poe:

> . . . an automaton constructed in such a way that it could play a winning game of chess, answering each move of an opponent with a countermove. A puppet in Turkish attire and with a hookah in its mouth sat before a chessboard placed on a large table. A system of mirrors created the illusion that this table was transparent from all sides. Actually, a little hunchback who was an expert chess player sat inside and guided the puppet's hand by means of strings. One can imagine a philosophical counterpart to this device. The puppet called "historical materialism" is to win all the time. It can easily be a match for anyone if it enlists the services of theology, which today, as we know, is wizened and has to keep out of sight.[1]

This image already contains all the ambiguity of the late Benjamin: Who is the real player? The puppet dressed as a Turk "called 'historical materialism'"? Or the hunchbacked dwarf, theology, who offers its "services" but moves the puppet's otherwise inert hands? And what do "theology" and "historical materialism" here represent?

As far as theology is concerned, it is not hard to answer. A nomad and a cabalist in disguise, Benjamin had believed from the beginning that the times required that he not devote himself to the traditional problems of his doctrine but plunge into and mimic mystical categories in the boundless world of the profane. Thus he had chosen, willy-nilly, the most disparate objects as cover for his innate esoteric knowledge: obscure baroque dramas, toy collections, the writings of psychopaths, evocations of urban landscapes (like the *passages* of Paris), hashish hallucinations. But in treating these materials, theology each time felt protected and concealed by a copious, curving shell. Now, instead, it had acquired its thinnest, most risky covering: that puppet dressed as a Turk, who *had* to win his match. To the symbolic eye, the image of the match already evoked the proximity of death.

But what, then, was this puppet? Here the answer gets complicated. Not only is the "historical materialism" of which the eighteen theses speak radically different from anything that has ever been called by that name, but in a way it is the *antithesis* of Marx's very theory and of the praxis that swore by that theory all over the world. Together, the theses constitute a devastating attack on what "liberal" historicists called "progress," what Marx called "development of the forces of production," and what German Social Democrats had celebrated for years with their most feeble-minded slogans: "Every day our cause becomes clearer and people get smarter" (Wilhelm Dietzgen). What was it that united them all, and not only in the idea of "progress" but in the connected sense of "work that ennobles" and nature as material to be exploited (and which "exists gratis," besides, observed the undaunted Josef Dietzgen)? The conception of time as a "homogeneous, empty" sequence.

With the pathos of fierce despair, Benjamin opposed this vision of history as a *continuum* tied by an uninterrupted thread, whether red, black, or purple. For him, "the catastrophe is progress, and progress is the catastrophe." In the face of History, a single gesture is called for: *Halt it.* And the only means for introducing this improbable discontinuity is that "*weak* Messianic power" with which "like every generation that preceded us, we have been endowed."[2] Seeking to restore "to the concept of the classless society its genuine Messianic face," Benjamin eliminated first the features of a muscular, benevolent, and rather obtuse working class in power. That class had been deprived by its leaders of the only true revolutionary force—memory—and been swindled into accepting in exchange faith in the future and the rising course of history.

"Nothing has corrupted the German working class so much as the notion that it was moving with the current," says the eleventh thesis.[3] For Benjamin, now, the oppressed are no longer the working class or the proletariat but a vaster and more silent mass: the dead, the "nameless" killed by History. Now it is a matter not of replacing one last time the personnel in charge of that cogwheel called History but of blowing up the wheel itself. The object of Benjamin's fury is nothing less than all of History. This is enough to separate him irrevocably from all theorists of socialism, who in their "ideals" have venerated the "locomotive of universal history" above everything else, while Benjamin would like to stop it by pulling the emergency brake. The only point on which Benjamin remained ambivalent was, as always, Marx himself, who in his image of the classless society had secularized the image of messianic time, with a gesture akin to Benjamin's theological practices. But Benjamin also knew that in Marx the messianic image, by being secularized, had come to be confused with that of an ordinary workers' club. It is one of Benjamin's obvious weaknesses that he pretended not to have noticed this dreadful mix-up. And this is just what makes certain pages from his last years stiff and wooden, pages in which he persisted in exercising a calling that physiologically did not suit him: that of "historical materialist." But having reached the testamentary threshold of his "Theses on the Philosophy of History," Benjamin has a flash that reestablishes stellar distances. He still speaks here, of course, in the name of "historical materialism," but now this concept has been completely emptied from within, by the hand of the dwarf hunchback and chess master.

According to Soma Morgenstern, Benjamin conceived the theses as a response to the Hitler-Stalin pact. It was in that spirit, at least, that he read them to Morgenstern. But there are no explicit references in the text. Benjamin gives the reason for this in the tenth thesis:

> The themes which monastic discipline assigned to friars for meditation were designed to turn them away from the world and its affairs. The thoughts which we are developing here originate from similar considerations. At a moment when the politicians in whom the opponents of Fascism had placed their hopes are prostrate and confirm their defeat by betraying their own cause, these observations are intended to disentangle the political worldlings from the snares in which the traitors have entrapped them. Our consideration proceeds from the insight that the politicians' stubborn faith in progress, their confidence in their "mass basis," and, finally, their servile integration in an uncontrollable apparatus have been three aspects of the same thing.[4]

The argument cuts both ways: The traitorous politicians may be not only the German Social Democrats, long an object of Benjamin's scorn, but also the Soviets, the newest target for his anger. Any doubt vanishes when one turns to the manuscript of the French version of the theses, written by Benjamin himself. Here the violent contraction of the German text loosens enough to allow unequivocal specifics: "As for ourselves, we start from the conviction that the fundamental vices of the politics of the left sustain each other. And among these vices we point primarily to three: blind faith in progress, a blind faith in the strength, rightness, and swift reactions that take shape in the masses; a blind faith in the party." The decisive word "party" is missing in the German text, but it echoes beneath it from beginning to end. It must surely have been very hard for Benjamin to sever his hopes of Russia, given that even in 1938 he had not dared to voice any objections to the Moscow trials.

But with the theses, Benjamin's "historical materialism" and "dialectics" finally *had* to withdraw to their natural surroundings: absolute solitude, where any possible connection with an existing praxis was lacking. The ugly slogan of his friend Bertolt Brecht ("The party has a thousand eyes, the individual only two") would no longer have any hold on him. Thus, as never before, there reemerges in the theses, almost raw, the fully paradoxical use that Benjamin reserved for the very terms he was preaching, not only "historical materialism" but also "dialectics." Adorno was not mistaken in reproaching Benjamin for not being "dialectical" enough, despite all his declarations of faith. Actually Benjamin's dialectics is something that was born and perhaps died with him. It too is an allegory, a reference to something *other* than what the word "dialectics" proclaims. How else is one to understand a dialectics that does not aim at any Hegelian or Marxian or in any way secular "overcoming" but fixes its gaze on a single point: the "Messianic cessation of happening"?[5] An enigmatic allusion, which Benjamin illuminated by referring to a subtle passage from Focillon on the "rapid felicity" of that moment when the beam of the scale "scarcely wavers," and we witness the "miracle of that hesitant immobility, the slight, imperceptible tremor that indicates to me that it is alive." A good "historical materialist" would have read these lines with perplexity and dismay.

When the Nazis occupied Paris in June 1940, Stalin had flags flown in celebration on the public buildings of Moscow. Between the ninth and the thirteenth of June, two million people fled south, Benjamin among them. He had succeeded, after much effort and delay, in getting a visa for the United States. Now there was a frontier to be crossed. In Marseilles, in November, he divided his supply of morphine with Arthur Koestler, "enough to kill a horse." On the morning of 26 September, he left with a small group to cross the Spanish border. They reached the frontier after twelve hours of painful hiking. But it had been closed on that very day. Their visas would no longer be accepted.

During the night, Benjamin took an overdose of morphine. Next morning, he sent for a woman friend and gave her a short letter for Theodor Adorno. Then he lost consciousness. His companions, after considerable negotiation, succeeded in crossing the frontier. The friend had Benjamin buried in the cemetery of Port Bou. A few months later, Hannah Arendt went looking for his grave, in vain: "The cemetery faces a small bay directly overlooking the Mediterranean; it is carved in stone in terraces; the coffins are also pushed into such stone walls. It is by far one of the most fantastic and most beautiful spots I have seen in my life."[6] Some years later, a grave would be shown, isolated from the others, with Walter Benjamin's name scrawled on the wooden enclosure. According to Scholem, it was an invention of the cemetery attendants, eager for tips. "Certainly the spot is beautiful, but the grave is apocryphal."[7]

Mythos

21 The Terror of Fables

Many of you will remember the chapter from Robert Musil's *The Man without Qualities* in which Ulrich reflects on an expression he has read in a sports article: "a racehorse of genius." That a racehorse should be called a "genius," thinks Ulrich, signifies something that involves the whole history of the world. And from this he draws the necessary conclusions: specifically, to take a year's leave of absence from his life as a mathematician—thus becoming entirely a "man without qualities."

But let us try to transpose Ulrich's experience to today: In all probability, we would not be reading the expression "a racehorse of genius." We would read something else: "a mythical racehorse." A few days ago, opening a newspaper, I saw a full-page ad for a car—which one, I don't remember. A picture of the automobile was accompanied by these words: "The total myth is born." Obviously, this sounds normal, just as "a racehorse of genius" sounded normal to Ulrich's contemporaries. Now we might ask ourselves: How did we arrive at this peculiar normality? How many centuries and millennia lie hidden behind the sports reporter's invention, or the ad man's? If we look at the common use of words, we realize immediately that the word "myth" survives primarily in two accepted meanings. On the one hand, it refers to an absolute, to something prodigious beyond which one cannot go. This is what the ad man is thinking when he chooses the expression "total myth" to designate the car he is glorifying. Thus, "mythical" here means something wrapped in the aura of the extreme. The second meaning is just the opposite: Everywhere we go, we meet people who declare that they do not believe in the "myth" of something or other, that they're opposed to it and hold it up to public disdain. Here "myth" simply takes on the meaning of "lie": generally an imaginative lie, accompanied by some emotion, which the clear mind must dispel and stamp out. I think that behind the distressing banality of these two accepted meanings of the word "myth," a long story lies hidden, and it is by no means banal. Quite the contrary: I would say that it throws open the very vortex of history. Certainly we will not get into it in this brief digression. Still, I should like to remind you of certain points that can be discerned behind the common, unconscious, and proud use of a word. And as a modest practical proposal, I would suggest for us all a means of self-defense: Use the word "myth" solely for the stories of gods and heroes called such by the ancients. This means abandoning forever the company of both ad men and debunkers, who—among other things—often coincide, like the hostile theologians in Jorge Luis Borges's story who discover in heaven that they are the same person.

The scandal over myth and its irrepressible lie is not simply one of the waste products of contemporary enlightenment. We find it everywhere in Greece, starting with Xenophanes. But there is *one* text in which the argument against myth is conducted with maximum authority and maximum force. It is Plato's *Republic.* This dialogue sheds light on everything that over the centuries has been stated to defend myth or to condemn it. One might even say that all that has been written on the subject since then is nothing but a series of glosses on a few lines from the *Republic.* In a famous passage in Book 10, Plato speaks of the "old quarrel between philosophy and poetry." And poetry means Homer. Indeed, the whole *Republic* can be read as a staged dispute between Plato and Homer, a dispute that has never ended and that even today invisibly guides our words. It is not, however, a literary dispute. For the Greeks, Homer is above all the first theologian, the first repository of wisdom about the gods and the world. In fact, Plato launches his attack on Homer in Book 2, well before Book 10, which deals with the function of poetry in the city. And here the argument is theological. Homer is bluntly accused of having composed "false myths." Whereas in Book 10 poets are condemned because they practice *mímēsis,* the dangerous art of imitation, here they are accused of "depicting images that in no way resemble the things they have tried to portray." The deception would thus reside in the divine stories themselves. But how can we believe that Plato was really disturbed by the adulteries, rapes, and other misdeeds of the gods? That would mean to read him like a Church Father or a Stoic moralist, whereas Plato is par excellence a metaphysician, and it is precisely on metaphysical grounds that he objects to the mythical tales.

Let us follow him now as he takes a decisive step. If Homer's stories were worthy of belief, what then would be the nature of the god? The god would be, says Plato, a *góēs,* a wizard, a magician capable of changing his appearance at will, deceiving us by roaming "in many forms." And here comes the metaphysical question: Should we believe that the god subjects himself to this incessant metamorphosis or that he has a "simple" form and "emerges" *(ekbaínei)* from himself less than any other? Here we have touched rock bottom in Plato's accusation: Homer, the enemy, is nothing but the representative of a realm, the realm of metamorphosis, and he is the bearer of the knowledge of metamorphosis. For philosophy, this is the enemy realm, the realm of ungovernable powers, whose witnesses—the poets—should be expelled from the city.

So when Plato simultaneously condemns mimetic poetry and Homeric myth, which is metamorphic and epiphanic, it is because a serious, invincible threat comes from these tales and forms. Unlike anyone before him, Plato was seized by a sort of giddy terror at the proliferation of images. The waves of the "boundless ocean of dissimilarity" were breaking all around him. If we try to limit the area of the quarrel with Homer, it would then be the area of appearance, of images, of simulacra, of *eídōla.* And *eídōlon,* "simulacrum," will here be the crucial word, just as idolatry was the crucial point in the quarrel between Judeo-Christianity and paganism. Now, myth is precisely a knowledge of the simulacrum through the simulacrum. Not only does the mythical tale not take a stand against the "boundless ocean of dissimilarity," but it would seem to glorify it, as if nothing could pass through the diversified barrier of appearance. And it is precisely in diversity, in that *poikilía* that rules in events on earth and that we already recognize when we raise our eyes to the stars—called by Plato "the ornaments *(poikílmata)* of the sky"—that the greatest danger lies hidden. The simulacrum, in fact, seduces one to imitation. The man who looks at the simulacrum is tempted to become the simulacrum. And if the wheel of simulacra appears diversified and perverse, this man will become—as it says in the *Republic*—not merely a poet but a *góēs,* a wizard, exactly like the god he celebrates. It is in this word that, for Plato, the enemy is condensed, be he god or poet.

Plato's city expels not only a certain type of man but a certain type of god: the Homeric gods, to be precise. As for the man to be expelled, Plato calls him not primarily a poet but a "man skillfully able to transform himself into everything." From that, one can see that Plato's opposition to the practice of metamorphosis takes precedence over his rejection of a certain use of words. And this practice is revealed precisely in the skill of anyone who treats simulacra by transforming himself into them. Therefore, hidden behind the opposition to poetry looms another, where the realm of words is even abandoned and two antagonistic kinds of knowledge clash. Plato alludes here to the trauma, the rift in the history of knowledge, that occurs when instead of saying "*a* is transformed into *b*," one says "*a* is *b*."

The first form, necessarily narrative, is the one in which knowledge is displayed wherever we find myths, and there is no civilization that does not contain some knowledge of this kind. On the other hand, predicative knowledge (in the form "*a* is *b*") appears rather late and only in a few places, one of which is archaic Greece. The final comparison would thus be this: on one side, a knowledge that today we would call algorithmic, that is, a chain of statements, of signs linked to the verb "to be"; on the other, a metamorphic knowledge, all inside the mind, where knowledge is an emotion that modifies the knowing subject, a knowledge born from the image, from the *eídōlon,* and culminating in the image, without ever being separated from it or admitting a knowledge higher than itself; a knowledge driven by an inexhaustible force, which, however, has the grace to offer itself as a literary device; that is, analogy.

In this mortal duel, when the predicative form of knowledge became dominant, one of its first concerns was to develop a theory of myth that would discredit its cognitive power. The first symptom of the terror of fables was thus the elaboration of some sort of theoretical reconstruction of their origin. The function of such an exorcising enterprise was above all to obliterate the idea that the myth itself had been born as an all-embracing and self-sufficient theory. What Plato was accomplishing by condemning Homer was therefore a grandiose attempt to undermine a whole form of knowledge. But let us look closely at the dangers of imitation: The mythical stories, by their nature, seduce the soul to imitate them, as though they inevitably belonged to the circulation of simulacra. And how did this process of imitation occur? I will give two examples, chosen from the two ends of the mythical range, which fundamentally coincide.

The first is from Homer. That the gestures of myth are models for human actions is attested for the first time in the *Iliad:* Achilles looks at Priam. He is about to restore to him the corpse of Hector, wrapped in linen and lying on a bed. But the night must still pass before the father can see him. So Achilles invites Priam to eat. What argument will he find to convince the petrified old man? Achilles begins to speak of the children of Niobe. Pierced by the arrows of Apollo and Artemis, they lay abandoned for nine days. Everything around them lay still, like coagulated blood. Niobe and all the other human beings remained motionless. Such was the will of Zeus. "Then, on the tenth day, they were buried by the gods, sons of Uranos." The gods came down silently from Olympus and dug a grave for six young women and six young men. "Then Niobe remembered food, since she had grown tired of weeping." Later she was transformed into a rock.

Achilles continues to speak to Priam: "Well, even we, divine old man, think about food." Perhaps in other texts, equally old and today lost, one might find similar scenes. Before performing a gesture, a hero remembers a previous gesture that formed part of a story of the gods. And that memory gave him the form for his action and the strength to carry it out. But the *Iliad,* for the Greeks, was the origin. Each of its lines can be read as something being said for the first time. Thus, mythical exemplariness is stated once and for all on this occasion: Two desperate men, one old and one young, must persuade themselves to eat. The gesture that then came to Achilles' mind was that of Niobe, she who had seen two gods kill all her children and then all the gods descend from heaven to bury them. First they kill us, then they bury us. Everything the gods wanted to tell us about themselves was contained in that image, that story. Now it would have to be repeated, just as it would later be repeated countless other times by others who perhaps did not even know its name—the gesture of Niobe.

The second example that I would like to offer you is a story of the Bushmen of the Kalahari, collected in 1879 by Wilhelm Bleek. Here, the one who speaks is not the bravest and mightiest of the Achaeans but a wretched nomadic hunter, hounded by blacks and whites, about four feet seven inches tall, and like all his people, able to count only to three. The following text demonstrates his relations with Canopus, a prominent star in Bushman mythology:

> My grandfather used to speak to Canopus as soon as the star rose. He would say: "You will give me your heart, which is full; you will take my heart, with which I feel desperately afflicted. So that I too can be full, like you. For you look full of food and so you are not little. For I am hungry.

You will give me your stomach, with which you are satisfied. You will take my stomach, so that you too may be hungry. Give me also your arm and take my arm, with which I do not kill. For I miss the target. You will give your arm."

Achilles and the Bushman thus act with a common premise. They think every action acquires meaning insofar as it conceals a double within, a mental epiphany, an exemplary action that once and for all gives form to the gesture: an action that may have occurred on the veldts of heaven or among the cliffs of Anatolia but that envelops every other similar action in its light, forever.

No one, I think—friend or foe—has ever been so lucid about myth as Plato. And no one—I think—has practiced myth in such an ambivalent way. One point, however, remains steady: His condemnation of Homer, the stubborn rejection expressed in Books 2 and 10 of the *Republic,* was the crucial event in our history, as far as the understanding of myth is concerned—or rather, as far as the nonunderstanding of myth is concerned. One might say that, from then until today, the most diverse theorists, each in his own way and sometimes at a distance of centuries, have been anxious to obey Plato's injunction. They have been philologists and theologians, antiquaries and poets, historians and archaeologists.

But before alluding to them, I should like to return for a moment to Plato's ambivalence. In the *Phaedo* he states a position quite the opposite of the one set forth in the *Republic.* Speaking of myths, Socrates says, "Beautiful indeed is this risk, and we somehow need to be enchanted with these things [i.e., with the fables themselves]." Knowledge by simulacra appears here as a sort of spell to which the mind subjects itself: a dangerous and beautiful enchantment, a risk we must accept because the knowledge that comes to us by this path would not be attainable in any other way.

Now let us go back to the *Republic.* After Plato's condemnation, one might say that the mythical tale was put under house arrest, or at best on probation. That the ancient fables were absurd, immoral, perverse, and childish has been repeated countless times over the centuries, primarily, of course, on the Christian side. But the noble Neoplatonic allegories, which reach their peak with Proclus, also served to enfeeble them by making them pious and obedient to a philosophical design. And finally, when ranks of learned mythographers began to make headway among scholars of classical antiquity, science too obeyed Plato's condemnation, confining mythical events, with desperate and often comical diligence, to unsuitable and inadequate spheres. Wilhelm Roscher's *Lexikon,* an enormous and magisterial work of mythography, bears obvious signs of this. There we find upright scholars doing their best to trace fables back to atmospheric phenomena, to disparate forms of clouds and dawns and thunderstorms. Just as, starting with Wilhelm Mannhardt, the other deadening word, "fertility,"came along as something to trace every image back to. Shortly thereafter, another obsession, the obsession with ritual, would appear, still with the same purpose of corralling and classifying the promiscuity of images. And in our own day, the last imposing attempt to systematize myth, that of Claude Lévi-Strauss, appears as the work of a Linnaeus of images, chiefly eager to conceive what myth could *not* conceive except unconsciously, that is, countless variations of the nature/culture opposition, a thought that might more accurately be attributed to Lévi-Strauss himself and to our whole period, dominated by society's superstitious faith in itself.

In the meantime, however, mythical simulacra have continued to act. But in what form? Ovid defined his *Metamorphoses* as *"carmen perpetuum,"* which we might translate as "endless enchantment," with an eye to the original meaning of *carmen.* This work, along with Nonnus's *Dionysiaca,* is the last surviving summa in which simulacra speak in the language of simulacra. Ovid's successors, by and large, did not sing but painted.

It is instructive to draw a comparison between Ovid's countless commentators and his illustrators. Among the commentators, beginning with the Ovid *moralisé* of the Middle Ages and then for century after century, there is a tenacious attempt to subject Ovid to a euhemerist, moralizing, or flatly narratological interpretation. Compare that with the illustrators of Ovid and the Greek fables. In Guido Reni's *Atalanta* or Gianlorenzo Bernini's *Apollo and Daphne,* in *Echo and Narcissus* by Nicolas Poussin (whom Bernini himself called a "great fabulist") or Rembrandt's *Rape of Proserpina,* in Titian's *Rape of Europa* or Carlo Saraceni's *Daedalus and Icarus,* in Francesco Furini's *Ulysses and Penelope* or Dosso Dossi's *Zeus Painting Butterflies,* it would seem that Ovid's *carmen* continues to be interwoven, without a thought to period and customs, as though the same knowledge of simulacra were transmitted silently from one to another or a tapestry of words was being continued on canvas and in marble. Thus fables, which when expressed in words had ended by terrifying people, have continued to be secretly contemplated. One would like to think that

European civilization found this honorable compromise to guarantee their survival by welcoming them into the irresponsible sphere of art.

Says Sallustius in *On the Gods and the World*, "For the world itself can be called myth, in that bodies and things appear in it, while souls and spirits are hidden in it." It was necessary to arrive at the end of paganism, with this obscure little Neoplatonic treatise, to come upon a definition of myth so dazzling in its simplicity as to make all others seem fruitless. So when we look at the spectacle of the world around us, we already find ourselves in a myth. And now we can understand why mythical tales, even when they come down to us fragmented and mutilated, sound familiar and different from all other stories. These tales are a landscape; they are our landscape, hostile and inviting simulacra that no one has invented, which we continue to meet and which expect us only to recognize them. Thus now we can own up to what was—what is—that ancient terror that the fables continue to arouse. It is no different from the terror that is the first one of all: terror of the world; terror in the face of its mute, deceptive, overwhelming enigma; terror before this place of constant metamorphosis and epiphany, which above all includes our own minds, where we witness without letup the tumult of simulacra.

Now, if myth is precisely a sequence of simulacra that help to recognize simulacra, it is naive to pretend to interpret myth, when it is myth itself that is already interpreting us. It acts on us like the wooden image of Taurian Artemis: Orestes stole it from the shrine. He traveled a long way holding it tightly in his hands, and all the while he felt madness hanging over his head. Then one day, he thought he would try to live by himself and hid the statue in a thicket of reeds, not far from the Eurotas River. There the image lay for years. One day two young Spartans of royal blood, Astrabacus and Alopecus, discovered it accidentally when they entered the thicket. Upright, wreathed in branches, the statue stared at them. The two Spartans were driven mad, because they had no idea what they were seeing. This is the power of the simulacrum, which cures only those who know it. For others it is a sickness. Thus the myth: The power that arouses terror is also the only one that can cure it, as happened with Orestes. But only if it is recognized for what it is.

Notes

I. FATAL MONOLOGUE

1. Friedrich Nietzsche, *On the Genealogy of Morals,* tr. Walter Kaufmann and R. J. Hollingdale (New York, 1989), preface, para. 1, p. 15.

2. Friedrich Nietzsche, *Ecce Homo,* tr. Walter Kaufmann (New York, 1989), preface, para. 1, p. 217.

3. Ibid.

4. Nietzsche, *Genealogy of Morals,* preface, para. 2, p. 16.

5. Nietzsche to C. Fuchs, 14 December 1887.

6. Nietzsche to C. von Gersdorff, 20 December 1887.

7. Nietzsche to P. Gast [Heinrich Köselitz], 20 December 1887.

8. Friedrich Nietzsche, *Beyond Good and Evil,* section 281, tr. R. J. Hollingdale (New York, 1990), p. 213.

9. Nietzsche to R. von Seydlitz, 12 February 1888.

10. Nietzsche to G. Brandes, 2 December 1887.

11. Nietzsche to P. Deussen, 3 January 1888.

12. Ibid.

13. Nietzsche to P. Gast, 7 April 1888.

14. Nietzsche to P. Gast, 20 April 1888.

15. Nietzsche to A. Strindberg, 8 December 1888.

16. Nietzsche to J. Burckhardt, 6 January 1889, in *The Portable Nietzsche,* tr. Walter Kaufmann (New York: Viking, 1968), p. 686.

17. Friedrich Nietzsche, *Posthumous Fragments,* 1[67], July–August 1882. The *Posthumous Fragments* are cited by number and date as established by the Colli-Montinari edition.

18. Friedrich Nietzsche, *The Gay Science,* tr. Walter Kaufmann (New York: Vintage Books, 1974), 367, p. 324.

19. Martin Heidegger, *Nietzsche* (Pfullingen, 1961), vol. 1, p. 480.

20. Ibid., p. 475.

21. Martin Heidegger, *Was heisst denken?* (Tübingen, 1954), second part, passim.

22. Martin Heidegger, *Der Satz vom Grund* (Pfullingen, 1957), pp. 150ff.

23. Friedrich Nietzsche, *The Case of Wagner,* epilogue, tr. Walter Kaufmann (New York, 1967), p. 192.

24. Nietzsche, *Ecce Homo,* preface, para. 1.

25. Friedrich Nietzsche, "Maxims and Arrows," 38, in *Twilight of the Idols,* in *The Portable Nietzsche,* p. 472.

26. Ibid., 42.

27. Friedrich Nietzsche, *Die Dionysische Weltanschauung,* para. 3, in *Vorstufen der Geburt der Tragödie,* vol. 3 (Leipzig, 1928).

28. Nietzsche, *Posthumous Fragments,* 9[42], 1871 (for the projected work *Music and Tragedy*).

29. Ibid., 2[146], Autumn 1885–Autumn 1886.

30. Ibid., 1[36], Autumn 1885–Spring 1886.

31. "Nihil etiam tam multiplex esse poteșt aut dispersum, quod per illam, de qua egimus, enumerationem certis limitibus circumscribi atque in aliquot capita disponi non possit." René Descartes, *Regulae ad directionem ingenii,* 8.

32. Nietzsche, *Posthumous Fragments,* 6[184], Autumn 1880.

33. Ibid., 14[31], Spring 1888.

34. Friedrich Nietzsche, "How the 'True World' Finally Became a Fable," in *Twilight of the Idols.*

35. Nietzsche, *Posthumous Fragments,* 7[54], late 1886–Spring 1887.

36. Nietzsche to P. Gast, 13 November 1888.

37. John 19:2.

38. Respectively in Nietzsche, *Ecce Homo*: "Why I am a Destiny," para. 1, and "The Case of Wagner," para. 4.

39. Nietzsche, *Ecce Homo,* preface, para. 1.

40. Nietzsche to F. Overbeck, 13 November 1888.

41. Nietzsche to P. Gast, 16 December 1888.

42. Nietzsche, *Beyond Good and Evil,* 40.

43. Friedrich Nietzsche, "Assorted Opinions and Maxims," 360, part 1 of vol. 2 of *Human, All Too Human,* tr. R. J. Hollingdale (Cambridge: Cambridge University Press, 1986), p. 293.

44. Friedrich Hölderlin, *Anmerkungen zum Ödipus.*

45. Nietzsche, *The Gay Science,* 374.

46. Friedrich Hölderlin, *Frankfurter Plan* for *Der Tod des Empedokles.*

47. Nietzsche, *Ecce Homo,* "Why I Am So Wise," para. 1.

48. Friedrich Hölderlin, *Grund zum Empedokles.*

49. Nietzsche, "Why I Am So Wise," para. 5, in *Ecce Homo.* [Translation slightly altered.]

50. Hölderlin, *Grund zum Empedokles.*

51. Ibid.

52. Friedrich Nietzsche, "The Wanderer and His Shadow," part 2 of vol. 2 of *Human, All Too Human,* 185.

53. Friedrich Nietzsche, "Skirmishes of an Untimely Man," 36, in *Twilight of the Idols,* p. 537.

54. Nietzsche, "Why I Am a Destiny," para. 1, in *Ecce Homo*.

55. Nietzsche, *The Gay Science*, 367.

56. Ibid., 371.

57. Nietzsche to P. Gast, 13 and 18 November 1888.

58. Nietzsche to F. Overbeck, 13 November 1888.

59. Nietzsche to P. Gast, 9 December 1888.

60. Nietzsche to P. Gast, 16 December 1888.

61. Nietzsche to C. Fuchs, 27 December 1888.

62. Nietzsche to J. Burckhardt, 6 January 1889, in *The Portable Nietzsche*, p. 686.

63. Ibid.

64. Nietzsche to F. Avenarius, 10 December 1888.

65. Nietzsche to J. Burckhardt, 6 January 1889, in *The Portable Nietzsche*, p. 687. [Translation slightly altered.]

66. Nietzsche, *Posthumous Fragments*, 21[4], Autumn 1888.

67. Ibid., 16[89], Spring–Summer 1888.

68. Nietzsche to J. Burckhardt, 4 January 1889.

69. Nietzsche, *Posthumous Fragments* 2[132], Autumn 1885–Autumn 1886.

70. Nietzsche, *Posthumous Fragments* 24[1]2, October–November 1888.

71. Pierre Klossowski, "Don Juan selon Kierkegaard," *Acéphale* 3–4, (1937):28.

72. Pierre Klossowski, *Nietzsche et le cercle vicieux* (Paris, 1969), pp. 319–56.

73. Nietzsche to J. Burckhardt, 6 January 1889, in *The Portable Nietzsche*, p. 687.

74. Klossowski, *Nietzsche et le cercle vicieux*, pp. 345–47.

75. Nietzsche to J. Burckhardt, 6 January 1889, in *The Portable Nietzsche*, p. 686.

76. Nietzsche, *Posthumous Fragments*, 10[95], Autumn 1887.

77. Klossowski, *Nietzsche et le cercle vicieux*, p. 323.

78. Nietzsche, *Posthumous Fragments*, 1[70], July–August 1882.

79. Nietzsche to J. Burckhardt, 6 January 1889, in *The Portable Nietzsche*, p. 686.

80. Ibid, p. 687. In Italian in Nietzsche's letter.

81. C. A. F. Bernoulli, *F. Overbeck und F. Nietzsche*, (Jena, 1908), vol. 2, p. 307.

82. Nietzsche, *The Gay Science*, 359.

83. "On Truth and Lying in the Extramoral Sense," para. 1 (dissertation of 1873).

84. Ibid., para. 2.

85. Ibid., para. 1, 2.

86. Ibid.

2. THE SLEEP OF THE CALLIGRAPHER

1. Cf. the section "Lektüre," in Robert Walser, *Der Europäer* (Geneva, 1968).

2. Robert Walser, "Meine Bemühungen," in *Grosse kleine Welt*, ed. Carl Seelig (Zurich, 1937), p. 198.

3. Walter Benjamin, "Robert Walser," in *Gesammelte Schriften*, vol. 2, book 1, (Frankfurt, 1977), p. 327.

4. C. Seelig, *Wanderungen mit Robert Walser* (St. Gallen, 1957), p. 14.

5. R. Mächler, *Das Leben Robert Walsers* (Geneva, 1966), p. 104.

6. E. Rohde, "Sardinische Sage von den Neunschläfern," in *Kleine Schriften,* vol. 2, (Tübingen, 1901), pp. 197–209.

7. L. Massignon, *Les nuages de Magellan et leur découverte par les Arabes* (Paris, 1962), pp. 14–15; G. de Santillana and H. von Dechend, *Hamlet's Mill* (Boston, 1969), p. 269.

8. Santillana and Dechend, *Hamlet's Mill,* pp. 239, 418–19.

9. A. Jeremias, *Handbuch der altorientalischen Geisteskultur* (Berlin, 1929), p. 189.

10. M. Schneider, *El origen musical de los animales-símbolos en la mitología y la escultura antiguas* (Barcelona, 1946), p. 186.

11. H. Corbin, "Physiologie de l'homme de lumière dans le soufisme iranien," in *Ombre et Lumière* (various authors) (Bruges, 1961), p. 179.

12. Massignon, *Les nuages de Magellan,* p. 14.

13. Charbry, *Josaphaz, Set Dormanz und Petit Plet* (Heilbronn, 1879). Christian and Islamic sources for the legend of the Seven Sleepers in M. Huber, *Die Wanderlegende von den Siebenschläfern* (Leipzig, 1910); I. Guidi, "Testi orientali inediti sopra i Sette Dormienti in Efeso," in *Raccolta di scritti* (Rome, 1945) vol. 1, pp. 61–198.

14. L. Massignon, "Les 'Sept Dormants': Apocalypse de l'Islam" and "Le culte liturgique et populaire des Sept Dormants Martyrs d'Éphèse," in *Opera Minora* (Beirut, 1963), book 3, pp. 104–19 and 119–81.

15. L. Massignon, *Les temps dans la pensée islamique,* in *Opera Minora,* book 2, p. 607.

16. Robert Walser, "Minotauros," in *Maskerade* (Geneva, 1968), p. 199.

17. H. Güntert, *Calypso* (Halle, 1919), pp. 170–72.

18. R. Eisler, *Weltenmantel und Himmelszelt* (Munich, 1970), vol. 2, pp. 390–91.

19. Mächler, *Das Leben Robert Walsers,* p. 107.

20. Max Brod, *Streitbares Leben* (Munich, 1960), pp. 393–94.

21. Franz Kafka, *Briefe* (Frankfurt, 1958), p. 75.

22. Robert Musil, "Literarische Chronik," in *Tagebücher, Aphorismen, Essays und Reden* (Hamburg, 1955), p. 687.

23. Elias Canetti, "Kafka's Other Trial: The Letters to Felice," in *The Conscience of Words,* tr. Joachim Neugroschel (New York, 1979), p. 111.

24. Robert Walser, "Das Kind (III)," in *Poetenleben* (Geneva, 1967), p. 406.

25. Carl Seelig, *National-Zeitung* (Basel, 6 January 1957).

26. Robert Walser, "Theodor," in *Festzug* (Geneva, 1966), pp. 307–33.

27. T. Izutsu, *The Key Philosophical Concepts in Sufism and Taoism* (Tokyo, 1966), pp. 11–13.

28. Hugo von Hofmannsthal, "The Letter of Lord Chandos," tr. Tania Stern and James Stern, in *Selected Prose* (New York, 1952), p. 138.

29. Robert Walser, "Die Glosse," in *Maskerade* (Geneva, 1968), p. 296.

30. Mächler, *Das Leben Robert Walsers,* p. 47.

31. Jacket copy for the Italian edition of *Der Gehülfe* (The Assistant) (Turin, 1961).

3. DÉESSES ENTRETENUES

1. Bertolt Brecht, 1918, in *Gesammelte Werke,* vol. 7, p. 3.

2. Arthur Kutscher, *Frank Wedekind: Sein Leben und sein Werk* (Munich, 1927), vol. 2, pp. 130–31.

3. M. Granet, *La pensée chinoise* (Paris, 1934), p. 332.

4. *Les mémoires historiques de Se-ma Ts'ien,* ed. É. Chavannes, chap. 28.

5. Morhofius, *Polyhistor* (Lübeck, 1747), p. 348.

6. Karl Marx, *Marx Engels Werke* (Berlin, 1956–), vol. 23, pp. 91–93. (Hereafter *MEW.*)

7. Ibid., p. 90.

8. Karl Marx, *Capital,* in *MEW,* vol. 25, p. 838.

9. Marx, *Capital,* in *MEW,* vol. 23, p. 85.

10. Ibid., p. 62.

11. Ibid., p. 99.

12. Karl Marx, *Grundrisse* (Berlin, 1953), p. 391.

13. Marcel Mauss, "Essai sur le don," in *Sociologie et anthropologie* (Paris, 1960), p. 167.

14. Marx, *Auszüge aus Mill,* in *MEW,* Ergbd. 1, p. 446.

15. *Capital,* in *MEW,* vol. 23, p. 102.

16. Ibid.

17. Ibid., p. 146.

18. Ibid., pp. 102–3.

19. *Auszüge aus Mill,* in *MEW,* Ergbd. 1, p. 455.

20. Ibid., pp. 448, 449.

21. Marx, *Grundrisse,* p. 391.

22. G. W. F. Hegel, *Aphorismen aus dem Wastebook,* 1803–1806.

23. Marx, *Grundrisse,* p. 25.

24. Marx, *Capital,* in *MEW,* vol. 23, p. 58.

25. Marx, *Grundrisse,* pp. 117ff.

26. Pierre Klossowski, *La monnaie vivante* (Paris, 1970), p. [30].

27. Marx, *Auszüge aus Mill,* in *MEW,* Ergbd. 1, p. 461.

28. Marx, *Grundrisse,* p. 80.

29. Arthur Rimbaud, "Illuminations," in *Rimbaud: Complete Works, Selected Letters,* tr. Wallace Fowlie, (Chicago, 1966), pp. 253–55.

30. Marx, *Grundrisse,* p. 134.

31. Frank Wedekind, *Schloss Wetterstein,* act 1, scene 1.

4. ENAMEL SCAR

1. Gottfried Benn, *Epilog und lyrisches Ich,* in *Gesammelte Werke,* ed. D. Wellershoff, vols. 1–4 (Wiesbaden, 1958–61) [hereafter *GW*], vol. 4, p. 8. All passages quoted are by Benn.

2. Gottfried Benn, *Zur Problematik des Dichterischen,* in *GW,* vol. 1, p. 78.

3. Gottfried Benn, *Lebensweg eines Intellektualisten,* in *GW,* vol. 4, p. 38.

4. Letter of 27 October 1940, in *Briefe an F. W. Oelze 1932–1945* (Wiesbaden, 1977), p. 246.

5. Gottfried Benn, *Mein Name ist Monroe,* in *GW,* vol. 1, p. 401.

6. Letter of 11 April 1942, in *Briefe an F. W. Oelze 1932–1945,* p. 311.

7. Letter to Wellershoff of 22 November 1950, in Gottfried Benn, *Ausgewählte Brief* (Wiesbaden, 1957), p. 202.

8. Ibid., pp. 204–5.

9. Gottfried Benn, "Die Reise," in *GW,* vol. 2, p. 33.

10. Gottfried Benn, "Die Insel," in *GW,* vol. 2, p. 46.

11. Benn, *Lebensweg eines Intellektualisten,* p. 30.

12. Ibid., p. 37.

13. Gottfried Benn, *Probleme der Lyrik,* in *GW,* vol. 1, p. 515.

14. Gottfried Benn, *Zucht und Zukunft,* in *GW,* vol. 1, p. 457.

15. Benn, *Epilog und lyrisches Ich,* p. 11.

16. Letter to Nele Soerensen of 24 August 1949, in N. P. Soerensen, *Mein Vater Gottfried Benn* (Wiesbaden, 1984), p. 97.

17. Gottfried Benn, *Doppelleben,* in *GW,* vol. 4, p. 133.

18. Ibid., p. 133.

19. Gottfried Benn, *Roman des Phänotyp,* in *GW,* vol. 2, p. 171.

20. Benn, *Doppelleben,* p. 133.

5. ON THE FUNDAMENTALS OF THE COCA-COLA BOTTLE

1. [A beautiful and wicked sorceress in Torquato Tasso's *Gerusalemme liberata.* —Trans.]

2. ["Die Frage nach der Technik" and "Überwindung der Metaphysik," both in *Vorträge und Aufsätze,* 1954.—Trans.]

6. THE PERPETUAL WAR

1. Elias Canetti, "The New Karl Kraus," in *The Conscience of Words,* tr. Joachim Neugroschel (New York, 1979), pp. 218, 219.

2. Walter Benjamin, "Karl Kraus," in *Reflections: Essays, Aphorisms, Autobiographical Writings,* tr. Edmund Jephcott (New York, 1978), p. 260.

3. Elias Canetti, *The Torch in My Ear,* tr. Joachim Neugroschel (New York, 1982), p. 71.

4. Canetti, "The New Karl Kraus," p. 214.

5. Canetti, *The Torch in My Ear,* p. 71.

6. Karl Kraus, "Pro domo et mundo" (1912), in *Beim Wort genommen* (Munich, 1955), pp. 294–95.

7. Ibid., p. 297.

8. Karl Kraus, *Die letzten Tage der Menschheit* (Munich, 1957), pp. 726, 679.

9. Kraus, "Nachts" (1918), in *Beim Wort genommen,* p. 435.

10. Walter Benjamin, "Erfahrung und Armut," in *Gesammelte Schriften* (Frankfurt, 1977), vol. 2, book 1, p. 214.

11. Kraus, *Die letzten Tage der Menschheit,* p. 643.

12. Ernst Jünger, *In Stahlgewittern* (1920), in *Werke* (Stuttgart, n.d.), vol. 1, p. 11.

13. Ernst Jünger, *Die Totale Mobilmachung* (1930), in *Werke,* vol. 5, p. 133.

14. Ibid., pp. 125–26, 130, 132.

15. Canetti, "The New Karl Kraus," p. 217.

16. [References are to scene and line number—Trans.]

17. Elias Canetti, *Crowds and Power,* tr. Carol Stewart (New York, 1996), pp. 73–75.

18. Leopold Liegler, *Karl Kraus und sein Werk* (Vienna, 1920), pp. 57–58. This book is the first and unsurpassed monument of Krausian apologetics.

19. Kraus, *Die letzten Tage der Menschheit,* p. 659.

20. Karl Kraus, "Erfahrung," *Die Fackel,* nos. 381–383, September 1913, p. 43.

21. Kraus, *Die letzten Tage der Menschheit,* p. 9.

22. *Chuang-tzu,* III, 2.

23. Delivered on 19 November in Vienna and printed as the only text in no. 404 of *Die Fackel,* 5 December 1914.

24. Karl Kraus, "In dieser grossen Zeit," in *Weltgericht* (Munich, [1965]), p. 9.

25. Benjamin, "Karl Kraus," p. 243.

26. Canetti, "The New Karl Kraus," p. 217. [Translation slightly altered.]

27. Karl Kraus, *Briefe an Sidonie Nádherný von Borutin* (Munich, 1974), vol. 1, pp. 179–80.

28. Karl Kraus, "Notizen," *Die Fackel,* nos. 423–25, May 1916, p. 18.

29. [In English in original—Trans.]

30. Canetti, "The New Karl Kraus," p. 216.

31. Benjamin, "Karl Kraus," p. 269.

32. Kraus, *Die letzten Tage der Menschheit,* p. 501.

33. Ibid., p. 497.

34. Benjamin, "Karl Kraus," pp. 255–56.

35. Ibid., p. 256; Kraus, *Die letzten Tage der Menschheit,* p. 681.

36. Benjamin, "Karl Kraus," pp. 250, 253, 260.

37. Karl Kraus, "Kriegssegen," *Die Fackel,* nos. 706–11, December 1925, p. 29.

38. Kraus, *Die letzten Tage der Menschheit,* p. 385.

39. Gottfried Benn, *Roman des Phänotyp,* in *Gesammelte Werke* (Wiesbaden, 1962), vol. 2, p. 161.

40. Kraus, *Die letzten Tage der Menschheit,* pp. 495–96.

41. Ibid., p. 412.

42. Ibid., pp. 413, 409.

43. "Reklamefahrten zur Hölle," on the recording *Karl Kraus liest aus eigenen Schriften,* Lebendiges Wort, LW 17.

44. Karl Kraus, "Reklamefahrten zur Hölle," *Die Fackel,* nos. 577–82, November 1921, p. 97.

45. Ibid., p. 98.

10. A REPORT ON READERS OF SCHREBER

1. D. P. Schreber, *Denkwürdigkeiten eines Nervenkranken* nebst Nachträgen und einem Anhang über die Frage: "Unter welchen Voraussetzungen darf eine für geisteskrank erachtete Person gegen ihren erklärten Willen in einer Heilanstalt festgehalten werden?" (Leipzig, 1903).

2. D. P. Schreber, *Memoirs of My Nervous Illness,* ed. and with two essays by I. Macalpine and R. A. Hunter, (London, 1955), p. 369; Elias Canetti, *The Human Province,* tr. Joachim Neugroschel (New York, 1978), p. 119.

3. C. Pelman, review of Daniel Paul Streber *[sic], Denkwürdigkeiten eines Nervenkranken,* in *Allgemeine Zeitschrift für Psychiatrie* 60(1903): 657.

4. R. Pfeiffer, review of D. P. Schreber, *Denkwürdigkeiten eines Nervenkranken,* in *Deutsche Zeitschrift für Nervenheilkunde* 27(1904): 352–53.

5. C. G. Jung, "The Psychology of Dementia Praecox" (1907), in *Collected Works,* vol. 3, *The Psychogenesis of Mental Disease,* tr. R. F. C. Hull (New York, 1960), passim.

6. Sigmund Freud, "Further Remarks on the Defence Neuro-Psychoses" (1896), in *Collected Papers* (New York, 1959), vol 1, p. 169.

7. Sigmund Freud, *The Origins of Psycho-Analysis: Letters to Wilhelm Fliess, Drafts and Notes: 1887–1902,* ed. Marie Bonaparte, Anna Freud, Ernst Kris, tr. Eric Mosbacher and James Strachey (New York, 1954), letter 69, p. 216.

8. Jung, "Psychology of Dementia Praecox," p. 34.

9. *The Freud/Jung Letters,* ed. William McGuire, tr. Ralph Manheim and R. F. C. Hull (Princeton, 1974), p. 13.

10. Ibid, pp. 120–21.

11. Ibid., pp. 293–94.

12. *The Correspondence of Sigmund Freud and Sándor Ferenczi,* vol. 1, *1908–1914,* tr. Peter T. Hoffer (Cambridge, Mass., 1993), p. 221.

13. *Freud/Jung Letters,* p. 356.

14. J. Honegger, "Über paranoïde Wahnbildung," *Jahrbuch für psychoanalytische und psychopathologische Forschungen* 2(1910): 734–35.

15. Sigmund Freud, "Psycho-Analytic Notes upon an Autobiographical Account of a Case of Paranoia (Dementia Paranoides)," in *Collected Papers,* tr. Alix Strachey and James Strachey (New York, 1959), vol. 3, pp. 423–24.

16. Ibid., p. 444.

17. Ibid., p. 452.

18. Ibid., p. 467.

19. Ibid., p. 462.

20. *Freud/Jung Letters,* p. 471.

21. C. G. Jung, "The Content of the Psychoses" (1908/1914), supplement: "On Psychological Understanding," in *Collected Works,* vol. 3, *The Psychogenesis of Mental Disease,* p. 187.

22. Sabina Spielrein, "Über den psychologischen Inhalt eines Falles von Schizophrenie (Dementia praecox)," in *Jahrbuch für psychoanalytische und psychopathologische Forschungen* 3(1911): 396–97.

23. Eugen Bleuler, review of Freud, "Psychoanalytische Bemerkungen über einen autobiographisch beschriebenen Fall von Paranoia (Dementia paranoides)," *Zentralblatt für Psychoanalyse* 2(1912): 346.

24. Sigmund Freud, "On Narcissism: An Introduction" (1914), in *Collected Papers,* vol. 4, pp. 30–59; "A Case of Paranoia Running Counter to the Psycho-Analytical Theory of the Disease" (1915), in *Collected Papers,* vol. 2, pp. 150–61; "Certain Neurotic Mechanisms in Jealousy, Paranoia, and Homosexuality" (1922), in *Collected Papers,* vol. 2, pp. 232–43; "A Neurosis of Demoniacal Possession in the Seventeenth Century" (1923), in *Collected Papers,* vol. 4, pp. 436–72.

25. Walter Benjamin, "Bücher von Geisteskranken," in *Gesammelte Schriften* (Frankfurt, 1972), vol. 4, bk. 2, p. 616.

26. This information is from a personal letter from Elias Canetti, whom I here thank for allowing me to quote it.

27. Canetti, *The Human Province,* p. 120.

28. Elias Canetti, "The Case of Schreber: I/II," in *Crowds and Power,* tr. Carol Stewart (New York, 1984), p. 435.

29. Ibid., p. 443.

30. Ibid., pp. 449–50.

31. W. J. Spring, "Observations on World Destruction Fantasies," *Psychoanalytic Quarterly* 8(1939):48–56; R. P. Knight, "The Relationship of Latent Homosexuality to the Mechanism of Paranoid Delusions," *Bulletin of the Menninger Clinic* 4 (1940):149–59.

32. Melanie Klein, "Notes on Some Schizoid Mechanisms," in *Envy and Gratitude and Other Works, 1946–1963* (New York, 1984), pp. 22–24.

33. Maurits Katan, "Schreber's Delusion of the End of the World," *Psychoanalytic Quarterly* 18(1949): 60–66; "Schreber's Hallucinations about the 'Little Men,'" *International Journal of Psycho-Analysis* 31(1950): 32–35; "Further Remarks about Schreber's Hallucinations," *International Journal of Psycho-Analysis* 33(1952): 429–32; "Schreber's Prepsychotic Phase," *International Journal of Psycho-Analysis* 34(1953): 43–51; "The Importance of the Non-Psychotic Part of the Personality in Schizophrenia," *International Journal of Psycho-Analysis* 35(1954): 119–28.

34. Maurits Katan, "Schreber's Hereafter," *The Psychoanalytic Study of the Child* 14 (1959): 314–82.

35. A. C. Carr, "Observations on Paranoia and Their Relationship to the Schreber Case," *International Journal of Psycho-Analysis* 44 (1963): 195–200; R. Waelder, "The Structure of Paranoid Ideas," *International Journal of Psycho-Analysis* 32 (1951): 167–77; J. Nydes, "Schreber, Parricide, and Paranoid-Masochism," *International Journal of*

Psycho-Analysis 44 (1963): 208–12; P. M. Kitay, introduction and summary of the symposium on *Reinterpretations of the Schreber Case: Freud's Theory of Paranoia,* in *International Journal of Psycho-Analysis* 44 (1963): 191–94, 222–23; R. B. White, "The Mother-Conflict in Schreber's Psychosis," *International Journal of Psycho-Analysis* 42 (1961): 55–73; and "The Schreber Case Reconsidered in the Light of Psychosocial Concepts," *International Journal of Psycho-Analysis* 44 (1963): 213–21; H. F. Searles, "Sexual Processes in Schizophrenia," in *Collected Papers on Schizophrenia and Related Subjects* (London, 1965), pp. 429–42.

36. R. Stoller, "Faits et hypothèses: Un examen du concept freudien de bisexualité," *Nouvelle Revue de Psychanalyse* 7(Spring 1973): 135–55.

37. Schreber, *Memoirs of My Nervous Illness.*

38. Jacques Lacan, "On a Question Preliminary to Any Possible Treatment of Psychosis," in *Ecrits: A Selection,* tr. Alan Sheridan (New York, 1977).

39. Schreber, *Memoirs of My Nervous Illness,* pp. 381ff.

40. W. G. Niederland, "Three Notes on the Schreber Case," *Psychoanalytic Quarterly* 20 (1951): 579–91; "River Symbolism," parts 1 and 2, *Psychoanalytic Quarterly* 25 (1956): 469–504 and 26 (1957): 50–75; "Schreber: Father and Son," *Psychoanalytic Quarterly* 28 (1959): 151–69; "The 'Miracled-Up' World of Schreber's Childhood," *The Psychoanalytic Study of the Child* 14 (1959): 383–413; "Schreber's Father," *Journal of the American Psychoanalytic Association* 8 (1960): 492–99; "Further Data and Memorabilia Pertaining to the Schreber Case," *International Journal of Psycho-Analysis* 44 (1963): 201–7; F. Baumeyer, "New Insights in the Life and Psychosis of Schreber," *International Journal of Psycho-Analysis* 33(1952): 262; "Der Fall Schreber," *Psyche* 9 (1955): 513–36 (reprinted in *Denkwürdigkeiten eines Nervenkranken*—see note 42 below); "Noch ein Nachtrag zu Freuds Arbeit über Schreber," *Zeitschrift für psychosomatische Medizin und Psychoanalyse* 16 (1970): 243–45 (also reprinted in *Denkwürdigkeiten eines Nervenkranken*).

41. Alfons Ritter, *Schreber: Das Bildungssystem eines Arztes* (Erfurt, 1936).

42. D. P. Schreber, *Denkwürdikeiten eines Nervenkranken,* ed. P. Heiligenthal and R. Volk, with two articles by F. Baumeyer and a glossary of the "basic language" (Wiesbaden, 1973), pp. 341–66.

43. Lacan, "On a question," p. 221.

44. "Une étude: la remarquable famille Schreber," *Scilicet* 4 (1973): 287–321 (no author's name given).

45. M. Schatzman, *Soul Murder* (New York, 1973).

46. W. G. Niederland, "Schreber and Flechsig," *Journal of the American Psychoanalytic Association* 16 (1968): 740–48.

47. Lacan, "On a question," p. 179.

48. Freud, "Psycho-Analytic Notes upon an Autobiographical Account," p. 465.

49. Lacan, "On a question," p. 190.

50. Ibid., p. 217.

51. G. Rosolato, "Paranoïa et Scène Primitive" and "Repères pour la psychose," in *Essais sur le symbolique* (Paris, 1969), pp. 199–241 and 315–34; O. Mannoni, *Clefs pour*

l'imaginaire (Paris, 1969), pp. 75–79; M. Mannoni, *Le psychiatre, son "fou," et la psychanalyse* (Paris, 1970), pp. 165–85, 229–31, and *Éducation impossible* (Paris, 1973), pp. 21–32, 48–49, and passim.

52. D. P. Schreber, *Denkwürdigkeiten eines Nervenkranken,* ed. and with an essay by S. M. Weber (Frankfurt, 1973).

53. Gilles Deleuze and Félix Guattari, *Anti-Oedipus: Capitalism and Schizophrenia,* tr. Robert Hurley et al. (New York, 1977), p. 56.

54. Freud, "Psycho-Analytic Notes upon an Autobiographical Account," p. 439.

55. Deleuze and Guattari, *Anti-Oedipus,* p. 57.

56. Anthony Wilden, "Critique of Phallocentrism: Daniel Paul Schreber on Women's Liberation," in *System and Structure: Essays in Communication and Exchange* (London, 1972), p. 291.

57. Much has been published on Schreber since 1974, when this essay was written. But all of it follows more or less the paths that were already laid out. One ought, however, to single out a book written by a Dutch sociologist that offers an impressive mass of new information about Schreber and his family: Han Israëls, *Schreber: Father and Son,* tr. H. S. Lake (Madison, Conn., 1989).

11. ACCOMPANIMENT TO THE READING OF STIRNER

1. [Published in English as *The Ego and His Own,* tr. Steven T. Byington (London, 1907).—Trans.]

2. F. A. Lange, *Geschichte des Materialismus* (Iserlohn, 1866), p. 292; the judgment seems to have stuck, since we read "*Der Einzige,* a famous, or rather infamous, book," in W. E. Biermann, *Anarchismus und Kommunismus* (Leipzig, 1906), p. 52.

3. Ettore Zoccoli, *I gruppi anarchici degli Stati Uniti e l'opera di Max Stirner* (Modena, 1901), pp. 31–32.

4. Letter to M. Hildebrand, 22 October 1889, in *Marx Engels Werke* (Berlin, 1956ff.) [hereafter *MEW*], vol. 37, p. 293.

5. Documents of the Landesarchiv of Bautzen, cited by B. Andréas and W. Mönke, "Neue Daten zur *Deutschen Ideologie,*" *Archiv für Sozialgeschicht* 8(1968): 18–19.

6. *MEW,* vol. 27, pp. 11–13.

7. Karl Marx and Friedrich Engels, *The German Ideology,* in *MEW,* vol. 3, p. 168.

8. Quoted in W. Bolin, *Ludwig Feuerbach* (Stuttgart, 1891), p. 106.

9. All in *Ausgewählte Briefe von und an Ludwig Feuerbach* (Leipzig, 1904), vol. 2, p. 259.

10. Arnold Ruge, *Briefwechsel und Tagebuchblätter aus den Jahren 1825–1880* (Berlin, 1886), vol. 1, pp. 379, 381–82, 386.

11. Ibid., p. 429.

12. Max Stirner, *Der Einzige und sein Eigentum* (Stuttgart, 1972), pp. 153, 159.

13. Marx and Engels, *The German Ideology,* in *MEW,* vol. 3, p. 17.

14. Now in *Werke,* vol. 4, (Frankfurt, 1975), pp. 69–80.

15. In the form of a pamphlet, *Die letzen Philosophen* (Darmstadt, 1845), then collected in *Sozialistische Aufsätze 1841–1847* (Berlin, 1921), pp. 188–206.

16. In the *Norddeutsche Blätter* of March 1845; but next year, the eager Szeliga, a favorite laughingstock of Marx and Engels and of Stirner as well, tried to incorporate something of Stirner's in a pamphlet. At the end of the pamphlet, he states that it "testifies to a great lack of clarity to designate egoism as the enemy of universal reform; on the contrary, it is its precursor, its school of hard knocks"; *Die Universalreform und der Egoismus* (Charlottenburg, 1846), p. 27.

17. Max Stirner, "Recensenten Stirners," reprinted by J. H. Mackay in *Kleinere Schriften,* 2nd ed. (Berlin, 1914), pp. 343–96.

18. G. Edward [Max Stirner], "Die philosophischen Reaktionäre," reprinted in MacKay, *Kleinere Schriften,* pp. 401–15.

19. Dronke, *Berlin* (Frankfurt, 1846), vol. 2, p. 116.

20. Karl Rosenkranz, *Aus einem Tagebuch* (Leipzig, 1854), p. 133.

21. *MEW,* vol. 36, p. 39.

22. "Marx und der 'wahre' Sozialismus," *Die Neue Zeit,* 12, no. 2 (1895): 217.

23. Engels, Letter to Max Hildebrand, 22 October 1889, in *MEW,* vol. 37, p. 293.

24. *Ludwig Feuerbach und der Anfang der deutschen Philosophie* [1888], in *MEW,* vol. 21, p. 271.

25. Eduard Bernstein, "Die soziale Theorie des Anarchismus," *Die Neue Zeit* 10, no. 1 (1891–92): 421–28; Franz Mehring, *Geschichte der Sozialdemokratie* (Stuttgart, 1897), vol. 1, p. 203.

26. Friedmund von Arnim, "Die Auflösung des Einzigen durch den Menschen," *Die Epigonen* 4(1847): 180–251.

27. Fritz Mauthner, *Der Atheismus und seine Geschichte im Abendlande* (Stuttgart-Berlin, 1923), vol. 4, p. 216.

28. Kuno Fischer, "Moderne Sophisten," reprinted in *Die Epigonen* 5(1848): 279.

29. Ibid., p. 281.

30. Ibid., p. 300.

31. Max Stirner, "Die philosophischen Reaktionäre," p. 412.

32. In *Die Epigonen* 4(1847): 152.

33. "Every insignificant pamphlet published in Berlin or other provincial or district towns of German philosophy was ordered and read to tatters and smudges, and the leaves fell out in a few days, if only there was a mention of Hegel in it"; A. I. Herzen, *My Past and Thoughts,* tr. Constance Garnett (London, 1968), vol. 2, p. 398.

34. On Stirner's reception in Russia, see, first of all, P. V. Annenkov, *The Extraordinary Decade: Literary Memoirs,* tr. Irwin R. Titunik (Ann Arbor, Mich., 1968), pp. 211–14; also copious references in T. G. Masaryk, *The Spirit of Russia* (London, 1919); P. Scheibert, *Von Bakunin zu Lenin* (Leiden, 1956); M. Malia, *Alexander Herzen and the Birth of Russian Socialism* (Cambridge, Mass., 1961); A. Walicki, *Un'utopia conservatrice* (Turin, 1973).

35. Eduard von Hartmann, *Philosophie des Unbewussten* (Berlin, 1869), pp. 611–12.

36. F. A. Lange, *Geschichte des Materialismus,* p. 292.

37. K. Joël, *Philosophenwege* (Berlin, 1901), p. 229.

38. J. H. MacKay, *Max Stirner: Sein Leben und sein Werke* (Berlin, 1898); later expanded in successive editions: Treptow, 1910, and Charlottenburg, 1914.

39. Some useful supplementation and correction of Mackay's data can be found in various studies and documents collected by D. Dettmeiyer, ed., in *Max Stirner* (Lausanne, 1979).

40. H. G. Helms, *Die Ideologie der anonymen Gesellschaft* (Cologne, 1966), pp. 510–600.

41. K. Mühsam, *Der Leidensweg Erich Mühsam* (Zurich-Paris, 1935), pp. 13–31.

42. He dreamed of Ascona becoming "a meeting place for persons who by the nature of their individuality are unsuited ever to become useful members of capitalistic human society"; Erich Mühsam, *Ascona* (Locarno, 1905), p. 57.

43. Rolf Recknagel, *Beiträge zur Biographie des B. Traven* (Berlin, 1977).

44. Karl Löwith, *Das Individuum in der Rolle des Mitmenschen* (Munich, 1928), pp. 169–80.

45. Martin Buber, *Die Frage an den Einzelnen* (Berlin, 1936), pp. 9–27.

46. Thinking, of course, of *L'être et le néant,* in *Existentialism, Marxism, and Anarchism* (London, 1949), p. 24.

47. Günther Anders, "Nihilismus und Existenz," *Die Neue Rundschau,* 1947, pp. 58–62.

48. Albert Camus, *L'Homme révolté* (Paris, 1951), pp. 84–88.

49. Henri Avron, *Aux sources de l'existentialisme: Max Stirner* (Paris, 1954).

50. R. W. K. Patterson, *Max Stirner: the Nihilistic Egoist* (Oxford, 1971).

51. Ernst Schultze, "Stirner'sche Ideen in einem paranoischen Wahnsystem," *Archiv für Psychiatrie und Nervenkrankheiten* 36 (Berlin, 1903): 793–818.

52. Ludwig Binswanger, *Grundformen und Erkenntnis menschlichen Daseins* (Zurich, 1942).

53. Reprinted along with other short writings by Panizza in *Die kriminelle Psychose* (Munich, 1978), pp. 119–77.

54. Zoccoli, *I gruppi anarchici degli Stati Uniti e l'opera di Max Stirner.*

55. Ettore Zoccoli, *L'anarchia* (Turin, 1907), pp. 7–69.

56. Letter to Cesare Berti, 3 November 1911, from Forlì prison, in *Opera omnia,* vol. 4 (Florence, 1952), p. 258.

57. *Opera omnia,* vol. 6 (Florence, 1953), p. 331.

58. Ibid., vol. 14 (Florence, 1954), p. 194.

59. Paolo Orano, *Il fascismo* (Rome, 1940), vol. 2, p. 240.

60. Julius Evola, Introduction to *L'Internationale ebraica, I "protocolli" dei "savi anziani" di Sion* [Protocols of the Elders of Zion] (Rome, 1937), pp. xix–xx. This is the slightly varied and revised version—and Stirner's name is part of the revision—of another list of great conspirators of Hebraism offered by Evola a few months earlier: Marx, Heine, Börne, Freud, Nordau, Lombroso, Reinach, Durkheim, Einstein, Zamenhof, Offenbach,

Sullivan—obviously thinking of *The Mikado* as a document of Judaic infiltration—Schönberg, Stravinsky, Wassermann, Döblin; in Julius Evola, *Tre aspetti del problema ebraico* (Rome, 1936), pp. 38–39.

61. Eugenio Garin, *Cronache di filosofia italiana* (Bari, 1959), p. 166.

62. For example, D. Koigen, *Zur Vorgeschichte des modernen philosopischen Sozialismus in Deutschland* (Bern, 1901).

63. Sidney Hook, *From Hegel to Marx* (London, 1936), p. 165.

64. Cesare Luporini, *L'ideologia tedesca* (Rome, 1977), pp. xi–lxxxviii.

65. [In Italian the names of eminent men are sometimes preceded by the definite article.—Trans.]

66. Luporini, *L'ideologia tedesca,* p. xxiv.

67. Max Nettlau, *Bibliographie de l'anarchie* (Paris-Brussels, 1897), pp. 35–36.

68. Georgy Plekhanov, *Anarchismus und Sozialismus* (Berlin, 1894), pp. 17–26.

69. Paul Eltzbacher, *Der Anarchismus* (Berlin, 1900), pp. 246–66.

70. Dronke, *Berlin,* vol. 2, p. 125.

71. Mauthner, *Der Atheismus und seine Geschichte,* vol. 4, pp. 201–7.

72. Carl Schmitt, *Ex Captivitate Salus* (Cologne, 1950), pp. 80–82.

73. Mauthner, *Der Atheismus und seine Geschichte,* vol. 4, p. 215.

74. Ibid., p. 210.

14. ON PUBLIC OPINION

1. Karl Kraus, *Die Fackel* 167 (26 October 1904): 9.

2. Karl Kraus, "In dieser grossen Zeit" (1914), in *Weltgericht* (Munich, 1965), p. 13.

3. G. W. Leibniz, "Drôle de pensée touchant une nouvelle sorte de Représentations," in *Politische Schriften* (Darmstadt, 1931), vol. 1.

4. Karl Kraus, "Sprüche und Widersprüche," reprinted in *Beim Wort genommen* (Munich, 1955), p. 134.

5. Karl Kraus, "Pro domo et mundo," reprinted in *Beim Wort genommen,* p. 236.

6. Ibid., p. 285.

7. Karl Kraus, "Heine und die Folgen" (1910), in *Untergang der Welt durch schwarze Magie* (Munich, 1960), p. 205.

8. Kraus, "Pro domo et mundo," p. 238.

9. Kraus, "Sprüche und Widersprüche," p. 122.

10. Kraus, "Pro domo et mundo," p. 284.

11. Kraus, "Sprüche und Widersprüche," p. 121.

12. Karl Kraus, *Die Sprache* (Munich, 1954), p. 381.

13. Karl Kraus, "Der sterbende Mensch," in *Worte in Versen* (Munich, 1959), p. 59.

14. Karl Kraus, "An meinen Drucker," in *Worte in Versen,* p. 463.

15. Karl Kraus, "Herbstzeitlose" (1915), in *Untergang der Welt durch schwarze Magie,* p. 413.

16. Kraus, *Die Sprache,* p. 341.

17. All quotations from the pre-Socratics are from Diels-Kranz, *Die Fragmente der Vorsokratiker,* 11th ed. (Berlin, 1964).

18. Friedrich Nietzsche, "How the 'True World' Finally Became a Fable," in *Twilight of the Idols,* in *The Portable Nietzsche,* tr. Walter Kaufmann (New York, 1954), p. 486.

19. Karl Kraus, "Warum die Fackel nicht erscheint," in *Die Fackel,* nos. 890–905, end of July 1934, p. 24.

20. Léon Bloy, *Exégèse des lieux communs* (1902) (Paris, 1953), p. 11.

21. Kraus, *Die Sprache,* p. 438.

22. Léon Bloy, *Exégèse des lieux communs (Nouvelle Série)* (1913) (Paris, 1953), p. 333.

23. Kraus, "Warum die Fackel nicht erscheint," p. 9.

24. This poem, entitled "Über die Bedeutung des zehnzeiliges Gedichtes in der 888. Nummer der Fackel," was published for the first time in *Stimmen über Karl Kraus* (Vienna, 1934), pp. 11–12.

25. Karl Kraus, *Die dritte Walpurgisnacht* (Munich, 1952), p. 9.

26. Walter Benjamin, "Karl Kraus," in *Reflections: Essays, Aphorisms, Autobiographical Writings,* tr. Edmund Jephcott (New York and London, 1978), p. 249.

27. Kraus, *Die dritte Walpurgisnacht,* p. 20.

28. Kraus, "Sprüche und Widersprüche," p. 70.

29. Kraus, *Die Sprache,* p. 227.

30. Kraus, *Die dritte Walpurgisnacht,* p. 280.

15. A CHINESE WALL

1. Robert Scheu, *Karl Kraus* (Vienna, 1909), pp. 4–5.

2. Robert Musil, *The Man without Qualities,* vol. 1, tr. Sophie Wilkins (New York, 1996), p. 28.

3. *Die Fackel,* no. 1, April 1899, p. 1.

4. Ibid., p. 7.

5. *Die Fackel,* nos. 232–33, October 1907, p. 43. "I have long sought the means to make myself unbearable to my contemporaries," wrote Léon Bloy—along with Søren Kierkegaard the most essential reference point in considering Kraus's relations with the new society—in the first issue of *Le Pal,* March 1885, a short-lived publication that constitutes one of the more significant precedents of *Die Fackel.* Moreover, both Bloy and Kraus recalled the same publication, Henri Rochefort's *La Lanterne* (1868–69).

6. Karl Kraus, "Nach zwanzig Jahren," in *Worte in Versen* (Munich, 1959), p. 253.

7. Walter Benjamin, "Karl Kraus," in *Reflections,* tr. Edmund Jephcott (New York and London, 1978), p. 239.

8. P. Schick, *Karl Kraus* (Reinbeck, 1965), p. 28.

9. *An der schönen blauen Donau* [On the Beautiful Blue Danube]—was a fortnightly publication presenting literature and music, where Hofmannsthal published under the pseudonym of Loris Melikov and Arthur Schnitzler under that of Anatol.

10. Karl Kraus, "Sprüche und Widersprüche" (1909), in *Beim Wort genommen* (Munich, 1955), p. 144.

11. *Briefwechsel zwischen George und Hofmannsthal* (Munich, 1953), p. 7.

12. Ibid., p. 241.

13. P. de Mendelssohn, *S. Fischer und sein Verlag* (Frankfurt, 1970), p. 195.

14. "Zur Überwindung des Naturalismus" is the title of Bahr's essay, to which the youthful Kraus replied with the article "Zur Überwindung des Hermann Bahr," in *Die Gesellschaft,* 5 May 1893, pp. 627–36.

15. As Kraus wrote in a review of Hofmannsthal's *Gestern:* "For us in Austria, however, to think of overcoming naturalism would be biting irony, an amusing paradox. *No longer to have* the naturalism that *we do not yet have* would mean to get rid of something we do not possess"; *Die Gesellschaft,* 6 June 1892, p. 800.

16. Quoted in Mendelssohn, *S. Fischer und sein Verlag,* p. 195.

17. K. Kraus, *Die demolirte Literatur* (Vienna, 1897), p. 37.

18. Hermann Broch, *Hofmannsthal und seine Zeit* (Munich, 1964), p. 51.

19. [A reference to Schnitzler's 1901 novel *Lieutenant Gustl*—Trans.]

20. "*Glatte Worte, bunte Bilder, / Halbes, heimliches Empfinden, / Agonies, episodes,*" from Hofmannsthal's introduction to Schnitzler's *Anatol.* The second quotation is taken from a review written in 1892, likewise of *Anatol,* that Hofmannsthal never published; it was found among his papers and was published in *Die Neue Rundschau* 4 (1971): 795–97. This review ends with a sentence that demonstrates Hofmannsthal's perfect awareness, from the beginning, of the Viennese syndrome: "Amid the nervous chatter of the figures, the Medusa-like character of life emerges from the shadows: What is senseless, enigmatic, solitary, the deaf and lifeless misunderstanding between those who love; the dark conscience, as of a fault committed; the presentiment at dawn of escaped infinities, of smothered, dissipated wonders; and the many things that fall like frost and rust on overly refined souls."

21. Broch, *Hofmannsthal,* p. 20.

22. Quoted in H. Kohn, *Karl Kraus. Arthur Schnitzler. Otto Weininger* (Tubingen, 1962), p. 14.

23. Benjamin, "Karl Kraus," p. 253. The sentence was quoted for the first time by Benjamin in his essay on Kraus; it does not appear in Brecht's writings. Werner Kraft assumes that it was said in conversation.

24. Karl Kraus, "Der Fall Riehl" (1906), in *Sittlichkeit und Kriminalität* (Munich [1963]), p. 228.

25. Kraus, "Nachts" (1918), in *Beim Wort genommen,* p. 341.

26. Karl Kraus, "Heine und die Folgen" (1910), in *Untergang der Welt durch schwarze Magie* (Munich, 1960), p. 191.

27. Adolf Loos, "Ornament und Verbrechen" (1908), in *Sämtliche Schriften* (Vienna, 1962), vol. 1, p. 283.

28. T. W. Adorno, "Rückblickend auf den Surrealismus," in *Noten zur Literatur* (Frankfurt, 1958), p. 160.

29. Kraus, "Heine und die Folgen," p. 191.

30. Hermann Broch, "Einige Bemerkungen zum Problem des Kitsches," in *Dichten und Erkennen* (Zurich, 1955), p. 297.

31. Karl Kraus, "Nachwort zu Heine und die Folgen" (1911), in *Untergang der Welt,*
p. 217.

32. Kraus, "Heine und die Folgen," p. 188.

33. Ibid., p. 200.

34. Sir Thomas Browne, *Hydriotaphia,* note e, at end.

35. On Kraus and Wittgenstein: E. Heller, in "Wittgenstein und Nietzsche," in *Die
Reise der Kunst ins Innere* (Frankfurt, 1966), pp. 233–63, mentions the connection between
the works of these two; his themes are taken up and expanded by W. Kraft in "Ludwig
Wittgenstein und Karl Kraus," in *Rebellen des Geistes* (Stuttgart, 1968), pp. 102–34; and
then by J. Bouveresse, *La parole malheureuse* (Paris, 1971), pp. 18 ff., 32 ff. Wittgenstein
had an immense admiration for Kraus: When he decided to entrust Ludwig von Ficker,
editor of the magazine *Der Brenner,* with the sum of 100,000 crowns to be distributed
to writers in difficulty—Trakl, Rilke, Else Lasker-Schüler, and a few others were later
chosen—Wittgenstein specified that his decision had been taken "on the basis of words
that Kraus wrote about you in *Die Fackel* and on the basis of words that you wrote about
Kraus": cf. Ludwig Wittgenstein, *Briefe an Ludwig von Ficker* (Salzburg, 1969), p. 12. The
first publisher to whom Wittgenstein offered the *Tractatus* was Jahoda, publisher of *Die
Fackel,* and when it was rejected, he wrote to Paul Engelmann, "I should very much like
to know what Kraus says about it." For these and other details, see P. Engelmann, *Letters
from Ludwig Wittgenstein with a Memoir* (Oxford, 1967), pp. 122–32. It is curious to note
that Kraus had had a violent argument with Wittgenstein's father, Karl, an influential
columnist on economics for the *Neue Freie Presse,* in the early years of *Die Fackel*: cf. no.
65, p. 16; no. 67, pp. 12–16; and no. 71, pp. 11–12.

On Kraus and Schoenberg: Schoenberg wrote this dedication for Kraus, on a copy
of *Harmonielehre*: "I learned from you more than one should if one wants to remain independent"; the text is quoted in Schoenberg's response to *Rundfrage über Karl Kraus*
(Innsbruck, 1917), p. 21. In *Die Fackel,* nos. 272–73, p. 34, Kraus printed a letter from
Schoenberg challenging a critic; in no. 300, p. 9, he reproduced a page from the manuscript score of Schoenberg's *Buch der hängenden Gärten*; in no. 374, pp. 24–25, he defend-
ed Schoenberg after a concert that had caused scandal. A comparison between Kraus and
Schoenberg was made as early as 1934 by Ernst Krenek, in *23,* the music journal edited by
Willi Reich and modeled after *Die Fackel,* in a text later republished, along with two others about Kraus, in *Zur Sprache gebracht* (Munich, 1958), pp. 172–74, 224–39. Krenek
clearly illustrates how the conception of language in Kraus is also valid as a reference
point for the musical practice of the composers of the school of Vienna. Kraus, on the
other hand, always remained aloof to this music. On Kraus and Freud: The mocking hos-
tility toward psychoanalysis revealed in Kraus's aphorisms has an interesting factual background. *Die Fackel,* no. 191, p. 8, carried a positive review by Otto Soyka of Freud's *Three
Contributions on the Theory of Sexuality,* at a time (1905) when psychoanalysis was still in
disrepute; when the brawl broke out with Fliess over priority in the theory of original bisexuality, Freud, in January 1906, wrote Kraus a letter beginning with these words: "The
partial coincidence of your conceptions and aspirations with mine must be the reason
why I have been able to find my name repeatedly cited in *Die Fackel*"; Kraus took Freud's

side in the dispute; cf. no. 210, pp. 26–27. In 1908, in the midst of his attack on Harden, Kraus cited a letter of support that Freud had sent him at the time of the Hervay case (1904)["Leontine von Hervay, accused of bigamy and evil practices"]: "A reader, who cannot be your supporter all that often, congratulates you on the penetration, the courage, and the ability to recognize the large in the small as shown by your article on the Hervay case"; *Die Fackel,* nos. 257–58, p. 40.

On Kraus and Loos: Alone among the great Viennese language figures, Loos was always a great friend of Kraus. Together with the lovable and incorrigible Peter Altenberg, they formed a diversified trio united by immense mutual esteem. From the beginning of *Die Fackel,* Kraus speaks in Loos's favor; cf. issue 29, p. 19. In the first volume of aphorisms and in "Heine und die Folgen," the affinities of substance and intention between the two are clearly stated, and they are mentioned continually in all the following years. In 1930, Kraus dedicated his book of *Zeitstrophen* to Loos with these words: "To Adolf Loos, pure counterimage of the world here depicted." Finally, it was Kraus who spoke at Loos's grave: The famous issue 888 of *Die Fackel,* the thinnest, contained, besides the three pages of the speech, only Kraus's marvelous last poem, an allusion to his silence in the face of Nazism: "Man frage nicht, was all die Zeit ich machte." As for Loos, he had saluted Kraus in *Rundfrage über Karl Kraus,* published by Ficker in Innsbruck in 1917, with praise that is general but that corresponds to his absolute faith in his friend: "He stands on the threshold of a new epoch, and to humanity, so long separated from God and nature, points out the path."

36. Leo Spitzer, "Das synthetische und das symbolische Neutralpronomen im Französischen," in *Stilstudien* (Munich, 1961), vol. 1, p. 202.

37. Karl Kraus, "Es" (1921), in *Die Sprache* (Munich, 1954), p. 77.

38. Gottfried Benn, "Nietzsche—nach fünfzig Jahren," in *Gesammelte Werke,* vol. 1 (Wiesbaden, 1962), p. 492.

39. Karl Kraus, *Die chinesische Mauer* (1909) (Munich, 1964), p. 279.

40. Kraus, "Maximilian Harden" (1907), in *Die chinesische Mauer,* p. 56.

41. Kraus, "Der Löwenkopf" (1913), in *Untergang der Welt,* pp. 186–87.

42. Kraus, "Girardi" (1908), in *Die chinesische Mauer,* p. 138.

43. Kraus, "Pro domo et mundo" (1912), in *Beim Wort genommen,* p. 238.

44. Maurice Blanchot, *L'entretien infini* (Paris, 1969), p. 229.

45. Jean Paul, *Vorschule der Aesthetik,* para. 45.

46. Kraus, "Sprüche und Widersprüche," p. 161.

47. Karl Kraus, "Meine Wiener Vorlesung," in *Die Fackel,* nos. 303–4, May 1910, p. 37.

48. Kraus, "Sprüche und Widersprüche," p. 117.

49. Meng Tien was the general to whom the emperor Huang-ti entrusted the completion of the Great Wall. His words, to be taken in a geomantic sense, are reported by Sseu-Ma Ts'ien, *Shih-chi,* chap. 88. On Meng Tien, see J. J. L. Duyvendak, *De grote chinese muur* (Leiden, 1953), pp. 15, 33–34; O. F. von Möllendorf, "Die Grosse Mauer von China," *Zeitschrift der Deutschen Morgenländischen Gesellschaft* 35(1881): 92–97.

50. Elias Canetti, "Karl Kraus: The School of Resistance," in *The Conscience of Words,* tr. Joachim Neugroschel (New York, 1979), p. 35.

51. Quoted by S. von Radecki in *Wie ich glaube* (Cologne, 1953), pp. 23–24.

52. Canetti, "Karl Kraus," p. 36.

53. Kraus, "Druckfehler" (1920), in *Die Sprache,* pp. 52–53.

54. Kraus, "Pro domo et mundo," p. 279.

55. Kraus, "Nachts," p. 433.

56. Karl Kraus, "Rechenschaftsbericht," in *Die Fackel,* nos. 795–99, December 1928, p. 3.

57. Kraus, "Sprüche und Widersprüche," p. 45.

58. Ibid., p. 26.

59. T. W. Adorno, "Sittlichkeit und Kriminalität," in *Noten zur Literatur III* (Frankfurt, 1965), p. 77.

60. Kraus, "Sprüche und Widersprüche," pp. 44–45.

61. Benjamin, "Karl Kraus," p. 258.

62. Ibid., p. 257.

63. Kraus, "Prozess Veith" (1908), in *Die chinesische Mauer,* pp. 13–14.

64. Kraus, "Sprüche und Widersprüche," p. 48.

65. Friedrich Nietzsche, *Beyond Good and Evil,* tr. R. J. Hollingdale (Harmondsworth, Eng., 1990), para. 75, p. 92.

66. Kraus, *Die chinesische Mauer,* pp. 280–81.

67. Ibid., p. 283.

68. Ibid., p. 284.

69. Kraus, "Sprüche und Widersprüche," p. 71.

70. Kraus, *Die chinesische Mauer,* pp. 286–87, 289.

71. Kraus, "Nachts," p. 427.

72. "Du bleibst am Ursprung: Ursprung ist das Ziel." Kraus, "Der sterbende Mensch," in *Worte in Versen* (Munich, 1959), p. 59.

73. William Gilbert and Arthur Sullivan, *Patience,* in *Treasury of Gilbert and Sullivan,* ed. M. Green (New York, 1961), p. 225.

74. Ibid., p. 226.

75. Kraus, "Nachts," p. 328.

76. Kraus, "Pro domo et mundo," p. 291.

77. "Ich bin nur einer der Epigonen / die in dem alten Haus der Sprache wohnen." Kraus, "Bekenntnis," in *Worte in Versen,* p. 79.

78. Benjamin, "Karl Kraus," p. 258. [Translation slightly altered.]

79. Kraus, "Perversität" (1903), in *Sittlichkeit und Kriminalität,* p. 302.

80. Kraus, "Nestroy und die Nachwelt" (1912), in *Untergang der Welt . . . ,* p. 226.

81. Kraus, "Pro domo et mundo," p. 297.

82. Walter Benjamin, "Einbahnstrasse" (1928), in *Gesammelte Werke,* vol. 4, book 1, Frankfurt, 1972, p. 138.

83. Benjamin, "Karl Kraus," p. 250.

84. There were more than seven hundred of these readings; they were held, between 1910 and 1936, primarily in Vienna but also in various German cities, in Czechoslovakia, in Paris, and twice in Trieste. They took place mostly in regular theaters: Kraus read from his own works or those of other writers he liked. In his last years, he recited, always alone and at a reading desk, whole operettas by Offenbach and whole plays by Shakespeare. A complete list of readings appears in O. Kerry, *Karl-Kraus-Bibliographie* (Munich, 1970), pp. 78–83.

85. Canetti, "Karl Kraus," p. 30.

86. "For the incomprehensible and unforgettable thing (unforgettable to anyone who experienced it, even if he lived to be three hundred) was that this law *glowed:* it radiated, it scorched and destroyed"; ibid., p. 31.

87. Ibid., pp. 37–38.

88. Benjamin, "Einbahnstrasse," p. 121.

89. Karl Kraus, "Sakrileg an George oder Sühne an Shakespeare," in *Die Fackel,* nos. 885–87, December 1932, p. 46.

90. Kraus, "Todesfurcht," in *Worte in Versen,* pp. 375–76, ll. 31–32.

91. "Doch hängen in blutig gespürter Verkettung / an meiner Gestalt die vielen Gestalten / die du zu bewahren mir vorbehalten, / und in dem schmerzbeseligten Bund / unzählige Stimmen an meiner Mund"; Kraus, "Bange Stunde," in *Worte in Versen,* p. 239.

92. H. Kann, "Erinnerungen an Karl Kraus," in *National-Zeitung,* 23 April 1944, Sunday supplement.

93. Walter Benjamin, "Goethes Wahlverwandtschaften," in *Gesammelte Schriften* (Frankfurt, 1978), vol. 1, bk. 1, p. 139.

94. Benjamin, "Karl Kraus," p. 259.

95. "Gebannt steh'ich auf diesem Fleck / und kann nicht zurück und kann nicht weg"; Kraus, "Bange Stunde," in *Worte in Versen,* p. 238.

96. Walter Benjamin, "On the Mimetic Faculty," in *Reflections: Essays, Aphorisms, Autobiographical Writings,* tr. Edmund Jephcott (New York and London, 1978), p. 333.

97. Karl Kraus, "In dieser grossen Zeit" (1914), in *Weltgericht* (Munich, 1965), p. 9.

98. Ibid.

99. Kraus, "Apokalypse" (1908), in *Untergang der Welt,* p. 11.

100. Kraus, "Girardi," p. 137.

101. To quote Robert de Montesquiou's phrase in *Les Chauves-souris* (Paris, [1892]), p. 31.

102. Karl Kraus, "Maximilian Harden," pp. 60–61.

103. Karl Kraus, "Die Einacter," in *Die Fackel,* no. 1, April 1899, p. 25. The history and nature of the incompatibility between Kraus and Hofmannsthal are complex questions that bear thinking about. A description of their relations can be found in Arntzen, "Karl Kraus und Hugo von Hofmannsthal," *Sprache im technischen Zeitalter* 26 (1968): 147–63.

104. Karl Kraus, "Maximilian Harden. Ein Nachruf," in *Die Fackel,* nos. 242–43, January 1908, p. 24.

105. Karl Kraus, "Aus der Branche" (1911), in *Literatur und Lüge* (Munich, 1958), p. 69.

106. Karl Kraus, "Literatur oder Man wird doch da sehn" (1921), in *Dramen* (Munich, 1967), p. 13.

107. "Der Lächler," in *Die Fackel,* nos. 557–60, January 1921, p. 17. Kraus's attitude toward German-language writers of the avant-garde became stinging only with the war and was especially so afterward. Indeed, it is clear today that the war, except in rare cases, either killed those writers or spared them to reveal their hitherto-disguised banality. But as far as Kraus is concerned, one should note that, before 1911, he had published pieces by Jacob van Hoddis and Albert Ehrenstein in *Die Fackel.* His great admiration for Else Lasker-Schüler and Georg Trakl always remained unchanged.

108. T. W. Adorno, *Minima Moralia,* tr. E. F. N. Jephcott (London, 1974), p. 144.

109. Benjamin, "Karl Kraus," p. 247.

110. Quotation printed in *Die Fackel,* nos. 852–56, May 1931, p. 60.

111. Benjamin, "Einbahnstrasse," p. 121.

112. Kraus, *Die chinesische Mauer,* p. 290.

113. Kraus, "Pro domo et mundo," p. 284.

114. The episode is related by Kurt Wolff in *Autoren / Bücher / Abenteuer* (Berlin, 1969), pp. 86–87, and gave rise to Kraus's essay "Schändung der Pandora," in *Die Sprache,* pp. 54–59.

115. Marcel Granet, "Quelques particularités de la langue et de la pensée chinoises," in *Études sociologiques sur la Chine* (Paris, 1953), p. 146 note.

116. Marcel Granet, *La pensée chinoise* (Paris, 1934), p. 329.

117. Marcel Granet, *Danses et légendes de la Chine ancienne* (Paris, 1959), vol. 2, p. 593.

118. Walter Benjamin, "Über den Begriff der Geschichte," in *Gesammelte Schriften* (Frankfurt, 1974), vol. 1, bk. 2, p. 694.

119. Karl Kraus, *Die letzten Tage der Menschheit* (Munich, 1957), pp. 681, 9, 10.

120. "Wie leer ist es hier / an meiner Stelle. / Vertan alles Streben./ Nichts bleibt von mir / als die Quelle, / die sie nicht angegeben"; Karl Kraus "Grabschrift," in *Worte in Versen,* p. 516.

121. Kraus, "In dieser grossen Zeit," p. 11.

122. Max Brod, *Streitbares Leben* (Munich, 1960), p. 154.

123. Kraus, "Pro domo et mundo," p. 274.

124. Kraus, "In dieser grossen Zeit," p. 11.

125. *David Hilberts Gesammelte Abhandlungen* (Berlin, 1935), vol. 3, p. 163.

126. G. Goblot, "Les parents de Karl Kraus," *Études Germaniques* 5, no. 1 (1950): 47.

127. Kraus, "Grimassen über Kultur und Bühne" (1908), in *Die chinesische Mauer,* pp. 149–50; partially reprinted in "Sprüche und Widersprüche," p. 98.

128. T. W. Adorno, "Hoffmanns Erzählungen in Offenbachs Motiven," in *Moments musicaux* (Frankfurt, 1964), p. 47.

129. Karl Kraus, "Offenbach-Renaissance," in *Die Fackel,* nos. 757–58, April 1927, p. 47.

130. Kraus, *Die letzten Tage der Menschheit,* p. 9.

131. Karl Kraus, "Vorwort" (to *La Créole*), in *Die Fackel,* no. 916, November 1935, p. 6.

132. Kraus, "Offenbach-Renaissance," p. 46.

133. Benjamin, "Karl Kraus liest Offenbach," in *Gesammelte Werke,* vol. 4, bk. 1, p. 517.

134. "Denn die hat nach jenem Duft gerochen / womit Eros meinen Traum gesegnet"; Karl Kraus, "Frauenlob," in *Worte in Versen,* p. 497.

135. Kraus, "Sprüche und Widersprüche," p. 97.

136. Kraus, "Frauenlob," in *Worte in Versen,* p. 497.

137. Kraus, "Nachts," p. 338.

138. Ibid., p. 452.

16. THE PRACTICE OF PROFANE ILLUMINATION

1. Walter Benjamin, "Surrealism," in *Reflections: Essays, Aphorisms, Autobiographical Writings,* tr. Edmund Jephcott (New York and London, 1978), p. 190.

17. BRECHT THE CENSOR

1. Walter Benjamin, "Conversations with Brecht," in *Reflections: Essays, Aphorisms, Autobiographical Writings,* tr. Edmund Jephcott (New York and London, 1978), p. 212.

2. Bertolt Brecht, "Difficult Times," translated by Michael Hamburger, in *Bertolt Brecht: Poems 1913–1956,* various translators, ed. John Willett and Ralph Manheim (New York: Methuen, 1976), p. 449.

19. THE SIREN ADORNO

1. [*Minima Moralia: Reflections from Damaged Life* was finally published in an English translation by E. F. N. Jephcott in 1974. Since 1978 it has been reprinted several times by Verso Editions, London and New York.—Trans.]

20. AN APOCRYPHAL GRAVE

1. Walter Benjamin, "Theses on the Philosophy of History," in *Illuminations,* tr. Harry Zohn (New York, 1969), p. 253.

2. Ibid., p. 254.

3. Ibid., p. 258.

4. Ibid.

5. Ibid., p. 263.

6. Quoted in Gershom Scholem, *Walter Benjamin: The Story of a Friendship,* tr. Harry Zohn (New York, 1988), p. 226.

7. Ibid.

Note on Texts

The texts translated for this volume originally appeared in the following books and publications.

"Fatal Monologue," in Friedrich Nietzsche, *Ecce Homo* (Milan, 1969).

"The Sleep of the Calligrapher," in Robert Walser, *Jakob von Gunten* (Milan, 1970).

"Déesses entretenues," in Frank Wedekind, *Mine-Haha* (Milan, 1975).

"Enamel Scar," in Gottfried Benn, *Cervelli* (Milan, 1986).

"On the Fundamentals of the Coca-Cola Bottle," *Corriere della Sera*, 31 October 1976.

"The Perpetual War," in Karl Kraus, *Gli ultimi giorni dell'umanità* (Milan, 1980).

"The Forty-Nine Steps," *L'Espresso*, 4 July 1971.

"The Superior Man and the Absolute Cocotte," *Corriere della Sera*, 14 December 1978.

"The Ordeal of Impossible Words," *Corriere della Sera*, 2 February 1979.

"A Report on Readers of Schreber," in D. P. Schreber, *Memorie di un malato di nervi* (Milan, 1974).

"Accompaniment to the Reading of Stirner," in Max Stirner, *L'unico e la sua proprietà* (Milan, 1979).

"Prelude to the Twentieth Century," *Corriere della Sera*, 5 February 1980.

"Hiding Places," *Corriere della Sera*, 17 June 1979.

"On Public Opinion," *Adelphiana*, 1971.

"A Chinese Wall," in Karl Kraus, *Detti e contraddetti* (Milan, 1972).

"The Practice of Profane Illumination," *Corriere della Sera*, 25 March 1978.

"Brecht the Censor," *Corriere della Sera,* 21 March 1976.

"The Ancient Egyptian Character of Art," *L'Espresso,* 10 January 1971.

"The Siren Adorno," *Corriere della Sera,* 2 December 1976.

"An Apocryphal Grave," *Corriere della Sera,* 26 September 1980.

"The Terror of Fables," *Corriere della Sera,* 4 November 1990.